A Teaching Hymnal

Art for Faith's Sake
A Brehm Center Series

The Brehm Center for Worship, Theology, and the Arts has designed this series of publications to promote the creation of resources for the church at worship. It fosters the creation of two types of material, what may be called primary and secondary liturgical art.

Like primary liturgical theology, classically understood as the actual prayer and practice of people at worship, primary liturgical art is that which is produced to give voice to God's people in public prayer or private devotion. Secondary liturgical art, like secondary theology, is written reflection on material that is created for the sake of the prayer, praise, and meditation of God's people.

The series presents both worship art and theological and pedagogical reflection on the arts of worship. The series title *Art for Faith's Sake*[1] indicates that, while some art may be created for its own sake, a higher purpose exists for arts that are created for use in prayer and praise.

Series Editors

Clayton J. Schmit

J. Frederick Davison

Editorial Staff

Editors: Joseph A. Novak and C. E. Weber

Music Editor: Scott Blasco

Hymn Editors: David Lemley and Joanie Frymire

Liturgical Editors: Jeffrey Frymire and Michelle Baker-Wright

Copy Editors: Karin Culp, Kyrie Schmit, and Jennifer Hill

---

1. "Art for Faith's Sake" is a phrase coined by art collector and church musician Jerry Evenrud, to whom we are indebted.

A Teaching Hymnal

Ecumenical and Evangelical

GENERAL EDITOR

Clayton J. Schmit

PUBLISHED BY THE

Brehm Center for Worship, Theology, and the Arts

AND

 CASCADE *Books* · Eugene, Oregon

A TEACHING HYMNAL
Ecumenical and Evangelical

Art for Faith's Sake

Cascade Books
An Imprint of Wipf and Stock Publishers
199 W. 8th Ave., Suite 3
Eugene, OR 97401

www.wipfandstock.com

PAPERBACK ISBN: 978-1-60899-279-8
HARDCOVER ISBN: 978-1-4982-8804-0

Cataloguing-in-Publication data:

Names: Schmit, Clayton J., general editor.

Title: A teaching hymnal : ecumenical and evangelical / edited by Clayton J. Schmit.

Description: Eugene, OR: Cascade Books, 2018 | Series: Art for Faith's Sake | Includes bibliographical references and index.

Identifiers: ISBN 978-1-60899-279-8 (paperback) | ISBN 978-1-4982-8804-0 (hardcover)

Subjects: LCSH: Hymns. | Prayers. | Liturgy.

Classification: M2119 T3 (print)

Manufactured in the U.S.A.   05/11/18

For our students

Contributing Authors and Artists

Michelle Baker-Wright

Scott Blasco

Jeffrey Frymire

Joanie Frymire

Jennifer Hill

Todd E. Johnson

David Lemley

Joseph A. Novak

Amy C. Schifrin

Clayton J. Schmit

Kyrie Schmit

C. E. Weber

Edwin M. Willmington

Contents

Part III: Essays and Resources

Foreword

The order of worship that had been handed to us as we entered the sanctuary listed the number in the hymnbook where the hymn could be found. But the words were also on display on the large overhead screen. My wife and I focused on the screen, as did most others in the large congregation. But I noticed that a middle-aged couple standing in the pew just across the aisle reached for the hymnbook in the pew rack, and then fixed their eyes on the page as they sang.

I don't mind looking up at the screen while I sing in church. Indeed, there is something good about being able to lift up our eyes—and even our arms—when we sing praises to God. At the same time, however, I know that the couple across from us in church was holding a precious gift in their hands—one that in many congregations is almost completely lost.

My predecessor in the Fuller presidency, David Allan Hubbard, had a memorable way of describing that gift. Hymnbooks, he said, are important repositories of the theological and spiritual memories of the church, offered to us there in poetic form. That is an important observation. Many of those important memories will be lost to us if we completely abandon the use of hymnals. And that is not even to mention what we lose by the fact that the screen typically does not give us the clues about how to sing in harmony!

This fine book is a wonderful gift to those of us who worry about these losses. While this *Teaching Hymnal* would have been a marvelous resource at any time in the past, it is especially important today. In teaching worship in college and seminary classrooms, as well as providing resources for the folks in local congregations who plan worship services, there is so much that we could once take for granted that we can no longer assume.

But to praise this book as giving us resources that we might otherwise lose is not to see it as a mere corrective for worrisome trends in the present day church. Exciting things have been happening in worship over the past several decades. There is much that is associated with "contemporary worship" that has enhanced the liturgical life of the Christian community. And this book acknowledges that, embracing all the good things we have been learning about what it means to be a multigenerational worshipping community in the twenty-first century. This is a book for and about the ages—including one that is both for and about the age in which we live!

Richard J. Mouw
Fourth President of Fuller Theological Seminary

Introduction

This resource has arisen out of two needs. The first is a need for materials that teach worship leaders and seminary students about the use of worship resources. The second need is for resources that can be used in the practice of worship in a Christian educational setting, specifically, for classroom devotions and for university and seminary worship experiences of various dimensions. While developed originally for the students of Fuller Theological Seminary in Pasadena, California—and to whom it is dedicated—it is hoped that the *Teaching Hymnal* may find broader use among those in the church who seek to understand how hymnals and service books function and those who desire to understand the power of music, poetic language, and the arts to express prayer, lament, and praise.

This hymnal includes much less and much more than a standard hymnal. Musically, there is less: the collection contains fewer hymns and songs than standard hymnals. Because exhaustive collections occur elsewhere, the attempt here is to include sufficient material to teach the use of church music and to provide a reasonable corpus of songs for worship in an educational setting. The musical selections contained here are chosen from three sources: traditional hymns and songs common to the ecumenical church, hymns and songs that represent musical idioms common in the global church, and material selected from among recent compositions. The newer materials attempt to demonstrate idioms of praise and prayer that represent a practical range of what is being used in churches today. Because the space for congregational songs in this book is limited, there is much that is missing. Favorite contemporary songs by famous composers and writers are not included. We have made the editorial choice of selecting new songs that represent popular worship idioms written by composers among our student and local communities.

In terms of worship resources, there is more than is typically found in service books. We include here traditional indexes, appendices, collections of prayers, occasional services, and so forth. But, we also include materials designed specifically for teaching. Among these are materials on the use of hymnal indexes and meters, sources of songs and hymns, instructions on common forms of prayer, annotated services and liturgical resources, a glossary of worship terms, and teaching essays.

The *Teaching Hymnal* is divided into three sections. Part I contains hymns and songs and their sources. Most occupy two pages in order to provide space for stories about the origin of each text and tune. These stories are provided alongside the music for ease of use as a teaching tool and a source of inspiration for those who sing the songs. Alternative hymn settings are indicated in cases where a hymn text is commonly sung to more than one tune. The musical material is arranged according to liturgical use. The hymn and song section contains the usual indexes (index of first lines and common names, sources of text and music, and metrical index). There are also four appendices: acknowledgments of sources and copyrights, a reference guide for the use of the common hymn page, a guide for the use of hymn meter to make tune substitutions, and an explanation of copyright and public domain.

Part II of the *Teaching Hymnal* contains services of worship that can be used as worship resources in classrooms and chapels. They can also be used as teaching models and templates for students as they seek to design services of worship. A service of marriage and a funeral service are contained in this section specifically for use in teaching seminary students to preside over such occasions.

Part III of the *Teaching Hymnal* contains essays and resources such as ecumenical worship texts, prayer resources, and instructional material. These materials relate to planning for corporate worship and the thoughtful execution of worship leadership roles.

The list of contributors to this project is a long one. Thanks go to the team of editors that have collaborated to bring this project forward. They are listed as "editorial staff" on the title page. I am also grateful to the long list of people who have contributed hymn and song texts, tunes and musical settings. They are indicated on the musical pages. There are many people who have provided graphic design, texts of liturgical material, essays and teaching resources, and copy editing expertise. The list of those to whom we are grateful is found on the Contributing Authors and Artists page in the front matter of the book. Especially to be noted are the authors and composers of traditional hymns and worship resources that have served the church for generations, even centuries. Much is owed to their inspirational and timeless contributions to the worship of the church. Their work demonstrates the ageless power of the arts to give voice to the countless Christian communities worldwide that have sung their songs and spoken their prayers and liturgies. It is on their shoulders all contemporary worship artists and worship leaders stand.

Special thanks are due to the Brehm Center for Worship, Theology, and the Arts and its innovative leaders including J. Frederick Davison, Kathleen Tiemobul, and Nate Risdon. Similarly, I wish to thank Lynn Swaya and the Henry Luce Foundation for the generous grant that has enabled this project to proceed. Deep appreciation goes to Chris Spinks and the editorial team at Wipf and Stock/Cascade Books. They were early, eager, and generous supporters of this project and have brought it to life in its present, beautiful form. I am also especially grateful to three persons from Fuller Seminary: Todd E. Johnson, the William K. and Delores Brehm Chair of Worship, Theology, and the Arts for invaluable advice on matters liturgical; Edwin

M. Willmington, Director of the Fred Bock Institute of Music for guidance in musical considerations; and former Fuller President Richard J. Mouw for his exuberant devotion to the hymnody of the church and his thoughtful words that stand as the foreword to this work. As always, I am deeply grateful for the love, support, and joyful partnership of Carol L. Vallely, attorney, teacher, and wife. Finally, we together wish to acknowledge the leadership of Bill and Dee Brehm and thank them for the vision and generosity that created the Brehm Center for Worship, Theology, and the Arts at Fuller Seminary.

Clayton J. Schmit

Pentecost 2016

Part I: Hymns and Songs for Worship

Service Music

Kyrie

Service Music

Hallelujah

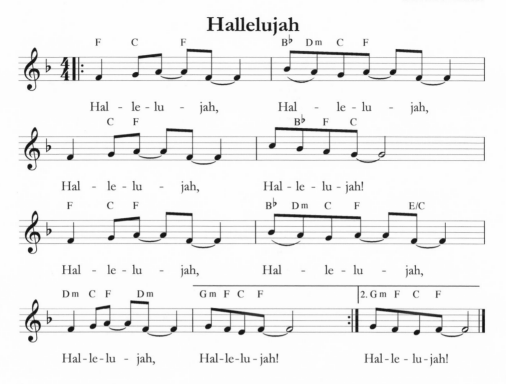

Hal - le - lu - jah, Hal - le - lu - jah,

Hal - le - lu - jah, Hal - le - lu - jah!

Hal - le - lu - jah, Hal - le - lu - jah,

Hal - le - lu - jah, Hal - le - lu - jah! Hal - le - lu - jah!

Service Music

Return to the Lord

Text: Mark G. Anzelon
Tune: Mark G. Anzelon
Text & tune ©1999 Mark G. Anzelon

Service Music

Holy, Holy

Ho - ly, ho - ly__ ho - ly Lord,

Hea - ven and earth__ are__ full__ of__ your glo - ry,

Ho - ly, ho - ly,__ ho - ly Lord,

God of pow'r__ and__ might.__

Text: Mark G. Anzelon
Tune: Mark G. Anzelon
Text & Tune © 1998 Mark G. Anzelon

Service Music

Lord, Let Your Word Come Alive

Lord,   let your Word   come a - live   in our hear-ing.

Lord,   let your Word   be   a - live in our   hearts.

Text: Clayton J. Schmit
Tune: Clayton J. Schmit
Text and Tune © 2007 Clayton J. Schmit

Caribbean Hallelujah

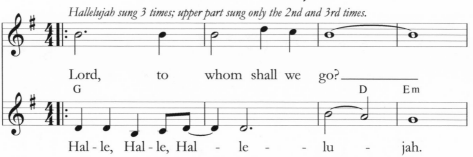

Hallelujah sung 3 times; upper part sung only the 2nd and 3rd times.

Lord, to whom shall we go?

Hal - le, Hal - le, Hal - le - lu - jah.

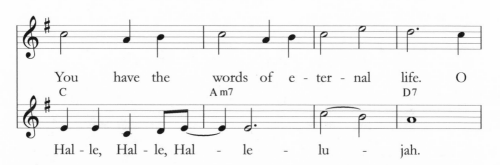

You have the words of e - ter - nal life. O

Hal - le, Hal - le, Hal - le - lu - jah.

Lord, to whom shall we go? Hal - le -

Hal - le, Hal - le, Hal - le - lu - jah, Hal - le -

2nd time, begin here

lu - jah, Hal - le - lu - jah. O

lu - jah, Hal - le - lu - jah.

Text: John 6:68
Tune: adapt. Clayton J. Schmit
Arrangement © 1990 Clayton J. Schmit

Advent

O Come, O Come, Emmanuel

1. O come, O come, Em - man - u - el, and ran-som cap - tive
2. O come, O Wis - dom from on high, who or-dered all things
3. O come, O come, great Lord of might, who to your tribes on
4. O come, O Branch of Jes - se's stem, un - to your own and

Is - ra - el that mourns in lone - ly ex - ile
might - i - ly; to us the path of knowl - edge
Si - nai's height in an - cient times you gave the
res - cue them! From depths of hell your peo - ple

here un - til the Son of God ap - pear.
show and teach us in its ways to go.
law in cloud and maj - es - ty and awe.
save, and give them vic - tory o'er the grave.

Re-joice! Re-joice! Em-man - u-el shall come to you, O Is - ra - el.

Text: *Psalteriolum Cantionum*, Köln, 1710
Tune: French processional, 15th cent.

VENI, EMMANUEL
888888

Advent

5. O come, O Key of David, come,
  and open wide our heav'nly home;
  make safe the way that leads on high
  and close the path to misery.
  Refrain

6. O come, O Dayspring, come and cheer;
  O Sun of justice, now draw near.
  Disperse the gloomy clouds of night,
  and death's dark shadows put to flight.
  Refrain

7. O come, O King of nations, come,
  O Cornerstone that binds in one;
  refresh the hearts that long for you;
  restore the broken, make us new.
  Refrain

O Come, O Come Emmanuel

For centuries, the evening services of Christians have been characterized by the singing of the Hymn of Mary, often known by its Latin title the Magnificat. A small sung portion, known as the antiphon, proceeds and follows the singing of the Magnificat. Antiphons were propers, meaning that they changed from service to service. The Magnificat antiphons of Advent, which directly preceed Christmas, are known as the "O Antiphons" because they each start with the interjection "O" as a form of direct address. These antiphons were paraphrased sometime in the 13th century to make this hymn which is widely considered the archetypal Advent hymn.

Originally used as a 15th century French processional, VENI, EMMANUEL was first attached to this hymn in 1854. It has been edited by John Mason Neale, Thomas Helmore, and countless others to produce the version presented here. There are a few different versions which are widely published still today. The most notable difference between versions of this tune is within the refrain. Some end the phrase containing "Emmanuel" on its last syllable while others, including this one, keep the phrase moving as the sentence structure suggests.

Advent

Come, Thou Long-Expected Jesus

1. Come, thou long-ex-pect-ed Je-sus, born to set thy
2. Is-rael's strength and con-so-la-tion, hope of all the
3. Born thy peo-ple to de-liv-er, born a child and
4. By thine own e-ter-nal Spir-it rule in all our

peo-ple free; from our fears and
earth thou art: dear de-sire of
yet a king, born to reign in
hearts a-lone; by thine all-suf-

sins re-lease us, let us find our rest in thee.
ev-ery na-tion, joy of ev-ery long-ing heart.
us for-ev-er, now thy gra-cious king-dom bring.
fi-cient mer-it raise us to thy glo-rious throne.

Text: Charles Wesley, 1707-1788
Tune: C. F. Witt, 1660-1716
adapted by Henry J. Gauntlett, 1805-1876

STUTTGART
8 7 8 7

Advent

Come, Thou Long-Expected Jesus

This messianic hymn by Charles Wesley appeared in *Hymns for the Nativity of Our Lord* (1744).

Christian F. Witt composed STUTTGART and included it in *Psalmodia Sacra* (1715). The German composer and hymn compiler was an organist and Kapellmeister at court in Gotha.

Christmas

Joy to the World!

1. Joy to the world, the Lord is come! Let earth re-
2. Joy to the earth, the Sav-ior riegns! Let all their
3. No more let sin and sor-row grow, nor thorns in-
4. He rules the world with truth and grace, and makes the

ceive her King. Let ev-er-y heart pre-pare him
songs em-ploy, while fields and floods, rocks, hills, and
fest the ground; he comes to make his bless-ings
na-tions prove the glo-ries of his right-eous-

room, and heav'n and na-ture sing, and heav'n and na-ture
plains re-peat the sounding joy, re-peat the sound-ing
flow far as the curse is found, far as the curse is
ness and won-ders of his love, and won-ders of his
and heav'n and na-ture sing,

and

Text: Isaac Watts, 1674-1719 (Ps. 98:4-9)   ANTIOCH
Tune: Arr. from G.F. Handel, 1685-1741, by Lowell Mason, 1792-1848   CM with repeat

Christmas

sing,   and   heav'n   and   heav'n   and   na - ture   sing.
joy,   re - peat,   re - peat   the   sound-ing   joy.
found,   far   as,   far   as   the   curse   is   found.
love,   and   won - ders,   won - ders   of   his   love.

heav'nand nature   sing

Joy to the World

While often considered a Christmas hymn, this hymn was not originally intended to be one. Instead, Isaac Watts wrote it as a metrical paraphrase of the second half of Psalm 98. Watts attributed the theme of the hymn as "the Messiah's coming and kingdom" which lends itself to the Advent season. However, it is almost universally used as a Christmas hymn.

Lowell Mason modified an English tune to create ANTIOCH for "Joy to the World" and since then they have been closely associated. Mason attributed the tune to G. F. Handel but modern scholarship has indicated more complicated origins. The opening musical line is originally derived from the melody of Handel's "Glory to God," from *Messiah*. At the words "let heaven and nature sing" the melody derives from the introduction to Handel's "Comfort Ye," also from *Messiah*.

Christmas

O Come, All Ye Faithful

1. O come, all ye faith-ful, joy-ful and tri-um-phant! O
2. God of God, Light of Light e-ter-nal,
3. Sing, choirs of an-gels, sing in ex-ul-ta-tion,
4. Yea, Lord, we greet thee, born this hap-py morn-ing;

come ye, O come ye to Beth-le-hem!
lo, he ab-hors not the Vir-gin's womb;
sing, all ye ci-ti-zens of heaven a-bove:
Je-sus, to thee be all glo-ry given;

Come and be-hold him, born the King of an-gels;
Son of the Fa-ther, be-got-ten, not cre-at-ed;
"Glo-ry to God, all glo-ry in the high-est!"
Word of the Fa-ther, now in flesh ap-pear-ing;

Text: John F. Wade, c. 1711-1786; tr. composite
Tune: John F. Wade, c. 1711-1786

ADESTE FIDELES
irregular

Christmas

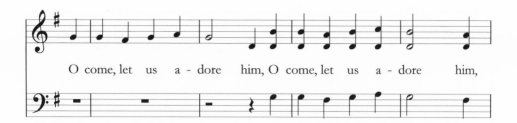

O come, let us a - dore him, O come, let us a - dore him,

O come let us a - dore him, Christ the Lord!

O Come All Ye Faithful

"Adeste Fideles" is a Latin hymn written by John Francis Wade sometime after 1743. It was translated into English first by Frederick Oakeley in 1841. The version presented here is a composite translation based on Oakeley's. This popular Christmas carol is often utilized as the opening hymn to the Christmas season.

Wade also composed the original tune ADESTE FIDELES to accompany his Latin hymn and the tune and text have remained wedded for their entire existence. Wade seems to have combined the Gregorian style plainchant common to Latin hymns with the newer more evangelical style of hymns popular in Wales.

Christmas

Away in a Manger

Text: American, 1885
Tune: American, 19th cent.

AWAY IN A MANGER
11 11 11 11

Christmas

Away in a Manger

This popular Christmas carol is a perennial favorite. It has been ascribed to Martin Luther though recent scholarship has determined this to be false. Rather the hymn has its anonymous origins in 19th century North America.

Written by James Murray, AWAY IN A MANGER is best heard as a lullaby in a lilting waltz. While this tune is perhaps the most well-known, this hymn can also be sung to CRADLE SONG by William Kirkpatrick.

Christmas

Alexander's Carol

1. Sing to our sov - ereign Sav - ior Christ Je - sus,
2. This is the day we've wait - ed and longed for,
3. Light years from now the cos - mos re - sounds with

born in a sta - ble low - - ly.
day of sal - va - tion glor - - ious.
glad an - thems ne - ver end - - ing.

Shep - herds a - dore him, wise men come laud him,
So we re - joice to lift up our voice and
Sta - ble-born babe, al - might - y to save, this

Text: Charles L. Bartow
Tune: Charles L. Bartow
Text & tune © 1987 Charles L. Bartow

ALEXANDER'S CAROL
irregular

Christmas

Mar - y's son, God's child, ho - ly.
join in the might - y cho - rus.
is your de - served thanks - gi - ving.

Shout for joy, all you an - gel choirs. Peo - ple of

earth, your prais - es of - fer now; for this

Christmas

bless - ed babe,   full   of God's love   and   grace,

is   bring - ing to   old   and   young,   wo-men, men,   the

pow - er to be   God's child - ren,   reign - ing in life   and

Christmas

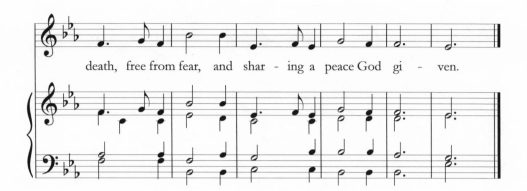

death, free from fear, and shar - ing a peace God gi - ven.

Alexander's Carol

This carol was composed in gratitude and anticipation of the birth of the author's first grandchild, Alexander Marshall. The text and melody came to him on a leisurely walk along the Mircale Mile in San Rafael, California. The birth of the grandchild was in January; the carol, while composed in the Christmas season, has Advent overtones that anticipate the child's birth.

The tune was prompted by a fragment of the opening of a piano sonata by Mozart. Concluding his walk, the author promptly sang the completed carol to his wife.

Christmas

Hark! The Herald Angels Sing

1. Hark! The her-ald an-gels sing, "Glo-ry to the new-born King; peace on hearth and mer-cy mild, God and sin-ners rec-on-ciled!" Joy-ful, all ye na-tions, rise; join the tri-umph of the skies;
2. Christ, by high-est heaven a-dored, Christ, the ev-er-last-ing Lord! Late in time be-hold him come, off-spring of the vir-gin's womb. Veiled in flesh the God-head see; hail the in-car-nate De-i-ty,
3. Hail the heaven-born Prince of Peace! Hail the Sun of Right-eous-ness! Light and life to all he brings, risen with heal-ing in his wings. Mild, he lays his glo-ry by, born that we no more may die,

Text: Charles Wesley, 1707-1739, alt.
Tune: Felix Mendelssohn, 1809-1840

MENDELSSOHN
7 7 7 7 D and refrain

Christmas

with   the an-gel - ic   hosts pro-claim,   "Christ is   born in   Beth-le-hem!"
pleased   as   man with   us   to dwell,   Je - sus,   our Em - man - u - el.
born   to   raise the   lost on earth,   born to   give them sec-ond birth.

Hark! The her-ald   an-gels sing,   "Glo-ry   to   the   new-born King!"

Hark! The Herald Angels Sing

Charles Wesley began to write the first version of this hymn as "Hark, how all the welkin rings/Glory to the King of kings." The more familiar version appeared in George Whitefield's *A Collection of Hymns for Social Worship*, (1753).

MENDELSSOHN, also known by several other titles, was taken from Felix Mendelssohn's *Festgesang an die Künstler*. Op. 68. It was written to celebrate the 400th anniversary of printing in 1840. It was first published as the setting for Wesley's hymn in 1857.

Christmas

O Little Town of Bethlehem

1. O little town of Beth-le-hem, how still we see thee lie!
2. For Christ is born of Mar - y, and, gath-ered all a - bove
3. How si - lent - ly, how si - lent-ly the won-drous gift is giv'n!
4. O ho - ly Child of Beth-le-hem, de-scend to us we pray;

A - bove thy deep and dream-less sleep the si - lent stars go by;
while mor-tals sleep, the an - gels keep their watch of won-d'ring love.
So God im-parts to hu - man hearts the bless-ings of his heav'n.
cast our our sin, and en - ter in, be born in us to - day.

yet in thy dark streets shin - eth the ev - er - last-ing light.
O morn-ing stars, to - geth - er pro - claim the ho - ly birth,
No ear may hear his com - ing; but in this world of sin,
We hear the Christ-mas an - gels the great glad tid-ings tell;

The hopes and fears of all the years are met in thee to-night.
and prais-es sing to God the King, and peace to all the earth!
where meek souls will re-ceive him, still the dear Christ en - ters in.
Oh, come to us, a - bide with us, our Lord Em - man - u - el!

Text: Phillips Brooks, 1835-1893   ST. LOUIS
Tune: Lewis H. Redner, 1831-1908   8 6 8 6 7 6 8 6

O Little Town of Bethlehem

Phillips Brooks traveled to Bethlehem in 1865 where he attended a Christmas Eve service at the Church of the Nativity. The trip is thought to have inspired this hymn which was written for Brooks' Sunday school group in 1868. It was used for the Sunday school's Christmas service that year and has become a favorite Christmas carol.

Lewis Redner wrote ST. LOUIS for this text at Brooks' request. It was used at the first public singing of this hymn. Despite this, the tune FOREST GREEN has often been used to sing this hymn.

Christmas

The Wonder of God's Grace

1. When the cold was in the air and the
2. When the ba - by ceased his cry at the
3. When the an - gels in the night lit the

mo - ther full of care, bore the Babe in a sta - ble there in
low - ing lul - la - bye, as he lay in a man - ger there in
hea - vens with their light as they told of the ba - by born in

Beth - le - hem; when the hand - maid of the Blest fed the
Beth - le - hem; when the shep - herds knelt to pray for the
Beth - le - hem; when the na - tal star a - bove marked the

Sa - vior at her breast, then the world knew the won - der of God's
One u - pon the hay, then the world knew the won - der of God's
birth - place of God's love, then the world knew the won - der of God's

Text: Clayton J. Schmit
Tune: Clayton J. Schmit
Text & tune © 1993 Clayton J. Schmit

TOMAHAWK
irregular

Christmas

The Wonder of God's Grace

This Christmas carol was written at the request of the composer's home congregation, Grace Lutheran Church in Tomahawk, Wisconsin, for the celebration of the congregation's one-hundredth anniversary in 1993. The use of the word "grace" creates an intentional word play on the name of the congregation.

The tune TOMAHAWK was created originally for the text. The composer's intention was to attempt to create a tune that reflected the northern European folk character of the people of the congregation.

Christmas

Angels from the Realms of Glory

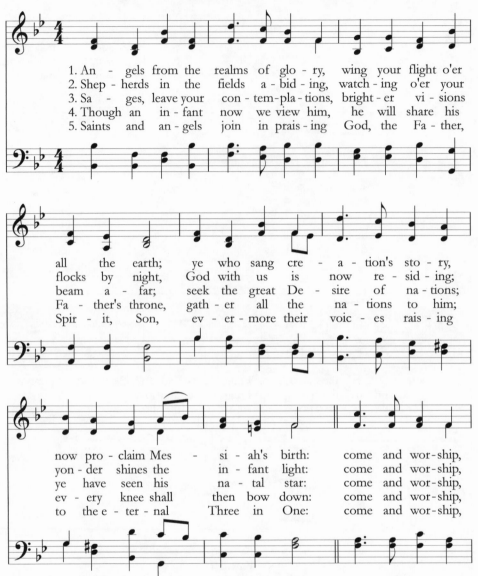

1. An - gels from the   realms of glo - ry,   wing your flight o'er
2. Shep - herds in the   fields a - bid - ing,   watch - ing o'er your
3. Sa - ges, leave your   con - tem - pla - tions,   bright - er   vi - sions
4. Though an   in - fant   now we view him,   he will share his
5. Saints and an - gels   join in prais - ing   God, the   Fa - ther,

all   the   earth;   ye who sang cre - a - tion's sto - ry,
flocks   by   night,   God with us   is   now   re - sid - ing;
beam   a - far;   seek the great De - sire   of   na - tions;
Fa - ther's throne,   gath - er   all   the   na - tions to him;
Spir - it,   Son,   ev - er - more their   voic - es   rais - ing

now pro - claim Mes   -   si - ah's birth: come and wor - ship,
yon - der shines the   in - fant light: come and wor - ship,
ye   have   seen his   na - tal   star: come and wor - ship,
ev - ery   knee shall   then bow down: come and wor - ship,
to   the e - ter - nal   Three   in   One: come and wor - ship,

Text: James Montgomery, 1771-1854, alt.
Tune: Henry Smart, 1813-1879

REGENT SQUARE
878787

Christmas

come   and   wor - ship,   wor - ship   Christ,   the   new-born   King!

Angels From the Realms of Glory

The text first appeared as "Nativity" in *The Sheffield Iris*, December 24, 1816, penned by the paper's editor James Montgomery. Montgomery was a poet whose work often addressed abolitionist concerns, and a significant contributor to English hymnody. It appeared in *A Selection of Psalms and Hymns for Public and Private Use* (1819), and was later revised and published in Montgomery's *The Christian Psalmist* (1825).

REGENT SQUARE was written by Henry Smart for *Psalms and Hymns for Divine Worship* (1867). The tune was named for the publisher's congregation, Regent Square Church, the English Presbyterian cathedral in London. The tune was composed for Horatius Bonar's "Glory be to God the Father."

Christmas

Angels We Have Heard On High

1. An - gels we have heard on high, sweet - ly sing - ing
2. Shep - herds, why this ju - bi - lee? Why your joy - ous
3. Come to Beth - le - hem and see him whose birth the

o'er the plain. And the moun - tains in re - ply
strains pro - long? What the glad - some ti - dings be
an - gels sing; come, a - dore on bend - ed knee

ech - o - ing their joy - ous strain.
which in - spire your heav - 'nly song? Glo - - -
Christ the Lord, the new - born King.

- - - - - - - - - - - - ri - a

Text: French carol; tr. "Crown of Jesus," 1862
Tune: French Carol

GLORIA
7 7 7 7 and refrain

Christmas

Angels We Have Heard On High

This French carol, "Les anges dans nos campagnes," was first published in
Nouveau ecueil de cantiques (1855). The text's origin is unknown, although
believed to date from the eighteenth century (as noted by Jan R.H. de Smidt,
Les Noels et al tradition popularie, 1932). The popular English translation
"Angels We Have Heard on High" first appeared in *Crown of Jesus Music*
(1862). Its author is also unknown.

GLORIA appeared with the original French publication, also likely an
eighteenth century composition. It occurred with other translations of the
French text. The tune is also known as IRIS.

Christmas

Silent Night, Holy Night!

1. Si - lent night, ho - ly night. All is calm,
2. Si - lent night, ho - ly night! Shep - herds quake
3. Si - lent night, ho - ly night! Son of God,

all is bright round yon vir - gin moth-er and child.
at the sight; glo - ries stream from heav-en a - far,
love's pure light ra - diant beams from thy ho - ly face,

Ho - ly In - fant so ten - der and mild, sleep in heav - en-ly
heav'n-ly hosts sing al - le - lu - ia! Christ the Sav - ior is
with the dawn of re - deem - ing grace, Je - sus, Lord, at thy

peace, sleep in heav - en - ly peace.
born! Christ the Sav - ior is born!
birth, Je - sus, Lord, at thy birth.

Text: Joseph Mohr, 1792-1849; tr. John F. Young, 1820-1885   STILLE NACHT
Tune: Franz Gruber, 1787-1863   irregular

Christmas

Silent Night, Holy Night!

This much loved Christmas carol has one of the most well-known stories of origin. The organ at St. Nikolaus Church in Oberndorf, Germany was out of order on Christmas Eve in 1818. One of the parish priests, Joseph Mohr, scrambled to provide music for the services that evening. He quickly wrote this hymn, passed it to the parish musician, Franz Gruber, who wrote the tune and arranged it for two voices, choir, and guitar. Since its original performance, it has been copied, translated, and arranged countless times. The English version we have here was translated by John Young in 1887.

Christmas

Infant Holy, Infant Lowly

1. In - fant ho - ly, in - fant low - ly, for his bed a cat - tle stall;
2. Flocks were sleep-ing, shep-herds keep-ing vig - il   till the morn-ing new

ox - en low-ing, lit - tle know-ing Christ the child is Lord of all.
saw the glo - ry, heard the sto - ry, tid - ings of a gos - pel true.

Swift-ly wing-ing an - gels sing-ing, bells are ring-ing, tid - ings bring-ing:
Thus re-joic - ing, free from sor-row, prais-es voic-ing, greet the mor - row:

Christ the child is Lord of all! Christ the child is Lord of all!
Christ the child was born for you! Christ the child was born for you!

Text: Polish carol; tr. Edith M.G. Reed, 1885-1933, alt.
Tune: Polish carol

W ZLOBIE LEZY
87878877

Infant Holy, Infant Lowly

This Polish Christmas carol may date as far back to the 13th century. It was translated into English in 1877 by Edith Reed. Reed dedicated her life to educating children in music. During her life she edited music magazines for children and wrote two Christmas plays.

W ZLOBIE LEZY is the original Polish tune which accompanied this hymn. The tune is structured like a mazurka, a Polish folk dance. During the Romantic period of classical music, the mazurka became a popular composition form for solo piano with the works of Chopin perhaps being the most characteristic. In many ways, this tune has been restrained by performance practice which has more often than not presented this tune in a slow tempo. The hymn, however, may best be sung in its original intended lively tempo.

Epiphany

Jesus is the Light of the World

Je - sus   is the light   of the world,   Je - sus   is the light of the world,

Je - sus   is the light   of the world,   Come on and let Him shine on you.

Text: Mark G. Anzelon
Tune: Mark G. Anzelon
Text & tune © 1998 Mark G. Anzelon

JESUS IS THE LIGHT OF THE WORLD
irregular

Epiphany

Jesus is the Light of the World

An electrical engineer who writes and sing faith based songs, Mark Anzelon serves as music director of Lutheran Church in the Foothills in La Cañada, California. This text, with its tune, was written for use in worship in 1988 in the style of "contemporary" Christian music.

Lent and Holy Week

O Sacred Head, Now Wounded

1. O sa-cred head, now wound-ed, with grief and shame weighed
2. My Lord, what you did suf-fer was all for sin-ners'
3. What lan-guage shall I bor-row to thank you, dear-est

down, now scorn-ful-ly sur-round-ed with thorns, your on-ly
gain; mine, mine was the trans-gres-ion, but yours the dead-ly
Friend, for this, your dy-ing sor-row, your mer-cy with-out

crown. O sa-cred head, what glo-ry and bless-ing you have
pain. So here I kneel, my Sav-ior, for I de-serve your
end? Lord, make me yours for-ev-er, a loy-al ser-vant

known! Yet, though de-spised and gor-y, I claim you as my own.
place; look on me with your fa-vor and save me by your grace.
true, and let me nev-er, nev-er out-live my love for you.

Text: Anon. Latin
Tune: Hans L. Hassler, 1564-1612

PASSION CHORALE
7 6 7 6 D

Lent and Holy Week

O Sacred Head Now Wounded

First popularized by Paul Gerhardt in German, this hymn has been a staple of Passion Week hymnody for centuries. Based on the Latin poem *"Salve, mundi salutare,"* "O Sacred Head" is full of Passion imagery and rich language. Though first translated into English by James Waddell Alexander in 1831, the version here is a composite translation.

PASSION CHORAL is often known by its German name HERZLICH TUT MICH VERLANGEN. It was originally a German secular song adapted by Hans Leo Hassler in 1601 for this hymn. The original tune flits between two and three subdivisions of the tactus (the "pulse" of the peice), common in Reformation era hymnody. The version presented here is the isometric version most popular today. J. S. Bach used this version extensively in his St. Matthew Passion.

Lent and Holy Week

Ah, Holy Jesus

1. Ah,   ho - ly   Je - sus,   how have you of - fend - ed,
2. Who   was the   guilt - y?   Who brought this up - on   you?
3. For   me, dear   Je - sus,   was your in - car - na - tion,
4. There-fore, dear   Je - sus,   Since I can-not   pay   you,

that mor-tal judg-ment has   on   you de - scend-ed?   By   foes de-
It   is my 'trea-son, Lord, that has un - done you. 'Twas I, Lord
your mor-tal sor-row,   and your life's ob - la - tion; your death of
I   do a - dore you   and will ev - er   pray you, think on your

rid - ed   by your own re - ject - ed,   O   most af - flict - ed!
Je - sus,   I   it was de - nied you;   I   cru - ci - fied you.
an-guish   and your bit - ter pas - sion, for   my sal - va - tion.
pit - y   and your love un - swerv-ing,   not   my de - serv - ing.

Text: Johann Heermann, 1585-1647; tr. by Robert S. Bridges, 1844-1930   HERZLIEBSTER
Tune: Johann Crüger, 1598-1662   11 11 11 5

Lent and Holy Week

Ah, Holy Jesus

This German hymn by hymn writer Johann Heermann was based on a Latin meditation by Jean de Fécamp (d. 1078). Heermann, a prolific writer, marked a transition from the objective hymns of the Reformation to a period of more subjective hymns. The English text originally appeared in *The Yattendon Hymnal* (published in four parts, 1895-1899), translated by Robert Seymour Bridges, poet laureate of Britan.

Herzliebster Jesu first appeared, with harmonization, in a 1640 Berliner hymnal, Johann Crüger's *Neues vollkömliches Gesangbuch Augsburgischer Confession*. It suggests the influence of the 1534 Genevan Psalter's setting for Psalm 23, and the 1627 tune "Gelieben Freund" by Johann Hermann Schein. Schein was a theologically educated Lutheran chorister who devoted his later life to church music.

Lent and Holy Week

Ah, Friend, What Have You Done?

1. Ah friend, what have you done? Why have you for-sa-ken Him,
2. Ah friend, what have you done? Why have you for-sa-ken Him?
3. Ah friends, what have we done? Why have we for-sa-ken Him?
4. Ah friends, what can we do? How can we now ho-nor Him?

in the gar-den late that night, with a kiss? It
Bit-ter cold their looks that night by the fire. His
Near the heart of faith-ful-ness lin-gers fear. The
Bow we down and wor-ship on bend-ed knee. Con-

was the be-gin-ning. It was the end. Oh
Rock, His com-pan-ion; yet thrice by the dawn, oh
kiss of be-tray-al, de-ni-al and shame. Oh
fess our be-tray-als; a-mend our lives, and

Text: Clayton J. Schmit
Tune: Clayton J. Schmit
Text and Tune © 2007 Clayton J. Schmit

LILAC CAROL
irregular

Lent and Holy Week

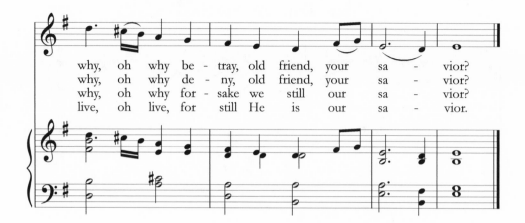

why, oh why be - tray, old friend, your sa - vior?
why, oh why de - ny, old friend, your sa - vior?
why, oh why for - sake we still our sa - vior?
live, oh live, for still He is our sa - vior.

Ah, Friend, What Have You Done?

The text for this hymn is a meditation on two events of the Passion: the betrayal of Jesus by his friend Judas and the denial of Jesus by his friend Peter. The text was composed as part of a choral presentation that interspersed musical reflections with episodes from the Passion story, the reading of which was an annual Palm Sunday tradition at Elim Lutheran Church in Petaluma, California.

The tune, LILAC CAROL, was originally composed as a folk-style song written for the composer's wife. Lilac refers to the original text which reads, in part, "Ah, see the lilacs, with beauty so rare."

Lent and Holy Week

Alas, And Did My Savior Bleed

1. A - las! And did my Sav - ior bleed, and did my Sov - ereign die? Would he de - vote that sa - cred head for sin - ners such as I?
2. Was it for sins that I have done he groaned up - on the tree? A - maz - ing pi - ty, grace un - known, and love be - yond de - gree!
3. Well might the sun in dark - ness hide and shut its glo - ries in when Christ, the might - y Mak - er, died for his own crea - tures' sin.
4. Thus might I hide my blush - ing face while his dear cross ap - pears, dis - solve my heart in thank - ful - ness, and melt mine eyes to tears.

Text: Isaac Watts, 1674-1748

Tune: Attr. to Hugh Wilson, 1766-1824

MARTYRDOM
CM

Lent and Holy Week

Alas, And Did My Savior Bleed

Isaac Watts' career as a hymn writer began with the challenge to write something he liked better than the psalmody in his Anglican congregation. This hymn appeared in *Hymns and Spiritual Songs* Bk II (1707) with the heading, "Godly Sorrow arising from the Sufferings of Christ." Changes to the text often attempt to contemporize Watts' "for such a worm as I" and to account for the theological issues of "When God, the mighty maker died."

MYRTYRDOM appears to come from a Scottish folk melody, "Helen of Kirkconnel," and was originally arranged in common time. A dispute over its current form determined Hugh Wilson (1766-1824) to be the original copyright owner. Wilson occasionally led the singing of psalmody in his Secession Church.

Easter

Christ the Lord Is Risen Today

1. Christ the Lord is   risen to - day!   Al - le - lu - ia!
2. Love's re-deem-ing   work is   done,   Al - le - lu - ia!
3. Lives a - gain our   glo - rious King;   Al - le - lu - ia!
4. Soar we now where Christ has   led,   Al - le - lu - ia!
5. Hail the Lord of   earth and heaven!   Al - le - lu - ia!

All   cre - a - tion, join to   say: Al - le - lu - ia!
Fought the fight, the bat - tle won;   Al - le - lu - ia!
Where, O death, is now your sting?   Al - le - lu - ia!
Fol - lowing our ex - alt - ed Head;   Al - le - lu - ia!
Ris - en Christ, tri - um - phant now;   Al - le - lu - ia!

Raise your joys and tri - umphs high; Al - le - lu - ia!
Death in   vain for - bids him rise; Al - le - lu - ia!
Once he   died, our souls to save; Al - le - lu - ia!
Made like him, like him we rise; Al - le - lu - ia!
Ris - en Christ, tri - um - phant now; Al - le - lu - ia!

Text: Charles Wesley, 1707-1788, alt.
Tune: attr. to J. Walsh, *Lyrica Davidica*, ca. 1708

EASTER HYMN
7 7 7 7 and alleluias

Easter

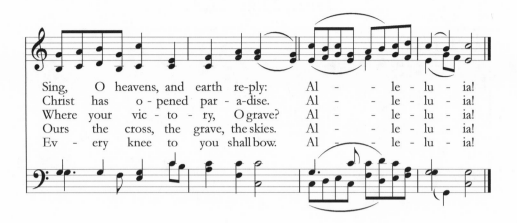

Sing, O heavens, and earth re-ply: Al - - le - lu - ia!
Christ has o - pened par - a-dise. Al - - le - lu - ia!
Where your vic - to - ry, O grave? Al - - le - lu - ia!
Ours the cross, the grave, the skies. Al - - le - lu - ia!
Ev - ery knee to you shall bow. Al - - le - lu - ia!

Christ the Lord Is Risen Today

Charles Wesley composed "Christ the Lord Is Risen Today" in the first year after his conversion. Wesley's hymn did not include the celebrative "Alleluia!" of its present form. Few contemporary hymnals include his final six stanzas, further highlighting events of the Passion and resurrection narratives. The "Alleluia!" refrain was likely added when the hymn was wedded to an older tune.

EASTER HYMN is also called Worgan. It first appeared in *Lyrica Davidica* around 1708, set to a similar text called "Jesus Christ is Risen Today," a Latin hymn from the fourteenth century, published by John Walsh. The tune has variously been ascribed to "Dr. Worgan" and Henry Edward Dibdin. The alternative text is featured below.

Jesus Christ is Risen Today

1. Jesus Christ is risen today, Alleluia!
   Our triumphant holy day, Alleluia!
   Who did once upon the cross, Alleluia!
   Suffer to redeem our loss, Alleluia!

2. Hymns of praise then let us sing, Alleluia!
   Unto Christ, our heavenly king, Alleluia!
   Who endured the cross and grave, Alleluia!
   Sinners to redeem and save. Alleluia!

3. But the pains which he endured, Alleluia!
   Our salvation have procurred; Alleluia!
   Now above the sky he's king, Alleluia!
   Where the angels ever sing. Alleluia!

Trinity

Holy, Holy, Holy

1. Holy, ho-ly, ho - ly! Lord   God Al - might - y!
2. Holy, ho-ly, ho - ly! All   the saints a - dore thee,
3. Holy, ho-ly, ho - ly! Though   the dark-ness hide thee,
4. Holy, ho-ly, ho - ly! Lord   God Al - might - y!

Ear - ly in the morn - ing our song shall rise to thee;
cast - ing down their gold - en crowns a - round the glass-y sea;
though the eye made blind by sins thy glo - ry may not see,
All   thy works shall praise thy name, in   earth and sky and sea;

ho - ly, ho - ly, ho - ly!   mer - ci - ful and might - y,
cher - u - bim and ser - a - phim   fall - ing down be - fore thee,
on - ly thou art ho - ly;   there is non be - side thee,
ho - ly, ho - ly, ho - ly!   mer - ci - ful and might - y,

Text: Reginald Heber, 1783-1826, alt.
Tune: John B. Dykes, 1823-1876

NICAEA
11 12 12 10

Trinity

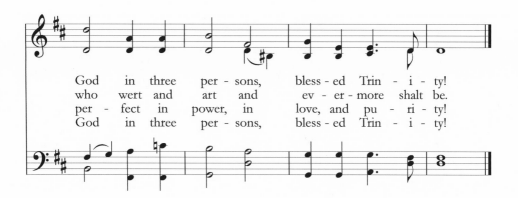

God in three per-sons, bless-ed Trin - i - ty!
who wert and art and ev-er-more shalt be.
per - fect in power, in love, and pu - ri - ty!
God in three per-sons, bless-ed Trin - i - ty!

Holy, Holy, Holy

This well known hymn of Reginald Heber's first appeared in *A Selection of Psalms and Hymns for the Parish Church of Banbury* (1826).

NICEA is aptly named for the Trinitarian council of 325. Written by John Bacchus Dykes, it was wedded to Heber's text in the 1861 edition of *Hymns Ancient and Modern*.

Christ the King

Crown Him with Many Crowns

1. Crown him with man-y crowns, the Lamb up-on his throne, while
2. Crown him the Lord of life, who tri-umphed o'er the grave, who
3. Crown him the Lord of peace; his-king-dom is at hand. From

heaven's e-ter-nal an-them drowns all mu-sic but its own! A-
rose vic-to-rious from the strife for those he came to save. His
pole to pole let war-fare cease and Christ rule ev-ery land! All

wake, my soul, and sing of him who died for thee, and
glo-ries now we sing who died and reigns on high; he
hail, Re-deem-er, hail, for thou hast died for me. Thy

hail him as thy match-less King through all e-ter-ni-ty.
died e-ter-nal life to bring, and lives that death may die.
praise and glo-ry shall not fail through-out e-ter-ni-ty.

Text: Matthew Bridges, 1800-1894; Godfrey Thring, 1823-1903   DIADEMATA
Tune: George J. Elvey, 1816-1893   SMD

Christ the King

Crown Him with Many Crowns

This text first appeared in Anglican hymn writer Matthew Bridges' *Hymns of the Heart* (1851). The hymn was first printed with a reference to Revelation 19:12. Bridges, who, shortly after is publication converted to Roman Catholicism in the wake of the Oxford Movement, later called the text "The Song of the Seraphs." Godfrey Thring was a hymn editor and publisher as well as a Anglican priest. He modified many texts for publication in his collections, such as *A Church of England Songbook*, 1880.

DIADEMATA was written for this hymn by George Job Elvey, appearing in an 1868 appendix to the popular Hymns Ancient and Modern (1816). Elvey was appointed by King William IV to St. George's Chapel, Windsor.

Word

A Mighty Fortress Is Our God

1. A might - y for - tress is our God, a bul - wark nev - er fail - ing; our help - er he, a - mid the flood of mor - tal ills pre - vail - ing. For still our an - cient foe does seek to work us woe; his
2. Did we in our own strength con - fide, our striv - ing would be los - ing, were not the right Man on our side, the Man of God's own choos - ing. You ask who that may be? Christ Je - sus, it is he; Lord
3. And though this world, with de - vils filled, should threat - en to un - do us, we will not fear, for God has willed his truth to tri - umph through us. The prince of dark - ness grim, we trem - ble not for him; his
4. That Word a - bove all earth - ly powers— no thanks to them— a - bid - eth; the Spir - it and the gifts are ours through him who with us sid - eth. Let goods and kin - dred go, this mor - tal life al - so; the

Text: Martin Luther, 1483-1546
Tune: Martin Luther

EIN FESTE BURG
8 7 8 7 6 6 6 6 7

Word

craft	and	power	are	great,	and	armed	with	cru -	el
Sa -	ba -	oth	his	name,	from	age	to	age	the
rage	we	can	en -	dure,	for	lo!	his	doom	is
bod -	y	they	may	kill:	God's	truth	a -	bid -	eth

hate,	on	earth	is	not	his	e - - -	qual.
same;	and	he	must	win	the	bat - - -	tle.
sure;	one	lit - tle	word	shall	fell		him.
still;	his	king - dom	is	for -	ev - - -		er!

A Mighty Fortress Is Our God

Luther based his German text, *"Ein' Feste Burg ist Unser Gott,"* on Psalm 46. Although not linked to any single occasion in his life, the hymn was considered the battle hymn of the Reformation. When discouraged by great opposition, Luther turned to friend Philip Melanchthon with the invitation, "Come, Philip, let us sing the Forty-sixth Psalm." The text was frequently translated into English, but its most popular American incarnation is by poet, pastor, and German scholar Frederic Henry Hedge, first appearing in 1852.

EIN FESTE BURG was possibly adapted by Luther, although many claim it is his original composition. The earliest preserved publication of the tune is from 1531.

Word

I Will Lift Up My Eyes to the Hills

Text: Clayton J. Schmit (Ps. 121)
Tune: Clayton J. Schmit
Text & tune © 2014 Clayton J. Schmit

I WILL LIFT UP MY EYES
irregular

Word

To verse 1, 2, 3 — Last Time

Lord who made the heav'ns and earth. earth.

Lord who made the heav'ns and earth. earth.

1. The Lord will guard your ev-'ry move and ne - ver look a -
2. The Lord who wat - ches o - ver you will shade you from the

way. The Lord who cares for Is - ra - el will
sun. It shall not smite you through the day, nor

Word

nei - ther slum-ber nor sleep.   3. The   Lord will keep you from
shall the moon by   night.

e - vil.   The   Lord   will keep you   safe.   The

Lord will watch you where-e'er you go, for   now and e -ver - more.

Word

I Will Lift Up My Eyes

This metrical setting of Psalm 121 was composed for use in worship at Elim Lutheran Church in Petaluma, California. Its composer served the congregation as associate pastor and choral director from 1986-1998.

Word

O Lord, my Heart Is Not Lifted Up

O Lord, my heart is not lift-ed

up;   my   eyes are not   raised   too

Text: Clayton J. Schmit (Ps. 131)
Tune: Clayton J. Schmit
Text & tune © 2010 Clayton J. Schmit

O LORD MY HEART IS NOT LIFTED UP
irregular

Word

Word

weaned child   in mo - ther's arms.   *All:*   But
mo - ment,   for - ev - er - more.   *All:*   O

I have calmed and qui - et - ed   my   soul   like   a
Is - ra - el your hope is   in   the   Lord   from this

To Refrain

weaned child   in mo-ther's arms.   O   O
mo - ment,   for - ev - er - more.   O   O

Word

O Lord my Heart Is Not Lifted Up

This metrical paraphrase and setting of Psalm 131 was originally prepared by the composer for use at a Duke Divinity School faculty retreat in 1999. Text and tune were composed simultaneously.

Word

Search Me, O God

1. Search me, O God, and know my heart and
2. With-in the womb's warm sol-i-tude you
3. If I should rise on wings of dawn, or
4. How pre-cious are your thoughts, O Lord, as

lead me in your way.   You know my thoughts, my
formed me as a child.   With-in the palm of
dwell a-cross the sea,   I find that you are
deep as a-ny sea;   Vast as the sand u-

ev-ery word; be with me all my days.
your right hand, I shall be safe-ly held.
al-ways there, you're ev-er near to me.
pon the shore, too won-der-ful for me.

Text: Janice Kibler and Clayton J. Schmit (Ps. 139)
Tune: Clayton J. Schmit
Text © 2010 Janice Kibler and Clayton J. Schmit
Tune: © 2010 Clayton J. Schmit

DINANE
irregular

Word

Search me, O God, and know my heart and lead me in your

way. Search me, O God, and know my heart and

lead me, lead me, lead me in your way.

Search Me, O God

This text grew out of a collaborative effort by students in Gracia Grindal's 1983 course at Luther Seminary on hymn text writing. The composer, along with Janice Kibler and others, contributed stanzas for a metrical paraphrase of Psalm 139 as a class assignment. Ultimately, the composer and Kibler developed the text as it is given here.

The tune, DINANE, is named for a member of the composer's family. It was composed the evening of the day that the original text was developed in the class. It was sung first at the seminary chapel service the following week.

Word

Have Mercy On Me, O God

1. Have mer - cy u - pon me, O God, ac - cord - ing
2. I hate my trans-gres-sions, O God, and I re -
3. For I have re - belled from my birth; my ve - ry
4. Cre - ate in my now a clean heart; re - new your
5. O - pen now my lips with praise and let my

to your lov - ing kind - ness, ac - cord - ing
pent my sins be - fore you. A - gainst you
bones have gone a - gainst you. O teach me
Spi - rit in me whol - ly. O cast me
mouth show forth your great - ness. Do not de -

to your ten - der mer - cy. Blot out my trans -
on - ly have I sinned. And done what is
all your truth in sec - ret And purge me with
not a - way to dark - ness And take not your
spise my bro - ken spi - rit; Have mer - cy u -

Text: Gracia Grindal (Psalm 51, adapted)
Tune: Clayton J. Schmit
Text © 1998 Gracia Grindal
Tune: © 1998 Clayton J. Schmit

KELLGREN
9 9 6 6 6

Word

gres - sions,   and wash me   tho - rough - ly.   O   cleanse me
e - vil   with - in your   sight,   O   God.   Wash   me   and
hys - sop;   and then I   shall   be   clean.   O   fill   me
Spi - rit   from me, O   Bles - sed One.   O   Lord,   re -
pon me,   O   God of   hosts,   I   cry.   Cleanse me   and

from   my   sin.
make   me   clean.
with   your   joy.
store   my   soul.
make   me   whole.

Have Mercy on Me

In 1983, hymn writer Gracia Grindal offered a Luther Seminary course on hymn text writing. The composer of KELLGREN was a student in the class, along with celebrated hymn writer, Rusty Edwards. Grindal provided musicians in the class with examples of her own metrical text paraphrasing, giving them the option to set them to music. This version of Psalm 51 was used later during the composer's pastoral work at Elim Lutheran Church in Petaluma, California to develop the tune KELLGREN. The tune is named for the senior pastor at the time, Timothy Kellgren.

Communion

Let Us Break Bread Together

1. Let us break bread to-geth-er on our knees;
2. Let us drink wine to-geth-er on our knees;
3. Let us praise God to-geth-er on our knees;

let us break bread to-geth-er on our knees.
let us drink wine to-geth-er on our knees.
let us praise God to-geth-er on our knees.

When I fall on my knees, with my face to the ris-ing

sun, O Lord, have mer-cy on me.

Text: African American spiritual
Tune: African American spiritual

BREAK BREAD TOGETHER
10 10 and refrain

Communion

Let Us Break Bread Together

This spiritual has obvious eucharistic overtones with references to breaking break and drinking wine. Kneeling can be seen as penitential, an image which works well with the phrase "O Lord, have mercy on me." It can also be seen as worshipful, as in "let us praise God together on our knees." Or it may simply be a reference to the way in which communion is sometimes received. The phrase "with my face to the rising sun" refers to the way some worship spaces are oriented with the people facing east.*

BREAK BREAD TOGETHER is a traditional spiritual melody. It gradually rises, suggesting imagery of the rising sun.

* Worship spaces began to be oriented to the east around the 4th century. This, in part, represented a desire to face Jerusalem during worship, the place of crucifixion and resurrection of Christ. Additionally, as pagan converts were brought into the Church during this time, some places chose to incorporate elements of pagan worship. Sun worship being common among pagans, the Church merely reappropriated worshipers' orientation toward the sun, baptizing the practice to represent Christian imagery.

Communion

Christ, You Are Known

Christ, you are known in the break-ing of the bread;
you give us hope for to-mor - row. Your love is shown in the

Text: Clayton J. Schmit
Tune: Clayton J. Schmit
Text & tune © 1998 Clayton J. Schmit

CHRIST YOU ARE KNOWN
irregular

Communion

free-ly flow-ing wine;   you give us hope for to-mor - row.

Christ, You Are Known

This communion song was composed for a synodical assembly in the Sierra Pacific Synod of the Evangelical Lutheran Church in America. The assembly theme was "Making Christ Known." The text reflects Lutheran sacramental theology which holds that Christ is both known and present in the bread and wine of communion.

The piece is intended to be sung as a cyclical chant, repeated as often as desired. It can be sung from memory by those going forward to receive the sacrament. The flute descant can be played by any C instrument.

The Hours

Abide With Me

1. A - bide with me, fast falls the e - ven - tide.
2. Swift to its close ebbs out life's lit - tle day;
3. I need your pres - ence ev - ery pass - ing hour.
4. I fear no foe with thee at hand to bless.
5. Hold now thy cross be - fore my clos - ing eyes.

The dark - ness deep - ens; Lord, with me a - bide.
earth's joys grow dim, its glo - ries pass a - way.
What but your grace can foil the tempt - er's power?
Ills have no weight, and tears no bit - ter - ness.
Shine through the gloom and point me to the skies.

When oth - er help - ers fail and com - forts flee,
Change and de - cay in all a - round I see.
Who like your - self my guide and strength can be?
Where is death's sting? Where, grave, thy vic - to - ry?
Heaven's morn - ing breaks and earth's vain shad - ows flee;

Text: Henry F. Lyte, 1793-1847
Tune: William H. Monk, 1823-1889

EVENTIDE
10 10 10 10

The Hours

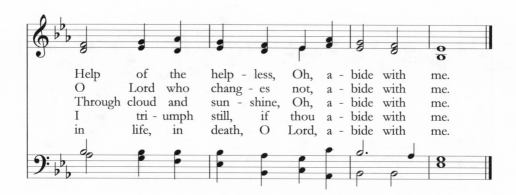

Help of the help-less, Oh, a - bide with me.
O Lord who chang - es not, a - bide with me.
Through cloud and sun - shine, Oh, a - bide with me.
I tri - umph still, if thou a - bide with me.
in life, in death, O Lord, a - bide with me.

Abide With Me

This hymn is frequently used at evening services, such as compline, as well as at funerals due to its use of metaphoric language. Here, a lifetime is compared to a single day in the sight of God, evocative of Psalm 90. While death is compared to the darkness of night, the hymn looks forward to the morning dawn of new life in Christ. Other biblical references include an allusion to the Road to Emmaus story (Luke 24) where two disciples request Jesus to stay with them as the day is nearly over.

Though Henry Lyte, author of the text, wrote his own tune for this hymn, it is the tune EVENTIDE written by William Monk that has become the most associated with the hymn. The tune is contemplative and, while intended to be sung at a slow tempo, can easily be sung too slowly. Monk was an advocate of strong congregational singing and wrote his tunes with the intention that they be sung easily and vigorously.

Community in Christ

In Christ There Is No East or West

1. In Christ there is no east or west, in
2. For God in Christ has made us one from
3. It is by grace we are as-sured that
4. So, broth-ers, sis-ters, praise his name who
5. In Christ there is no east or west— he

him no south or north, but one great fel-low-
ev-ery land and race; he rec-on-ciled us
we be-long to him; the love we share in
died to set us free from sin, di-vi-sion,
breaks all bar-riers down; by Christ re-deemed, by

ship of love through-out the whole wide earth.
through his Son and met us with his grace.
Christ our Lord, the Spir-it works with-in.
hate, and shame, from spite and en-mi-ty.
Christ pos-sessed, in Christ we live as one.

Text: John Oxenham, 1852-1941

Tune: African American spiritual; adapt. Harry T. Burleigh, 1866-1949

MCKEE
CM

Community in Christ

In Christ There Is No East or West

John Oxenham is a pseudonym for William Arthur Dunkerley, the son of an English merchant. At various times in his life he lived in France, Scotland, and New York, often working as a publisher. After World War I he began to write novels, including fictional accounts of Christ's life. This hymn was first published in 1913 in the collection of poems *Bees in Amber*.

Originally an African American spiritual, MCKEE was adapted by Henry Burleigh for this text. A unique wedding of an English text with an African American tune has lent to the popularity of this hymn beyond the communities of its origin. Notice the so-called Scotch snap, characteristic of spirituals, in the second to last measure, deviating from the otherwise steady and predictable rhythm.

Community in Christ

Glorious Things of Thee Are Spoken

1. Glo - rious things of thee are spo-ken, Zi - on, cit - y of our God. He whose word can - not be bro - ken formed you for his own a - bode. On the Rock of A - ges found - ed, what can shake your sure re - pose? With sal -
2. See, the streams of liv - ing wa - ters, spring-ing from e - ter - nal love, well sup - ply thy sons and daugh - ters and all fear of want re - move. Who can faint while such a riv - er ev - er will their thirst as - suage? Grace which,
3. Round each hab - i - ta - tion hov-ering, see the cloud and fire ap - pear for a glo - ry and a cov - ering, show - ing that the Lord is near. Thus de - riv - ing from their glo - ry in your name. Fad - ing are the world's best ban - ner light by night and shade by day, safe they
4. Sav - ior, since of Zi-on's cit - y I through grace a mem-ber am, let the world de - ride or pit - y, I will glo - ry in your name. Fad - ing are the world's best plea - sures, all its boast - ed pomp and show; sol - id

Text: John Newton, 1725-1807, alt.
Tune: C. Hubert H. Parry, 1848-1918

RUSTINGTON
8 7 8 7 D

Community in Christ

va - tion's walls su - round - ed, thou mayest smile at all thy foes.
like the Lord, the giv - er, nev - er fails from age to age.
feed up - on the man - na which God gives them on their way.
joys and last - ing trea - sures non but Zi - on's chil-dren know.

Glorious Things of You are Spoken

While John Newton is most well-known for writing "Amazing Grace," this hymn is another of his notable compositions. First published in 1779, it is a paraphrase of Isaiah 33:20-21. Newton intended this hymn to be paired with another based on the call story of Jeremiah (Jeremiah 1:5). Both hymns end with sound reflections on God's grace, a theme throughout Newton's compositions.

RUSTINGTON is named for the town in which Hubert Parry died in 1918. The tune has an impressive range of a minor tenth with notable chromatic alterations in the melody. This contributes to the lyrical quality of through-composed tune which is easily sung by most, despite its wide range.

This hymn is also often sung to the tune AUSTRIA by Franz Joseph Hayden, 1732-1809. This tune, though named for Austria the country, is best known as the melody for Germany's national anthem.

Community in Christ

The Church's One Foundation

1. The church's one foun-da-tion is Je-sus Christ, her Lord;
2. E - lect from ev-ery na-tion, yet one o'er all the earth;
3. Though with a scorn-ful won-der the world sees her op-pressed,
4. Mid toil and trib-u-la-tion, and tu-mult of her war,

she is his new cre-a-tion by wa-ter and the Word.
her char-ter of sal-va-tion: one Lord, one faith, one birth.
by schisms rent a-sun-der, by her-e-sies dis-tressed,
she waits the con-sum-ma-tion of peace for-ev-er-more,

From heaven he came and sought her to be his ho-ly bride;
One ho-ly name she bless-es, par-takes one ho-ly food,
yet saints their watch are keep-ing; their cry goes up: "How long?"
till with the vi-sion glo-rious her long-ing eyes are blest,

with his own blood he bought her, and for her life he died.
and to one hope she press-es, with ev-ery grace en-dued.
and soon the night of weep-ing shall be the morn of song.
and the great church vic-to-rious shall be the church at rest.

Text: Samuel J. Stone, 1839-1900
Tune: Samuel S. Wesley, 1810-1876

AURELIA
7 6 7 6 D

Community in Christ

The Church's One Foundation

Samuel Stone, British clergyman, poet, and hymnwriter, wrote this hymn in 1866 as part of several other hymns dedicated to explicating the Apostles' Creed. This hymn was intended for the portion dealing with the "one, holy, catholic, and apostolic Church."

Composed in 1864 by Samuel S. Wesley, AURELIA has been joined to many different texts. Yet its paring with this hymn in 1868 is perhaps most well-known. It has a typical arc forms with the two middle phrases marking the high-points of the hymn while the first and last phrase are more grounded and lower.

Witness

What Wondrous Love Is This?

1. What wond-rous love is this, oh my soul, oh my soul! What

wond-rous love is this, oh my soul! What wondrous love is

this, that caused the Lord of bliss to bear the dread-ful curse for my

soul, for my soul, To bear the dread-ful curse for my soul!

Text: American folk hymn   WONDROUS LOVE
Tune: American folk hymn   12 9 6 6 12 9

2. When I was sinking down, sinking down, sinking down,
when I was sinking down, sinking down,
when I was sinking down beneath God's righteous frown,
Christ laid aside his crown for my soul, for my soul,
Christ laid aside his crown for my soul.

3. To God and to the Lamb I will sing, I will sing;
to God and to the Lamb I will sing;
to God and to the Lamb, who is the great I AM,
while millions join the theme, I will sing, I will sing;
while milliions join the theme, I will sing.

4. And when from death I'm free, I'll sing on, I'll sing on;
and when from death I'm free, I'll sing on;
and when from death I'm free, I'll sing and joyful be,
and through eterity I'll sing on, I'll sing on;
and Through eternity I'll sing on.

Witness

What Wondrous Love is This

First appearing in an 1811 Methodist hymnal, this anonymous hymn is an example of a shape-note hymn. In its orginal published form, each note-head has a particular shape which corresponds to the scale degree. In this minor key, square shapes are *do* and *so*, diamonds are *re*, triangles are *mi* and *la*, and circles are *fa* and *ti*. You will also notice that the melody is on the second staff, due to the fact that the melody is sung by both men and women. In performance practice, the melody is to be sung by half the women and tenors (down an octave). The top line is sung by the other half of the women and tenors (again down an octave). The bass line is sung normally. The resulting unique sound is characteristic of shape-note singing.

This simple, yet beautiful shape-note tune is typical of its genre. WONDROUS LOVE recieves its haunting character by using a pentatonic scale (five notes per octave), typical of much Southern and Appalachian hymnody.

Witness

I Love to Tell the Story

1. I love to tell the sto-ry of un-seen things a-bove, of
2. I love to tell the sto-ry; 'tis pleas-ant to re-peat what
3. I love to tell the sto-ry, for those who know it best seem

Je - sus and his glo - ry, of Je - sus and his love. I
seems, each time I tell it, more won-der-ful-ly sweet. I
hun - ger-ing and thirst-ing to hear it like the rest. And

love to tell the sto-ry be - cause I know 'tis true; it
love to tell the sto-ry, for some have nev - er heard the
when, in scenes of glo-ry I sing the new, new song, 'twill

sat - is - fies my long-ings as noth - ing else can do.
mes - sage of sal - va - tion from God's own ho - ly Word.
be the old, old sto - ry that I have loved so long.

Text: Katherine Hankey, 1834-1911   HANKEY
Tune: William G. Fischer, 1835-1912   7 6 7 6 D and refrain

Witness

I love to tell the sto-ry; 'twill be my theme in glo-ry to tell the old, old sto-ry of Je-sus and his love.

I Love to Tell the Story

Katherine Hankey was an English poet who was part of the Clapham Sect, a group of wealthy Anglican Evangelicals. Her poem "The Old, Old Story" included the text of this hymn. Notice that the text never elaborates on the contents of "the story;" in its original form it needed no elaboration as the rest of Hankey's poem explicated the story well. There are mixed feelings among church musicians concerning this hymn. Many find its accessible language appealing while others argue that it is a trite explication of evangelism.

William G. Fischer wrote the tune HANKEY, named after the composer of the text, specifically for this hymn. Fischer added the refrain.

Praise and Prayer

Oh, for a Thousand Tongues to Sing

1. Oh, for a thou - sand tongues to sing my great Re - deem - er's praise, the glo - ries of my God and King, the tri - umphs of his grace!
2. My gra - cious Mas - ter and my God, as - sist me to pro - claim, to spread through all the earth a - broad the ho - nors of your name.
3. The name of Je - sus charms our fears and bids our sor - rows cease; 'tis mu - sic in the sin - ner's ears, 'tis life and health and peace.
4. He breaks the power of can - celed sin, he sets the pris - oner free; his blood can make the foul - est clean; his blood a - vails for me.
5. He speaks, and, lis - tening to his voice, new life the dead re - ceive; the mourn - ful, bro - ken hearts re - joice; the hum - ble poor be - lieve.

6. Hear him, you deaf; you voiceless ones,
   your loosened tongues employ;
   you blind, bejold your Savior come;
   and leap, you lame, for joy!

7. To God all glory, praise, and love
   be now and ever given
   by saints below and saints above,
   the church in earth and heaven.

Text: Charles Wesley, 1707-1788
Tune: Carl G. Gläser; arr. by Lowell Mason, 1792-1872

AZMON
CM

Praise and Prayer

Oh, For a Thousand Tongues to Sing

This is perhaps the most famous hymn by Charles Wesley. He originally composed eighteen stanzas. Most modern published versions use what were originally Wesley's stanzas 7, 8, 9, 11, 13, and 1, in that order. The omitted stanzas are not lacking in quality; instead, the stanzas provided are the best of Wesley's original hymn logically arranged for congregational use.

Carl Gläser, a German composer, wrote a melody from which this tune is based. Lowell Mason modified it for use in an 1839 psalter. He initially called the tune AZMON but later renamed it DENFIELD. Nevertheless, the original name stuck, by which this hymn is known today.

Praise and Prayer

Come, Thou Almighty King

1. Come, thou al - might - y King, help us thy
2. Come, thou in - car - nate Word, gird on thy
3. Come, ho - ly Com - for - er, thy sa - cred
4. To thee, great One in Three, e - ter - nal

name to sing; help us to praise. Fa - ther all -
might - y sword; scat - ter thy foes. Let thine al -
wir - ness bear in this glad hour. Thou who al -
prais - es be hence ev - er - more! Thy sov - ereign

glo - ri - ous, o'er all vic - to - ri - ous,
might - y aid our sure de - fense be made,
might - y art, rule now in ev - ery heart,
maj - es - ty may we in glo - ry see,

come and reign o - ver us, An - cient of Days.
our soulds on thee be stayed; thy won - ders show.
and ne'er from us de - part, Spir - it of power.
and to e - ter - ni - ty love and a - dore.

Text: source unknown, c. 1757, alt.
Tune: Felice de Giardini, 1716-1796

ITALIAN HYMN
6 6 4 6 6 6 4

Praise and Prayer

Come, Thou Almighty King

Although its author is unknown, this hymn first appeared in collections rising from the Eighteenth century North American "Great Awakening." It was paired in tracts with works of the Wesleys, and later included in George Whitefield's collections. The hymn honors each member of the Trinity, and in its original tune reflected the British National Anthem.

The tune ITALIAN HYMN, also known as MOSCOW, was composed by accomplished Italian violinist Felice de Giardini. de Giardini began as a chorister at Milan Cathedral, and after unsuccessful work directing operas in Italy and England died in Russia. "Italian Hymn" is widely used across denominational hymnals.

Praise and Prayer

O Worship the King

1. O wor-ship the King all-glo-rious a-bove, O grate-ful-ly sing his power and his love: our shield and de-fend-er, the An-cient of Days, pa-
2. O tell of his might and sing of his grace, whose robe is the light, whose can-o-py space. His char-iots of wrath the deep thun-der-clouds form, and
3. Your boun-ti-ful care, what tongue can re-cite? It breathes in the air, it shines in the light; it streams from the hills, it de-scends to the plain, and
4. Frail chil-dren of dust, and fee-ble as frail, in you do we trust, nor find you to fail. Your mer-cies, how ten-der, how firm to the end, our
5. O mea-sure-less Might, un-change-a-ble Love, whom an-gels de-light to wor-ship a-bove! Your ran-somed cre-a-tion, with glo-ry a-blaze, in

Text: Robert Grant, 1779-1838 (Ps. 104)   LYONS
Tune: attr. to Johann Michael Haydn, 1732-1809   10 10 11 11

Praise and Prayer

vil - ioned in sple - dor and gird - ed with praise.
dark is his path on the wings of the storm.
sweet - ly dis - tills in the dew and the rain.
Mak - er, De - fend - er, Re - deem - er, and Friend!
true ad - o - ra - tion shall sing to your praise!

O Worship the King

This hymn is a metrical paraphrase of Psalm 104 composed by Robert Grant in 1833. Grant is thought by some to have composed his paraphrase by relying heavily on William Kethe's paraphrase of the same psalm. Others hold that Grant freely wrote this text.

LYONS in only one tune associated with this text. Both HANOVER and OLD 104TH are options. LYONS has been attributed to Johann Michael Haydn, the younger brother of noted classical composer Franz Joseph Haydn. It might also be the work of Joseph Martin Kraus, a Bavarian composer. LYONS has an ABCA' (whereas A' indicates a varriation of the original A section) structure with short singable phrases, making it a congregational favorite.

Praise and Prayer

Praise to the Lord, the Almighty

1. Praise to the Lord, the Al - might - ty, the King of cr -
   a - tion! O my soul praise him, for he is your
   health and sal - va - tion! Come, all who hear; broth - ers and
   sis - ers, draw near, join me in glad ad - o - ra - tion!

2. Praise to the Lord, who o'er all things is won - drous - ly
   reign - ing, and as on wings of an ea - gle, up -
   lift - ing, sus - tain - ing. Have you not seen all that is
   need - ful has been sent by his gra - cious or - dain - ing?

3. Praise to the Lord, who will pros - per your work and de -
   fend you; sure - ly his good - ness and mer - cy shall
   dai - ly at - tend you. Pon - der a - new what the Al -
   might - y can do as with his love he be - friends you.

4. Praise to the Lord! O let all that is in me a -
   dore him! All that has life and breath, come now with
   prais - es be - fore him! Let the a - men sound from his
   peo - ple a - gain. Glad - ly for - ev - er a - dore him!

Text: Joachim Neander, 1650-1680   LOBE DEN HERREN
Tune: *Ernewerten Gesangbuch*, 1665   14 14 4 7 8

Praise and Prayer

Praise to the Lord, the Almighty

Drawing on Psalms 103 and 150, this hymn is staple of German hymnody. Catherine Winkworth translated this hymn into English in 1863 and since then it has remained a standard.

While several versions of LOBE DEN HERREN exist, this is the most commonly sung in English. The melody was used by J. S. Bach in his Cantatas 57 and 137, as well as in other compositions.

Praise and Prayer

What a Friend We Have in Jesus

1. What a friend we have in Je-sus, all our sins and griefs to bear!
2. Have we tri-als and temp-ta-tions? Is there trou-ble an-y-where?
3. Are we weak and heav-y-lad-en, cum-bered with a load of care?

What a priv-i-lege to car-ry ev-ery-thing to God in prayer!
We should nev-er be dis-cour-aged— take it to the Lord in prayer.
Pre-cious Sav-ior, still our ref-uge— take it to the Lord in prayer.

Oh, what peace we of-ten for-feit; oh, what need-less pain we bear;
Can we find a friend so faith-ful who will all our sor-rows share?
Do your friends de-spise, for-sake you? Take it to the Lord in prayer.

all be-cause we do not car-ry ev-ery-thing to God in prayer!
Je-sus knows our ev-ery weak-ness— take it to the Lord in prayer.
In his arms he'll take and shield you; you will find a sol-ace there.

Text: Joseph M. Scriven, 1819-1886
Tune: Charles C. Converse, 1832-1918

CONVERSE
8 7 8 7 D

Praise and Prayer

What a Friend We Have in Jesus

While there are contending stories about the origin of this hymn, one thing is for certain: Joseph Scriven wrote this text at a time of great sorrow. It was written either at the death of his mother or fiancée, both of whom died in 1855. The repeated expression of bringing all to God in prayer is often misunderstood as an ability on the believer's part to enact human will by the work of prayer. Rather this hymn is meant to express the importance of praying to God in every need as an expression of faith.

Originally published under the pseudonym Karl Reden, CONVERSE was written by Charles Converse. It goes by various names including ERIE, FRIENDSHIP, and WHAT A FRIEND. It was first paired with this text in 1875.

Praise and Prayer

All Creatures of Our God and King

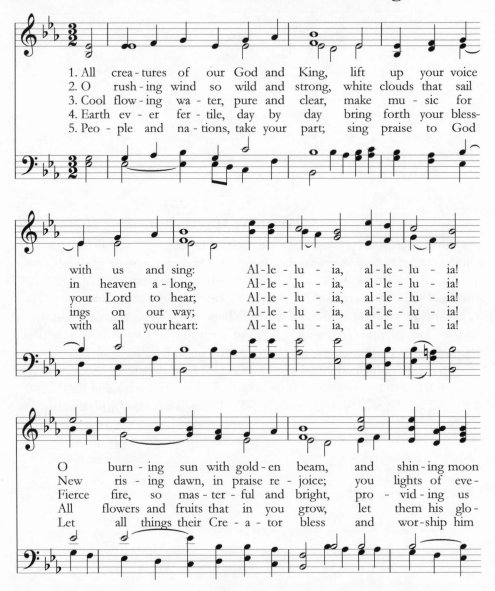

1. All crea-tures of our God and King, lift up your voice
2. O rush-ing wind so wild and strong, white clouds that sail
3. Cool flow-ing wa - ter, pure and clear, make mu - sic for
4. Earth ev - er fer - tile, day by day bring forth your bless-
5. Peo - ple and na - tions, take your part; sing praise to God

with us and sing: Al-le - lu - ia, al-le-lu - ia!
in heaven a - long, Al-le - lu - ia, al-le-lu - ia!
your Lord to hear; Al-le - lu - ia, al-le-lu - ia!
ings on our way; Al-le - lu - ia, al-le-lu - ia!
with all your heart: Al-le - lu - ia, al-le-lu - ia!

O burn - ing sun with gold-en beam, and shin-ing moon
New ris - ing dawn, in praise re - joice; you lights of eve-
Fierce fire, so mas-ter-ful and bright, pro - vid-ing us
All flowers and fruits that in you grow, let them his glo-
Let all things their Cre - a - tor bless and wor-ship him

Text: Francis of Assisi, 1182-1226
Tune: *Geistliche Kirchengesänge*, Köln, 1623

LASST UNS ERFREUEN
8 8 8 8 8 8 and alleluias

Praise and Prayer

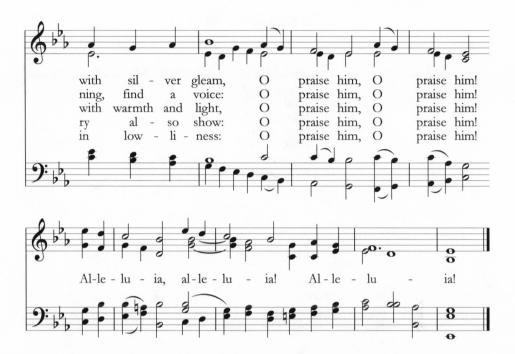

with   sil - ver gleam,   O   praise him,   O   praise him!
ning,   find   a   voice: O   praise him,   O   praise him!
with   warmth and light,   O   praise him,   O   praise him!
ry   al - so   show: O   praise him,   O   praise him!
in   low - li - ness: O   praise him,   O   praise him!

Al-le-lu - ia,   al-le-lu - ia!   Al-le-lu - ia!

All Creatures of Our God and King

This text is an adaptation of Francis of Assisi's "Canticle of the sun, and hymn of creation." St. Francis composed "Laudato si', mi Signor, con tutte le tue creature" to praise God for all created things, while he suffered with illness and blindness in a hut infested with field mice. Translator and hymn writer William Henry Draper, member of the Anglican clergy, paraphrased Francis' hymn for a Pentecost festival for children at Leeds sometime between 1899 and 1919. It was published in 1926 with the collection *Hymns of the Spirit*.

LASST UNS ERFREUEN appeared in Peter von Brachel's 1623 *Ausserlesene Catholische Geistliche Kirchengasänge* as the setting for an Easter hymn. It was likely a melody based on an earlier folk song. It appeared solely in Roman Catholic hymnals until *The English Hymnal* of 1906, where it was harmonized by Ralph Vaughan Williams.

Praise and Prayer

Beautiful Savior

1. Beau-ti-ful Sav-ior! King of cre-a-tion!
2. Fair are the mead-ows, fair are the wood-lands,
3. Fair is the sun-shine, fair is the moon-light,
4. Beau-ti-ful Sav-ior! Lord of the na-tions!

Son of God and Son of Man!
robed in flowers of bloom-ing spring;
bright the spar-kling stars on high;
Son of God and Son of Man!

Tru-ly I'd love thee, tru-ly I'd serve thee,
Je-sus is fair-er, Je-sus is pur-er;
Je-sus shines bright-er, Je-sus shines pur-er
Glo-ry and hon-or, praise, ad-o-ra-tion,

Light of my soul, my joy, my crown.
he makes our sor-rowing spir-it sing.
than all the an-gels in the sky.
now and for-ev-er-more be thine!

Text: *Gesangbuch*, Münster, 1677; tr. Joseph A. Seiss, 1823-1904
Tune: Silesian folk tune, 19th cent.

SCHÖNSTER JESU
5 5 7 5 5 8

Praise and Prayer

Beautiful Savior

"Schönster Herr Jesu" appeared in a Roman Catholic collection published in Münster, the *Munsterisch Gesangbuch*, 1677. "Beautiful Savior" is an 1873 translation by prolific hymn writer Joseph A. Seiss. Seiss was raised as a Moravian, and persisted in their hymn tradition after becoming a Lutheran minister. The alternate "Fairest Lord Jesus," first published in 1850, appears in many hymnals.

SCHONSTER HERR JESU is from a Silesian folk melody. Many Silesian peasants were Hussite refugees who quietly maintained their Protestant hymn tradition in the Glaz district (now southwestern Poland). The simplicity and natural imagery of the hymn reflect the disctric and its bucolic life. A version of the text and tune were first paired in a collection of sacred and secular folksongs of Silesia, in 1842.

Praise and Prayer

I'm So Glad Jesus Lifted Me

1. I'm   so   glad
2. Satan   had me bound,   Je-sus lift-ed me.
3. When I   was in   trouble,

I'm   so   glad
Satan   had me bound,   Je-sus lift-ed me.
When I   was in   trouble,

I'm   so   glad
Satan   had me bound,   Je-sus lift-ed me,   singing
When I   was in   trouble,

glo - ry,   hal - le - lu - jah!   Je-sus lift-ed me.

Text: African American spiritual
Tune: African American spiritual

JESUS LIFTED ME
irregular

Praise and Prayer

I'm So Glad Jesus Lifted Me

This hymn exemplifies the common call-and-response form used in African-American spirituals. A leader would improvise the opening line for each stanza and the congregation would respond each time with "Jesus lifted me." The simplicity of the tune and lyrics suggest it is part of a long standing oral tradition that extends back farther than its publication in any hymnal.

JESUS LIFTED ME employs only four notes: *ti*, *do*, *re*, and *mi*. Its simplicity allows for it to be easily taught. It can be sung accompanied or *a cappella* with clapping on the off-beat.

Praise and Prayer

Jesus Shall Reign

1. Je - sus shall reign wher - e'er the sun does its suc -
2. To him shall end - less prayer be made, and prais - es
3. Peo - ple and realms of ev - ery tongue dwell on his
4. Blessings a - bound wher - e'er he reigns: the pris - oners
5. Let ev - ery crea - ture rise and bring the high - est

ces - ive jour - neys run, his king - dom stretch from
throng to crown his head. His name like sweet per -
love with sweet - est song, and in - fant voic - es
leap to lose their chains, the wea - ry find e -
hon - ors to our King, an - gels de - scend with

shore to shore, 'til moons shall wax and wane no more.
fume shall rise with ev - ery morn - ing sac - ri - fice.
shall pro - claim their ear - ly bless - ings on his name.
ter - nal rest, and all who suf - fer want are blest.
songs a - gain, and earth re - peat the loud a - men.

Text: Isaac Watts, 1674-1748 (Ps. 72)   DUKE STREET
Tune: John Hatton, 1710-1793   LM

Praise and Prayer

Jesus Shall Reign

This hymn is a paraphrase of the latter half of Psalm 72. Naturally, the original psalm contains no mention of Jesus. The Christological addition was made by Isaac Watts, considered to be the father of English hymnody.

This tune is attributed to John Hatton. An English Presbyterian, he lived in Windle, Lancaster on Duke Street from which this tune derives its name. Nearly every phrase rises and falls in an arch, giving this tune an uplifting quality.

Praise and Prayer

Every Time I Feel the Spirit

Ev - 'ry time I feel the Spir - it mov - ing

in my heart, I will pray. Ev - 'ry time I feel the

Spir - it mov - ing in my heart, I will pray.

1. Up - on the moun - tain my Lord
2. All a - round me looked so
3. Jor - dan riv - er, chilly and

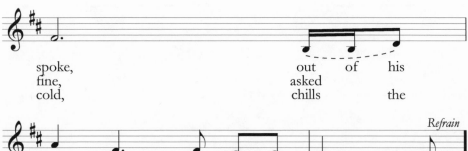

spoke, out of his
fine, asked
cold, chills the

mouth came fire and smoke.
my Lord if all was mine.
bod - y but not the soul.

Text: African American spiritual   EVERY TIME I FEEL THE SPIRIT
Tune: African American spiritual   irregular

Praise and Prayer

Every Time I Feel the Spirit

The structure of this spiritual suggests a common performance practice of spirituals: stanzas sung by a leader with the refrain sung by all. This would account for the variable syllabification on the stanzas which allows variations in rhythm to be improvised from verse to verse. Biblical imagery in the lyrics include references to the giving of the Law to Moses on the mountain of Sinai and the Jordan River, a common symbol for death in African American spirituals.

EVERY TIME uses lively rhythm and consistent syncopation throughout. This spiritual should be sung with vigor and benefits well from clapping or other percussion.

Praise and Prayer

Immortal, Invisible, God Only Wise

1. Im - mor - tal, in - vis - i - ble, God on - ly
2. Un - rest - ing, un - hast - ing, and si - lent as
3. To all life thou giv - est, to both great and
4. Thou reign - est in glo - ry, thou dwell - est in

wise, in light in - ac - ces - si - ble hid from our
light, not want - ing nor wast - ing, thou rul - est in
small, in all life thou liv - est, the true life of
light. Thine an - gels a - dore thee, all veil - ing their

eyes, most bless - ed, most glo - rious, the An - cient of
might; thy jus - tice like moun - tains high soar - ing a -
all; we blos - som and flour - ish like leaves on the
sight; our laud we would ren - der, O help us to

Days, al - might - y, vic - to - rious, thy great name we praise.
bove, thy clouds which are foun - tains of good - ness and love.
tree, and whith - er and per - ish, but naught chang - eth thee.
see, 'tis on - ly the splen - dor of light hid - eth thee.

Text: W. Chalmers Smith, 1824-1908, alt.

ST. DENIO
11 11 11 11

Tune: Welsh folk tune

Praise and Prayer

Immortal, Invisible, God Only Wise

Written by Scottish minister Walter Chalmers Smith, this hymn focuses on the unchanging nature of God. The fourth stanza is a composite of two other original stanzas.

ST. DENIO is a Welsh folk tune most likely from the 18th century. It was originally set to several secular texts, including one about a cuckoo bird. Its present form is a modification of the folk tune by Welsh musician John Roberts.

Praise and Prayer

Joyful, Joyful, We Adore Thee

1. Joy - ful, Joy - ful, we a - dore thee, God of glo - ry,
2. All thy works with joy sur - round thee, earth and heav'n re -
3. Thou art giv - ing and for - giv - ing, ev - er bless - ing,
4. Mor - tals, join the might - y chor - us which the morn - ing

Lord of love; hearts un - fold like flowers be - fore thee,
flect thy rays, stars and an - gels sing a - round thee,
ev - er blest, well - spring of the joy of liv - ing,
stars be - gan; Love di - vine is reign - ing o'er us,

open - ing to the sun a - bove. Melt the clouds of
cen - ter of un - bro - ken praise. Field and for - est,
o - cean depth of hap - py rest! Thou our Fa - ther,
bind - ing all with - in its span. Ev - er sing - ing,

sin and sad - ness, drive the dark of doubt a - way.
vale and moun - tain, flow - ery mead - ow, flash - ing sea,
Christ our broth - er, all who live in love are thine;
march we on - ward, vic - tors in the midst of strife;

Text: Henry Van Dyke, 1852-1933; st. 4 alt.
Tune: Ludwig van Beethoven, 1770-1827; arr. by Edward Hodges

HYMN TO JOY
8 7 8 7 D

Praise and Prayer

Giv - - - er	of	im -	mor - tal	glad - ness,	
chant - - ing	bird	and	flow - ing	foun - tain,	
teach	us	how to	love each	oth - er,	
joy - - - ful	mu - sic	leads	us	sun - ward,	

fill	us	with the	light	of	day!
call	us	to re -	joice	in	thee.
lift	us	to the	joy	di -	vine.
in	the	tri - umph	song	of	life.

Joyful, Joyful, We Adore Thee

Henry van Dyke was an American Presbyterian minister who, in his spare time, was an enthusiastic fisherman and naturalist. This hymn celebrates the joy and wonder of God observed through the natural world. The fourth stanza is a later addition.

In 1824, Ludwig van Beethoven's ninth and final symphony was first performed. Beethoven was completely deaf by this point in his life yet this symphony is widely considered Beethoven's greatest work. Unique to the symphony is the final movement which includes a choral section. The text was J. C. F. von Schiller's "Ode to Joy" which lends its name to the tune HYMN TO JOY. Elam Ives adapted the original symphonic and choral setting to make a hymn tune in 1846. This version retains Beethoven's rhythm which features syncopation (unexpected rhythm) at the beginning of the last line. The melodic phrase starts on fourth beat of the final measure of the previous phrase, anticipating the final line. Many hymnals eliminate the syncopation in an effort to make the hymn more easily sung.

Praise and Prayer

Praise God, from Whom All Blessings Flow

Praise God, from whom all bless - ings flow; praise him, all

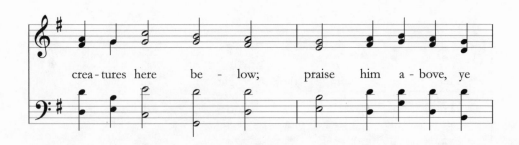

crea - tures here be - low; praise him a - bove, ye

heav-enly host; praise Fa-ther, Son, and Ho - ly Ghost. A - men.

Text: Thomas Ken, 1637-1711
Tune: attr. to Louis Bourgeois, 1510-1559

OLD 100TH
LM

Praise and Prayer

Praise God, from Whom All Blessings Flow

This short, simple hymn is commonly known as "The Doxology." Used frequently for meal blessings and offertories, it is the quintessential thanksgiving song of the English-speaking Church.

OLD 100TH was originally composed as a tune for a metrical paraphrase for Psalm 134. It was paired, however, with Psalm 100 in 1560, and thereby derived its name. It is the most beloved and most memorable of the songs originally copose for the Geneva Psalter.

Note the "Amen" afixed to the end of the hymn. There is a strong historical tradition of ending all hymns with prayer texts in a final Amen. In recent hymnals, this tradition has fallen away. It is retained here as an example of the tradition and because The Doxology is so often used as a meal time prayer.

Praise and Prayer

To God Be the Glory

1. To God be the glo - ry, great things he has done; so loved he the
2. O per - fect re - demp-tion, the pur-chase of blood, to ev - ery be-
3. Great things he has taught us, great things he has done, and great our re-

world that he gave us his Son, who yield - ed his life an a -
liev - er the prom-ise of God; the vil - est of - fend-er who
joic - ing through Je - sus the Son; but pur - er and high-er and

tone - ment for sin, and o-pened the life-gate that all may go in.
tru - ly be - lieves, that mo-ment from Je - sus a par-don re - ceives.
great - er will be our won-der, our glad-ness, when Je-sus we see.

Praise the Lord, praise the Lord; let the earth hear his voice! Praise the

Text: Fanny J. Crosby, 1820-1915
Tune: William H. Doane, 1832-1915

TO GOD BE THE GLORY
11 11 11 11 and refrain

Praise and Prayer

Lord, praise the Lord; let the peo-ple re-joice! O come to the Fa-ther through

Je-sus the Son, and give him the glo-ry; great things he has done.

To God Be the Glory

Frances "Fanny" Crosby is one of the most influential hymn writers in history. Despite the fact she was blinded as an infant, Crosby translated countless hymns into English and wrote over 8,000 hymns herself. She once said: "Do you know that if at birth I had been able to make one petition, it would have been that I was born blind? Because when I get to heaven, the first face that shall ever gladden my sight will be that of my Savior."

William Doane was the president of a woodworking machinery company. He was trained as a musician and pursued this avocation by writing and publishing numerous settings for hymn texts.

Praise and Prayer

When Morning Gilds the Sky

1. When morn - ing gilds the sky, our hearts a - wak - ing
2. To God, the Word on high, the hosts of an - gels
3. Let earth's wide cir - cle round in joy - ful notes re -
4. Be this, when day is past, of all our thoughts the
5. The let us join to sing to Christ, our lov - ing

cry: May Je-sus Christ be praised! In all our work and
cry: May Je-sus Christ be praised! Let mor - tals too up -
sound: May Je-sus christ be praised! Let air and sea and
last: May Je-sus Christ be praised! The night be - comes as
King: May Je-sus Christ be praised! Be this th'e - ter - nal

prayer we   ask his lov - ing care: May Je - sus Christ be praised!
raise their voice in hymns of praise: May Je - sus Christ be praised!
sky   from depth to height re - ply: May Je - sus Christ be praised!
day   when from the heart we say: May Je - sus christ be praised!
song through all the   a - ges long: May Je - sus christ be praised!

Text: *Katholisches Gesangbuch*, trans. Robert Bridges, 1844-1930
Tune: Joseph Barnby, 1838-1896

LAUDES DOMINI
6 6 6 6 6 6

Praise and Prayer

When Morning Gilds the Sky

Usually understood as a morning hymn due to its opening line, "When Morning Gilds the Sky" is an anonymous German hymn. It was originally published in English in 1828 with fourteen stanzas. Since then, it has been shortened to the version presented here which is best understood as a hymn of praise.

LAUDES DOMINI is one of over 200 hymn tunes written by Joseph Barnby. In many ways it is the least characteristic of his compositions yet is one of the few that has lingered on. Written originally in 1868 for an early translation of this hymn, it has become a popular tune.

Creation

For the Beauty of the Earth

1. For the beau-ty of the earth, for the glo-ry of the skies,
2. For the won-der of each hour of the day and of the night,
3. For the joy of hu-man love, broth-er, sis-ter, par-ent, child,
4. For your-self, best gift di-vine, to the world so free-ly given,

for the love which from our birth o-ver and a-round us lies,
hill and vale and tree and flower, sun and moon and stars of light,
friends on earth, and friends a-bove, for all gen-tle thoughts and mild,
a-gent of God's grand de-sign: peace on earth and joy in heaven.

Christ, our Lord, to you we raise this, our hymn of grate-ful praise.

Text: Folliott S. Pierpoint, 1835-1917, alt.
Tune: Conrad Kocher, 1786-1872

DIX
7 7 7 7 7 7

Creation

For the Beauty of the Earth

This text, the most well known of prolific English poet Folliott Sandford Pierpoint, was published in 1864. The hymn was included as a communion hymn in *Lyra Eucharistica*, 1864. Folliott was inspired by the spring blossoms in view near his hometown of Bath, England.

DIX, also known as TREUER HEILAND, was included in Conrad Kocher's *Stimmen aus dem Reiche Gottes*, published in1838 in Stuttgart. The present form of the hymn is an adaptation by William Henry Monk which appeared in *Hymns Ancient and Modern*, 1861, set to the text "As with gladness, men of old."

Creation

Great Is Thy Faithfulness

1. Great is thy faith-ful-ness, O God my Fa-ther; there is no
2. Sum-mer and win-ter and spring-time and har-vest, sun, moon, and
3. Par-don for sin and a peace that en-dur-eth, thy own dear

shad-ow of turn-ing with thee; thou chang-est not, thy com-
stars in their cours-es a-bove join with all na-ture in
pres-ence to cheer and to guide, strength for to-day and bright

pas-sions, they fail not; as thou hast been thou for-ev-er wilt be.
man-i-fold wit-ness to thy great faith-ful-ness, mer-cy and love.
hope for to-mor-row; bless-ings all mine, with ten thou-sand be-side!

Great is thy faith-ful-ness! Great is thy faith-ful-ness! Morn-ing by

Text: Thomas O. Chisholm, 1866-1960 (Lam. 3:22-23)
Tune: William M. Runyan, 1870-1957

FAITHFULNESS
11 10 11 10 and refrain

Creation

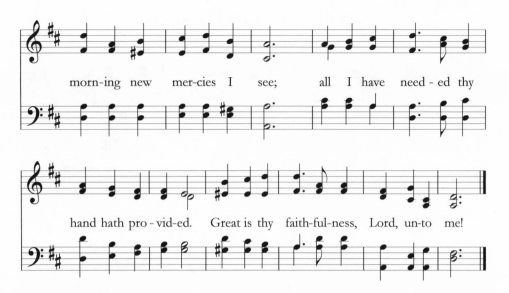

morn-ing new mer-cies I see; all I have need-ed thy

hand hath pro-vid-ed. Great is thy faith-ful-ness, Lord, un-to me!

Great Is Thy Faithfulness

Written by Thomas Chisholm in 1923, this gospel hymn is a favorite. The text combines the theme of the faithfulness of God with examples of that faithfulness found in creation. The opening line is from Lamentations 2:32 followed immediately by a quote from James 1:17.

FAITHFULNESS was written by William Runyan, a friend of Chisholm. As if to suggest the faithfulness of God who "changest not," the opening lines consists of repeated notes, establishing a foundation for the melody.

Creation

O God of the Mountain

O God of the moun-tain,   O Lord of the Height;   Trans-
O God of the moun-tain,   O Lord of the Word;   We
O God of the moun-tain,   O Lord of the Cloud;   From
O God of the moun-tain,   O Lord of the Plain;   your

fig - ur - ing vi - sion, glor - i - ous light;   U-
come to the mount to learn of the Lord.   No
earth comes a sigh in - creas - ing - ly loud.   For
glo - ry the cross, your po - wer the pain;   No

nit - ing the pro-phet, the Law, and the Son,   the
glo - ri - ous vi - sion is need - ed to - day;   your
hun - ger and jus - tice, the cry can be heard,   from
tent for a dwel - ling to stay on the height,   Lord,

Text: Clayton J. Schmit, 1992
Tune: Clayton J. Schmit
Text and Tune © 1992 Clayton J. Schmit

BERKELEY HEIGHTS
11 10 11 10 11 11

Creation

old   and the new   now joined in - to   one;   Re -
Word   is   the lamp   that lights our   way.   O
peo -   ple in need   who   thirst for your   Word.   Send
send   us   to share   your glo - ri - ous   light,   to

veal   to your peo - ple your   vi - sion to - day;   il -
teach   us   to   lis - ten, to   call on your name, that,
forth   from the moun - tain dis - ci - ples to   share the
bring   love and jus - tice, to   speak of God's Word; to

1. 2. 3.

lu -   mine the dark - ness,   turn night in - to   day.   2. O
changed on   the moun - tain,   we're ne - ver the same.   3. O
power   of   your sto - ry,   the   depth of your care.   4. O
go   from the moun - tain   to

Creation

serve the Lord,   to serve the Lord.

O God of the Mountain

In 1992, at the fortieth anniversary of the founding of Pacific Lutheran TheologicalSeminary, the school undertook a hymn search to commemorate the occasion. This hymn was written for that search and was selected as the winning entry. Because of the location of the seminary high atop the Berkeley, California hills, the author chose to write a meditation on the Transfiguration story.

The tune BERKELY HEIGHTS refers to the geographic placement of the seminary. The accompaniment was arranged to feature a stepping bass line, suggestive of climbing footseps.

Creation

God of Beauty, God of Artistry

1. God of beau-ty, God of ar-tis-try, Lord of mys-ter-y and
2. All cre-a-tion sings your prai-ses: rock and ri-ver, oak and
3. When we seek a place of beau-ty, None is fair-er than the
4. In our church-es, in our cha-pels, In our homes or on a

light; From your Word flows per-fect ge-ne-sis, All is
lark. So we, too, your gift-ed chil-dren, bear-ers
earth. Still, we long for sac-red spa-ces that re-
street; At the o-cean, in the for-est, an-y

good-ness in your sight. We are sac-red i-mi-
of the Mak-er's mark Long to loose i-ma-gi-
flect up-on your worth: Where your Word is spo-ken
place your peo-ple meet; There we'll praise you, God Cre-

ta-tions, to cre-ate is to o-bey. Sac-red
na-tion cel-e-brat-ing all you are. This is
clear-ly and pro-claimed through e-very art. The are
a-tor, There we'll tell of Christ, your Son, There we'll

Text: Clayton J. Schmit and William K. Brehm
Tune: *The Sacred Harp*, Philadelphia, 1884
Text © 2004 Clayton J. Schmit

BEACH SPRING
8 7 8 7 D

Creation

art   is   a - do - ra - tion flow-ing through i - ma - go Dei.
praise when   we cre - ate   in   so - li   De - o   glo - ri - a.
nave   and sanc-tu - a - ry: space for   beau - ty   set a - part.
feel   your Spi-rit's lead - ing   to   a - dore you Three - in - One.

God of Beauty, God of Artistry

This hymn text was written in 2004 to commemorate the seventy-fifth birthday of businessman, composer, and philanthropist, William K. Brehm. Its author drew imagery from an interview with Bill and wife Dee Brehm published in Theology, News, and Notes: Art for Faith's Sake (Fall 2001) titled "A Place for Beauty, Set Apart." The article and the hymn text reflect upon the Brehms' participation in, and generous support of worship arts at Fuller Theological Seminary in Pasadena, California.

BEACH SPRING is attributed to Benjamin Franklin White, co-editor with brother-in-law William Walker, of the hymn collection *Southern Harmony* (1835). This tune was first included in White's later shape-note* hymn collection (co-edited with Elisha James King,) Sacred Harp (1844).

* See an explanation of shape-note hyms at "What Wonderous Love is This?," p. 78.

Creation

This Is My Father's World

1. This is my Father's world, and to my lis-tening
2. This is my Father's world: the birds their car-ols
3. This is my Father's world: O let me ne'er for-

ears all na-ture sings and round me rings the
raise, the morn-ing light, the lil-y white, de-
get that though the wrong seems oft so strong, God

mu-sic of the spheres. This is my Fa-ther's
clare their mak-er's praise. This is my Fa-ther's
is the rul-er yet. This is my Fa-ther's

world; I rest me in the thought of
world; he shines in all that's fair; in the
world: why should my heart be sad? The

Text: Maltbie D. Babcock, 1858-1901
Tune: Franklin L. Sheppard, 1852-1930, adapt.

TERRA PATRIS
SMD

Creation

rocks and trees, of skies and seas— his
rust - ling grass I hear him pass; he
Lord is King, let heav - en ring! God

hand the won - ders wrought.
speaks to me ev - ery - where.
reigns; let earth be glad.

This Is My Father's World

This hymn was taken from one of Maltbie Babcock's poems originally published in 1901. Babcock's poem consisted of sixteen four-line verses. For each stanza of this hymn, two of Babcock's original stanzas have been combined with several omitted. The text is a meditation on the wonders of creation.

Franklin Sheppard wrote TERRA PATRIS for this hymn. He originally thought that he was merely arranging a tune taught to him by his mother but no such tune has been found. It is sometimes known as TERRA BEATA.

Justification

My Hope Is Built on Nothing Less

1. My hope is built on noth-ing less than
2. When dark-ness veils his love-ly vace, I
3. His oath, his cov-e-nant, his blood sus-
4. When he shall come with trum-pet sound, oh,

Je-sus' blood and right-eous-ness; no
rest on his un-chang-ing grace; in
tain me in the rag-ing flood; when
may I then in him be found, clothed

mer-it of my own I claim, but
ev-'ry high and storm-y gale my
all sup-ports are washed a-way, he
in his right-eous-ness a-lone, re-

Text: Edward Mote, 1797-1874
Tune: John B Dykes, 1823-1876

MELITA
8 8 8 8 8 8

Justification

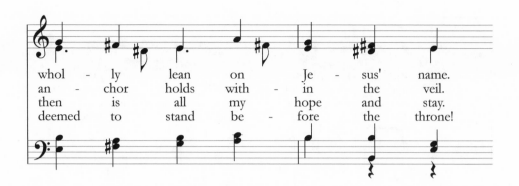

whol - ly lean on Je - sus' name.
an - chor holds with - in the veil.
then is all my hope and stay.
deemed to stand be - fore the throne!

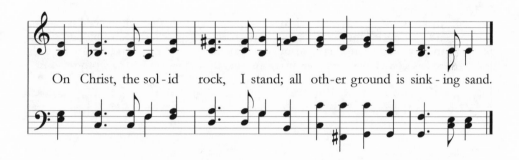

On Christ, the sol-id rock, I stand; all oth-er ground is sink-ing sand.

My Hope Is Build on Nothing Less

This hymn was composed by English Baptist minister Edward Mote and included, along with one hundred other compositions of Mote, in *Hymns of Praise: A New Selection of Gospel Hymns, combining all the Excellencies of our Spiritual Poets, with many Originals*, 1836. Mote composed the hymn upon visiting a dying woman in his congregation around 1834. The hymn originally began, "Nor earth, nor hell my soul can move."

John Dykes originally wrote this tune to accompany "Eternal Father Strong to Save." This other hymn extensively uses nautical imagery and has been adopted by many seafarers including the US Navy. As such, it is of little surprise that Dykes named the tune after island of Malta where the apostle Paul found safety after being shipwrecked (Acts 27:27-28:1). This text is also widely sung to the tune THE SOLID ROCK.

Justification

Just As I Am, Without One Plea

1. Just as I am, with-out one plea, but that thy blood was shed for me, and that thou bidd'st me come to thee, O Lamb of God I come, I come.
2. Just as I am, and wait-ing not to rid my soul of one dark blot, to thee, whose blood can cleanse each spot, O Lamb of God I come, I come.
3. Just as I am, though tossed a-bout with man-y a con-flict, many a doubt, fight-ings and fears with-in, with-out, O Lamb of God, I come, I come.
4. Just as I am, thou wilt re-ceive, wilt wel-come, par-don, cleanse, re-lieve; be-cause thy prom-ise I be-lieve, O Lamb of God, I come, I come.

Text: Charlotte Elliott, 1789-1871
Tune: William B. Bradbury, 1816-1868

WOODWORTH
LM

Justification

Just As I Am, Without One Plea

Although often associated with the evangelistic revivals of Dwight L. Moody and other evangelical preachers, Charlotte Elliot composed this text for *The Invalid's Hymn Book*, 1836. Elliot, suffering from a medical condition that confined her to bed rest all her life, contributed 112 hymns to the book. She meant to comfort and encourage others incapacitated by physical illness or disability through her hymns.

William Bradbury, organist and hymn tune writer, studied under another famous hymn tune writer from the Boston Academy of Music, Lowell Mason. Bradbury's WOODWORTH first appeared in the *Mendelssohn Collection*, 1849. It was set to a text called "The God of Love Will Sure Indulge."

Faith and Commitment

He Leadeth Me

1. He lead - eth me: O bless - ed thought! O
2. Some - times mid scenes of deep - est gloom, some -
3. Lord, I would clasp thy hand in mine, nor
4. And when my task on earth is done, when,

words with heav - enly com-fort fraught! What - e'er I do, wher-
times where E - den's flow-ers bloom, by wa - ters calm, o'er
ev - er mur - mur nor re - pine; con - tent, what - ev - er
by thy grace, the vic-tory's won, e'en death's cold wave I

e'er I be, still 'tis God's hand that lead - eth me.
trou - bled sea, still 'tis God's hand that lead - eth me.
lot I see, since 'til my God that lead - eth me.
will not flee, since God through Jor - dan lead - eth me.

He lead-eth me, he lead-eth me; by his own hand he lead - eth me:

Text: Joseph H. Gilmore, 1834-1918, alt.
Tune: William B. Bradbury, 1816-1868

HE LEADETH ME
LM and refrain

Faith and Commitment

his faith-ful fol-lower I would be, for by his hand he lead-eth me.

He Leadeth Me

Joseph Gilmore wrote these words as a psalm paraphrase in 1862 while supplying the pulpit at First Baptist Church of Philadelphia. He simply jotted the text down on a scrap of paper and passed it to his wife for safe-keeping. Gilmore never expected his wife to send the text to be published in a local Christian paper. There, it came to the attention of William Bradbury who wrote a tune and had it published. Later when Gilmore was supplying at another parish, he flipped through the hymnal to see what the congregation was singing that day and was surprised to find his own paraphrase of Psalm 23 published within.

HE LEADETH ME is a simple setting for this hymn. Written by William Bradbury in 1864. It utilizes an AA'BB' (where A' and B' represent varriation on their original phrases) form with the B' portion of the refrain using the same cadence from the A' section.

Faith and Commitment

Breathe on Me, Breath of God

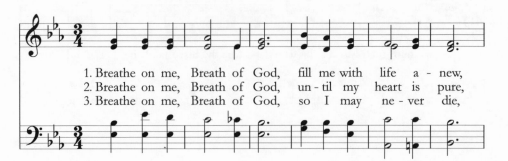

1. Breathe on me, Breath of God, fill me with life a - new,
2. Breathe on me, Breath of God, un - til my heart is pure,
3. Breathe on me, Breath of God, so I may ne - ver die,

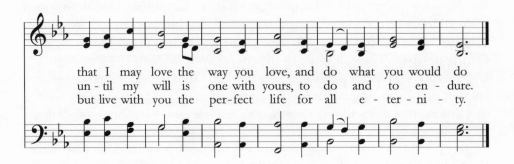

that I may love the way you love, and do what you would do
un - til my will is one with yours, to do and to en - dure.
but live with you the per - fect life for all e - ter - ni - ty.

Text: Edwin Hatch, 1835-1889   DURHAM
Tune: Aaron Williams, 1731-1776   SM

Faith and Commitment

Breathe on Me, Breath of God

Edwin Hatch grew up a British Nonconformist, but at age twenty joined the Church of England, and took Holy Orders six years later in 1859. Hatch was an esteemed scholar, but also remembered for his simple faith. His hymn "Breathe on Me, Breath of God" was based on John 20:22, the impartation of the Spirit through Jesus' breath on his disciples. It was first published privately in 1878, and later included in Hatch's posthumous *Towards Fields of Light*, 1890.

Accomplished organist and prolific church musician Henry Gauntlett is accredited with DURHAM, also known as DOVER and HAMPTON. Gauntlett's facility with music, acoustics, and organs drew the appreciation of Felix Mendelssohn, and he received a Doctor of Music degree from the Archbishop of Canterbury. It appeared, along with "Breathe on Me, Breath of God," in his *Congregational Psalmist Hymnal*, 1890.

Faith and Commitment

Come, Thou Fount of Every Blessing

1. Come, thou Fount of ev-ery bless-ing, tune my heart to sing thy
2. Here I find my great-est trea-sure; hith-er by they help I've
3. Oh, to grace how great a debt-or dai-ly I'm constrained to

grace; streams of mer-cy, nev-er ceas-ing, call for
come and I hope, by thy good plea-sure, safe-ly
be! Let thy good-ness, like a fet-ter, bind my

songs of loud-est praise. Teach me some me-lo-dious
to ar-rive at home. Je-sus sought me when a
wan-dering heart to thee: prone to wan-der, Lord, I

son-net, sung by flam-ing tongues a-bove. Praise the
strang-er, wandering from the fold of God. He, to
feel it, prone to leave the God I love; here's my

Text: Robert Robinson, 1753-1790

Tune: J. Wyeth, *Repository of Sacred Music*, Part II, 1813

NETTLETON

8 7 8 7 D

Faith and Commitment

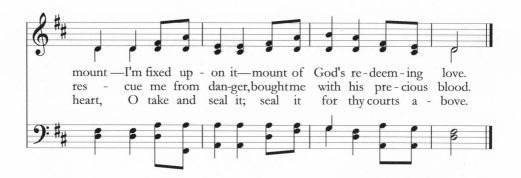

mount —I'm fixed up - on it—mount of God's re - deem - ing love.
res - cue me from dan-ger, bought me with his pre - cious blood.
heart, O take and seal it; seal it for thy courts a - bove.

Come, Thou Fount of Every Blessing

This hymn text was likely one of two compositions by Robert Robinson, probably about 1757. Robinson was a convert of George Whitefield, and wrote the hymn while a Baptist pastor in Cambridge. Robinson was a self-educated author of several books, including a noted early English Baptist history. The often altered line, "Here I raise my Ebenezer" refers to 1 Samuel 7:12, in which a stone raised by Samuel to mark the Lord's help.

The tune NETTLETON appeared anonymously with this text in John Wyeth's 1813 *Repository of Sacred Music, Part Second*.

Faith and Commitment

A Fuller Vision

1. A ful-ler vi-sion, Lord we seek, to see the realm of God at
2. A ful-ler vi-sion, Lord we seek, to see the world of hu-man
3. A ful-ler vi-sion, Lord we seek, to see, through death and rub-ble's

hand; a clear-er voice with which to speak, to spread your
need; a strong-er arm to bear the weak, a firm-er
dust, the work to do, the words to speak, and where to

Word in ev-ery land; a deep-er know-ledge of your
hand in ho-ly deeds; a clear-er call to fol-low
turn and whom to trust. Though moun-tains shake or build-ings

Text: Clayton J. Schmit
Tune: Clayton J. Schmit
Text & tune © 2007 Clayton J. Schmit

A FULLER VISION
LMD

Faith and Commitment

Word,   a firm-er   faith   in   Christ   our   Lord.   A ful-ler
you,   a love that shows   in   all   we   do.   A ful-ler
fall,   you are the Christ, still Lord   of   all.   A ful-ler

vi-sion, Lord we   seek   to be the   Church that   we   must be.
vi-sion, Lord we   seek   to be the   Church that   we   must be.
vi-sion, Lord we   seek   to be the   Church that   we   must be.

A Fuller Vision

The text for this hymn was developed by its author while serving on the faculty of Fuller Theological Seminary in 2000. It was an appreciative response to the gratifying work he found himself involved in at the school. The word play on "fuller" was intentional. Following the events of September 11, 2001, the third stanza was added as a reflection on the vivid images captured in the news of rubble, dust, and death. The stanza also evokes images from Psalm 46.

The hymn tune was composed by the author, developed at the time of the text's composition.

Faith and Commitment

When Peace Like a River

1. When peace like a riv - er at - tend - eth my way, when
2. Though Sa - tan shouldbuf - fet, though tri - als should come, let
3. My sin— oh, the bliss of this glo - ri - ous thought!— my
4. O Lord, haste the day when my faith shall be sight, the

sor - rows like sea bil - ows roll; what - ev - er my lot, thou hast
this blest as - sur - ance con - trol: that Christ has re - gard - ed my
sin, not in part, but the whole, is nailed to the cross, and I
clouds be rolled back as a scroll; the trump shall re - sound and the

taught me to say, "It is well, it is well with my soul."
help - less es - tate, and has shed his own blood for my soul.
bear it no more; praise the Lord, praise the Lord, O my soul!
Lord shall de - scend; e - ven so, it is well with my soul.

It is well   with my soul;
        it is well   with my soul;

Text: Horatio G. Spafford, 1828-1888   VILLE DU HAVRE
Tune: Philip P. Bliss, 1838-1876   11 8 11 9

Faith and Commitment

it   is   well,   it   is   well   with   my soul.

When Peace Like a River

Horatio Spafford lived a life full of tragedies. He lost a great deal of money in the Chicago fire of 1871. While they were traveling to Europe in 1873, his four daughters died when their ship sank. He lost another child to scarlet fever some years later. This hymn was written just after the death of his daughters, possibly even written at sea near where their ship sank.

VILLE DU HAVRE was written by Philip Bliss. Bliss was a family friend of the Spaffords and wrote the tune for this hymn. He named it after the French ship which sank resulting in the death of Spafford's daughters. It is a typical example of a 19th century melody, employing chromatic harmony.

Faith and Commitment

Lead On, O King Eternal

1. Lead on, O King e-ter-nal, the day of march has come; hence-
2. Lead on, O King e-ter-nal, 'til sin's fierce war shall cease, and
3. Lead on, O King e-ter-nal; we fol-low, not with fears, for

forth in fields of con-quest your tents will be our home. Through
ho-li-ness shall whis-per the sweet a-men of peace. For
glad-ness breaks like morn-ing wher-e'er your face ap-pears. Your

days of prep-a-ra-tion your grace has made us strong; and
not with swords' loud clash-ing or roll of stir-ring drums— with
cross is lift-ed o'er us, we jour-ney in its light' the

now, O King e-ter-nal, we lift our bat-tle song.
deeds of love and mer-cy the heav-enly king-dom comes.
crown a-waits the con-quest; lead on, O God of might.

Text: Ernest W. Shurtleff, 1862-1917
Tune: Henry T. Smart, 1813-1879

LANCASHIRE
7 6 7 6 D

Faith and Commitment

Lead On O King Eternal

Ernest Shurtleff was a Congregationalist minister in America and attended Andover Theological Seminary. For his graduation in 1888, he composed this hymn which was sung at the commencement ceremony. The text displays signs of commitment and vocation. God is depicted as a victorious king who leads an army of faithful, armed with the weapons of love, mercy, and grace.

LANCASHIRE was originally written for another hymn. It was first joined to "Lead on, O King Eternal" in 1905. It has the quality of a march which complements the martial nature of the text.

Faith and Commitment

Take My Life and Let It Be

1. Take my life and let it be
2. Take my hands and let them move
3. Take my voice and let me sing
4. Take my sil - ver and my gold;

con - se - crat - ed, Lord, to thee.
at the im - pulse of thy love.
al - ways, on - ly, for my King.
not a mite would I with - hold.

Take my mo - ments and my days;
Take my feet and let them be
Take my lips and let them be
Take my in - te - lect and use

Text: Frances R. Havergal, 1836-1879, alt.   PATMOS
Tune: William H. Havergal, 1793-1870   7 7 7 7

Faith and Commitment

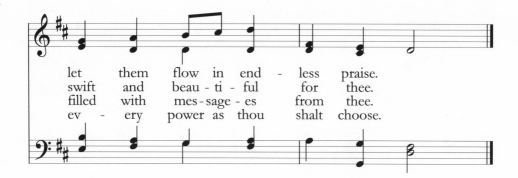

let them flow in end - less praise.
swift and beau - ti - ful for thee.
filled with mes - sage - es from thee.
ev - ery power as thou shalt choose.

5. Take my will and make it thing;
   it shall be no longer min.
   Take my heart - it is thine own;
   it shall be thy royal throne.

6. Take my love; my Lord, I pour
   at thy feet its treasure store.
   Take myself, and I will be
   ever, only, all for thee.

Take My Life and Let It Be

Frances Havergal wrote this hymn in 1874 after visiting a house for the elderly. Each verse asks God to take something from ourselves and use it for the glory of God. The poetry is moving and direct and, despite being over a hundred years old, the language has not needed to be updated in modern hymnals

It was Frances Havergal's father who composed this tune. While written before this hymn, PATMOS was intended to be the tune by which "Take my Life" was to be sung. William Havergal was an English minister. After being thrown from a carriage and sustaining a traumatic brain injury, he could no longer serve as a priest. He dedicated his life to church music, writing several anthems and hymn tunes.

Faith and Commitment

How Firm a Foundation

1. How firm a foun - da - tion, you saints of the
2. "Fear not, I am with you; O be not dis -
3. "When through the deep wa - ters I call you to
4. "When through fi - ery tri - als your path - way shall
5. "The soul that on Je - sus has leaned for re -

Lord, is laid for your faith in his ex - cel - lent
mayed, for I am your God and will still give you
go, the riv - ers of sor - row shall not o - ver -
lie, my grace all - suf - fi - cient shall be your sup -
pose I will not, I will not de - sert to its

Word! What more can he say than to you he has
aid; I'll strength - en you, help you, and cause you to
flow, for I will be with you in trou - ble to
ply; the flame shall not hurt you; I on - ly de -
foes; that soul, though all hell should en - deav - or to

Text: John Rippon, 1751-1836, *A Selection of Hymns*, alt.
Tune: early American

FOUNDATION
11 11 11 11

Faith and Commitment

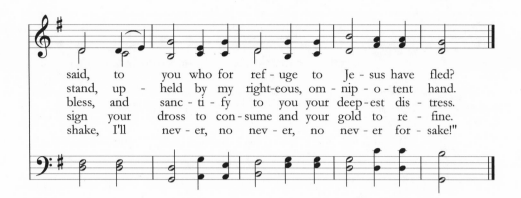

said,   to   you who for   ref - uge   to   Je - sus have   fled?
stand,   up - held   by my   right-eous, om - nip - o - tent   hand.
bless,   and   sanc - ti - fy   to   you your   deep - est dis - tress.
sign   your   dross to con - sume and your   gold to   re - fine.
shake,   I'll   nev - er,   no   nev - er,   no   nev - er   for - sake!"

How Firm a Foundation

While attributed to John Rippon's *A Selection of Hymns*, this hymn was simply signed with the letter "K." While there has been speculation, the hymn's actual author remains anonymous to this day. It is rich with biblical imagery including 2 Peter, Isaiah, and Hebrews. Note the change of voice in the hymn, from the general declaration of a believer to the voice of God speaking to us.

FOUNDATION is a pentatonic tune, built on five notes (d, e, g, a, and b). Its structure is AA'BA' (whereas A' indicates a varriation from the original phrase). These two factors make it an easily sung tune, contributing to the popularity of this hymn.

Faith and Commitment

Send Me

Send me,_____ send me,_____ send me.

If you think that I should or I could do an-y good, send me._____

Send me,_____ send me,_____ send me.

I know I don't de-serve it but I'll be your ser-vant. Send

me._____ Send I know I

don't de-serve it but I'll be your ser-vant. Send me._____ I know I

don't de-serve it but I'll be your ser-vant. Send me._____

Send Me

This song, adapted from Isaiah 6:8, was written by Gary Dreier, Lutheran pastor and musician. It was written for his daughter who was discerning her path of discipleship.

Text: Gary Dreier (Isaiah 6:8)
Tune: Gary Dreier
Text and Tune © 2006 Gary Dreier

Faith and Commitment

Into Your Hands

Into Your Hands

This song, adapted from Psalm 31:5, was written by Gary Dreier, Lutheran pastor and musician. The author was praying Psalm 31 when the melody for this verse occurred to him; he quickly wrote it down to capture the song.

Text: Gary Dreier (Psalm 31:5)
Tune: Gary Dreier
Text and Tune © 2002 Gary Dreier

Christian Hope

Guide Me, O Thou Great Jehovah

1. Guide me, O thou great Je - ho - vah, pil - grim through this bar - ren land. I am weak, but thou art might-y; hold me with thy power - ful hand. Bread of heav-en, bread of heav-en feed me 'til I want no more; feed me 'til I want no more.
2. O - pen now the crys - tal foun-tain, whence the heal - ing stream doth flow; let the fire and cloud - y pil - lar lead me all my jour - ney through. Strong de - liv - erer, strong de - liv - erer, be thou still my strength and shield; be thou still my strength and shield.
3. When I tread the verge of Jor - dan, bid my anx - ious fears sub-side; death of death and hell's de - struction, land me safe on Ca - naan's side. Songs of prais-es, songs of prais-es, I will ev - er give to thee; I will ev - er give to thee.

Text: William Williams, 1717-1791
Tune: John Hughes, 1873-1932

CWM RHONDDA
8 7 8 7 8 7

Christian Hope

Guide Me, O Thou Great Jehovah

William Williams made great contributions to Welsh hymnody, including this hymn "Arglwydd, arwain trwy'r anialwch," published in 1745. The English version of this hymn, was first published in 1772 or 1773 in *Lady Huntingdon's Collection of Hymns*, fifth edition. It was primarily based on the translation of Methodist revivalist Peter Williams.

CWM RHONDDA (pronounced "coom rontha") was written by John Hughes for a Welsh Baptist singing festival held in Rhondda, the heart of the mining district. It is variously dated as written in 1905 or 1907.

Christian Hope

Love Divine, All Loves Excelling

1. Love di - vine, all loves ex - cel - ling, joy of
2. Come, Al - might - y to de - liv - er, let us
3. Fin - ish, then, thy new cre - a - tion; pure and

heaven, to earth come down; fix in us thy hum - ble
all thy life re - ceive; sud - den - ly re - turn, and
spot - less let us be; let us see thy great sal -

dwell - ing, all thy faith - ful mer - cies crown. Je - sus,
nev - er, nev - er - more thy tem - ples leave. Thee we
va - tion per - fect - ly re - stored in thee: changed from

thou art all com - pas - sion, pure, un-bound - ed
would - be al - ways bless - ing, serve thee with thy
glo - ry in - to glo - ry, 'til in heaven we

Text: Charles Wesley, 1707-1788   HYFRYDOL
Tune: Rowland H. Prichard, 1811-1887   8 7 8 7 D

Christian Hope

love thou art; vis - it us with thy sal -
hosts a - bove, pray and praise thee with - out
take our place, 'til we cast our crowns be -

va - tion, en - ter ev - ery trem - bling heart.
ceas - ing, glo - ry in thy per - fect love.
fore thee, lost in won - der, love, and praise.

Love Divine, All Loves Excelling

Charles Wesley wrote this hymn, which is characteristically Methodist. This is most notable in the final stanza when the author prays "pure and spotless let us be," a reference to the Methodist doctrine of perfection. Yet the hymn is not reserved for Methodist use and is much loved in many faith traditions.

HYFRYDOL (pronounced HU-vru-dol) is a Welsh term meaning "good cheer." The tune was written before the composer was twenty years old. Though Prichard wrote many hymn tunes, he worked on the looms and died at age 28. This text may also be sung to the tune BEECHER.

Christian Hope

Blessed Assurance

1. Bless-ed as - sur - ance: Je-sus is mine! Oh, what a
2. Joy - ful con - fes - sion: I am his own! Fol - low - ing
3. Per - fect sub - mis - sion: all is at rest, I in my

fore-taste of glo-ry di - vine! Heir of sal - va - tion, pur-chase of
Je - sus, I'm nev-er a - lone. Born of his Spir - it, I am re-
Sav - ior am hap-py and blest; watch-ing and wait-ing, look-ing a-

God, born of his Spir - it, washed in his blood.
stored, chal - lenged to serve my Sav - ior and Lord.
bove, filled with his good - ness, kept in his love.

This is my sto - ry, this is my song, prais-ing my

Text: Fanny J. Crosby, 1820-1915
Tune: Phoebe P. Knapp, 1830-1908

ASSURANCE
9 10 9 9 and refrain

Christian Hope

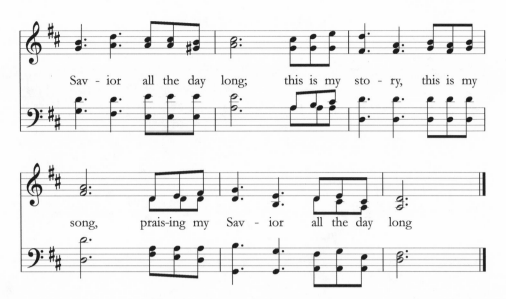

Sav - ior all the day long; this is my sto - ry, this is my song, prais-ing my Sav - ior all the day long

Blessed Assurance

The typical creative process for writing a hymn starts with the composition of the lyrics. Normally, after the lyrics have been finalized a tune is written or assigned for the text. This hymn, however, represents a reversal of that process. Musician Phoebe Knapp came up with the tune and played it for Fanny Crosby; Crosby in turn responded with this text. Together, they created this archetypal gospel song.

The tune ASSURANCE drives this hymn, both in the creative process of inspiring the text as well as in the singing. Note that the last beat in each measure consists of three eighth notes. This propels the hymn forward, each measure anticipating the next. Knapp produced over five hundred hymn tunes during her life and continued her collaborative friendship with Crosby for the rest of her life.

Christian Hope

In Remembrance

1. In re - mem - brance of one who was
2. So the Church in our time, break - ing
3. O Cre - a - tor of all! through the

touched by the Word, we the sto - ry re - call and the
free of her past saw the fin - est of gifts flow-ing
Spi - rit set free, now in Je - sus, may ours be a

Text: Martin Schaefer
Tune: Martin Schaefer
Text & tune © 1994 Martin Schaefer

IN REMEMBRANCE
12 12 13 12

Christian Hope

grace-gift she poured: from the   heart   of a   sis - ter,   from the
free - ly   at last!   In their   min - is-try   ser - ving,   by the
sto - ry   to see!   Bring-ing   hope   to your   peo - ple,   we are

depth   of   her   soul,   came   the   beau-ty   of   love   and a
Spir - it's sweet   pow'r,   wo - men   pour   heal-ing   oils   on a
bro - ken a - new,   as   we   pour   out   our

Christian Hope

fra - grance poured whole.
world's pain - ful hour.

2. So the
3. O Cre

life   and our whole heart to   you.

Christian Hope

In Remembrance

In 1994, at the twenty-fifth anniversary of the ordination of women in the Evangelical Lutheran Church in America, the denomination undertook a hymn search to celebrate the event. This hymn text and tune were composed for that occasion. While the hymn was not selected as the official commemorative hymn for the occasion, it was a runner-up and was used widely in worship in the Sierra Pacific Synod of the ELCA, the synodical home of the composer. "Marty" Schaefer is a Lutheran pastor and musician.

The optional descant can be played by any C instrument.

Christian Hope

All Hail the Power of Jesus' Name

1. All hail the power of Je - sus' name! Let an-gels pros-trate
2. O seed of Is - rael's cho - sen race now ran-somed from the
3. Let ev - ery tongue and ev - ery tribe re - spon-sive to his
4. Oh, that with all the sa - cred throng we at his feet may

fall. Bring forth the roy - al di - a - dem, and
fall, hail him who saves you by his grace, and
call, to him all maj - es - ty as - cribe, and
fall! We'll join the ev - er - last - ing song and

crown him Lord of all. Bring forth the roy - al
crown him Lord of all. Hail him who saves you
crown him Lord of all. To him all maj - es -
crown him Lord of all. We'll join the ev - er -

di - a - dem, and crown him Lord of all!
by his grace, and crown him Lord of all!
ty a - scribe, and crown him Lord of all!
last - ing song and crown him Lord of all!

Text: Edward Perronet, 1726-1792; alt. by John Rippon   CORONATION
Tune: Oliver Holden, 1765-1844   8 6 8 6 8 6

Christian Hope

All Hail the Power of Jesus' Name!

Edward Perronet, an early friend and colleague of John and Charles Wesley, composed "On the Resurrection, the Lord Is King" published in *The Gospel Magazine*, 1780. Originally a poem of eight verses, its was edited and amended by Rev. John Rippon in 1787 for *A Selection of Hymns, from the Best Authors intended to be an Appendix to Dr. Watt's Psalms and Hymns*. Rippon's version included the stanza "Oh that with yonder sacred throng. . ." and provided themes for each stanza: Angels, Martyrs, Converted Jews, Believing Gentiles, Sinners of Every Age, Sinners of Every Nation, and Ourselves. Rippon composed over 1000 hymns and published two collections.

The hymn tune CORONATION was composed by Oliver Holden in 1792 (the year of Perronet's death). Holden was a carpenter, a member of the Massachusetts House of Representatives, and a Puritan minister who composed this tune on an organ now preserved by the Bostonian Society. The tune MILES LANE, frequently an alternate for this text, was originally provided for this hymn in its 1779 printing. It was written by Perronet's close friend William Shrubsole.

Christian Hope

Deep River

Deep riv-er, my home is o-ver Jor-dan,

deep ri - ver, Lord, I

want to cross o - ver in - to camp-group.

1. Oh, don't you want to go to that
2. Oh, when I get to heav - en, I'll

gos - pel feast, that prom - ised
take my seat, and cast my

land where all is peace? Oh,
crown at Je - sus' feet. Oh,

Text: African American spiritual
Music: African American spiritual

DEEP RIVER
irregular

Christian Hope

Deep River

This spiritual employs the common image of the Jordan River as the line between life and death. The image points in two directions, one from the story of the Exodus and one from the story of Jesus' life. It is the Jordan that Israel must cross over in order to arrive at the Promised Land. It is also in the Jordan that Jesus is baptized. The spiritual points to the understanding that in baptism believers are joined in death and resurrecction with Christ. The reference to camp-ground is to the revival camp meeting site, typical of the second great awakening of the early 19th century.

DEEP RIVER is well known for its dark and somber mood, especially when the refrain is sung slowly. The melody contains a high F which is a half step higher than the normal upper limit in hymn singing. This melodic climax adds to the dramatic effect of the hymn.

Christian Hope

Rock of Ages, Cleft for Me

1. Rock of A - ges, cleft for me, let me hid my - self in thee; let the wa - ter and the blood, from thy riv - en side which flowed, be of sin the dou - ble cure: cleanse me from its guilt and pow'r.

2. Not the la - bors of my hands can ful - fill thy law's de - mands; could my zeal no res - pite know, could my tears for - ev - er flow, all for sin could not a - tone; thou must save, and thou a - lone.

3. Noth - ing in my hands I bring; sim - ply to thy cross I cling. Na - ked, come to thee for dress; help - less, look to thee for grace; foul, I to the foun - tain fly; wash me, Sav - ior, or I die.

4. While I draw this fleet - ing breath, when mine eye - lids close in death, when I soar to worlds un - known, see thee on thy judg - ment throne, Rock of A - ges, cleft for me, let me hide my - self in thee.

Text: Augustus M. Toplady, 1740-1778
Tune: Thomas Hastings, 1784-1872

TOPLADY
7 7 7 7 7 7

Christian Hope

Rock of Ages, Cleft for Me

Augustus Toplady was an English priest who wrote this hymn to accompany two articles published in 1776. During his life, Toplady wrote 130 hymns of which this is undoubtably the most well-known. In this hymn, the depiction of Christ as a rock of safety and protection draws on numerous biblical texts.

TOPLADY was written by Thomas Hastings for this hymn in 1832. It is named for Augustus Toplady, the author of the text.

Christian Hope

Steal Away

Steal a-way, steal a-way, steal a-way to Je - sus!

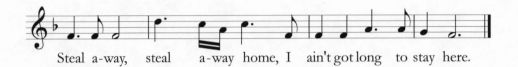

Steal a-way, steal a-way home, I ain't got long to stay here.

1. My   Lord   calls me,   he   calls me by   the thun-der; the
2. Green trees are bend-ing, poor sin-ners stand a - trem-bling; the
3. Tomb-stones are burst-ing, poor sin-ners stand a - trem-bling; the
4. My   Lord   calls me,   he   calls me by   the light-ning; the

trum-pet sounds with-in-a my soul, I ain't got long to stay here.

Text: African American spiritaul
Tune: African American spiritual

STEAL AWAY
irregular

Christian Hope

Steal Away

In an effort to control their slaves, white slave owners used the Bible and religious education to promote obedience. Part of this strategy was to prohibit independent slave worshiping communities. In many places, slaves were forbidden to lead or participate in Christian worship apart from established services. Yet, many slaves joined together in small, clandestine worship communities. These often took place out of earshot, in thickets near slave quarters. These became known as brush arbors. A slave had to "steal away" to the brush arbor for worship, which was hurried and secretive. This narrative is preserved in this spiritual which employs additional apocalyptic imagery throughout.

STEAL AWAY is structured in a way to suggest that the refrain was sung by all with the verses sung by a leader. The slow tempo of this tune suggests a wide range of leniency for improvisation.

Christian Hope

O God, Our Help in Ages Past

1. O God, our help in a-ges past, our hope for years to come,
2. Un-der the shad-ow of your throne still may we dwell se-cure;
3. Be-fore the hills in or-der stood or earth re-ceived its frame,
4. A thou-sand a-ges in your sight are like an eve-ning gone,

our shel-ter from the storm-y blast, and our e-ter-nal home:
suf-fi-cient is your arm a-lone, and our de-fense is sure.
from ev-er-last-ing you are God, to end-less years the same.
short as the watch that ends the night be-fore the ris-ing sun.

5. Time like an ever-rolling stream,
   soon bears us all away;
   we fly forgotten, as a dream
   dies at the op'ning day.

6. O God, our help in ages past,
   our hope for years to come,
   still be our guide while troubles last
   and our eternal home!

Text: Isaac Watts, 1674-1748 (Ps. 90)
Tune: Attr. to William Croft, 1678-1727

ST. ANNE
CM

Christian Hope

O God, Our Help in Ages Past

This popular hymn by Isaac Watts, the father of English hymnody, is a metrical paraphrase of Psalm 90. The opening line was originally "Our God, our help;" John Wesley changed the text to avoid the repetition.

ST. ANNE is one of the best known hymn tunes in the world. It was, however, originally written not for this text but for another metrical psalm paraphrase. The tune itself shares uncanny similarities with another tune by J. S. Bach, his "Prelude and Fugue in E-flat." The subject of the fugue closely resembles the opening phrase of ST. ANNE. Because of this, it is often known as the "St. Anne's Fugue" despite there being no evidence that they are related.

Trust and Guidance

Amazing Grace

1. A - maz - ing grace — how sweet the sound — that
2. 'Twas grace that taught my heart to fear, and
3. The Lord has prom - ised good to me, his
4. Through man - y dan - gers, toils, and snares I
5. When we've been there ten thou - sand years, bright

saved a wretch like me! I once was lost but
grace my fears re - lieved; how pre - cious did that
word my hope se - cures; he will my shield and
have al - read - y come; 'tis grace hath brought me
shin - ing as the sun, we've no less days to

now am found, was blind but now I see.
grace ap - pear the hour I first be - lieved!
por - tion be as long as life en - dures.
safe thus far, and grace will lead me home.
sing God's praise than when we'd first be - gun.

Text: John Newton, 1725-1807
Tune: American, 19th century

NEW BRITAIN
CM

Trust and Guidance

Amazing Grace

Amazing Grace first appeared in John Newton's *Olney Hymns*, 1779. The text was included under I Chronicles 17:16-17, entitled "Faith's review and expectation." Newton, remembered as a converted slave trader, was acquainted with the Wesleys and Isaac Watts. Newton and William Cowper's popular *Olney Hymns* had a great impact on Evangelical hymnody. The stanza beginning "When we've been there ten thousand years. . . " was likely composed by John P. Rees, probably incorporated among additions and improvisations in its use throughout nineteenth century camp meetings.

The tune NEW BRITAIN, also known as AMAZING GRACE, was a popular Southern tune of unknown origin. It first appeared in *Virginia Harmony* in 1831. Its present form was included in *Make His Praise Glorious*, 1900, credited to Edwin Othello Excell.

Trust and Guidance

When I Survey the Wondrous Cross

1. When I sur-vey the won-drous cross on which the Prince of glo-ry died, my rich-est gain I count but loss, and pour con-tempt on all my pride.

2. For-bid it, Lord, that I should boast save in the death of Christ, my God! All the vain things that charm me most, I sac-ri-fice them through his blood.

3. See, from his head, his hands, his feet, sor-row and love flow min-gled down. Did e'er such love and sor-row meet, or thorns com-pose so rich a crown?

4. Were the whole realm of na-ture mine, that were a pre-sent far too small. Love so a-maz-ing, so di-vine, de-mands my soul, my life, my all.

Text: Isaac Watts, 1674-1748 (Gal. 6:14)
Tune: Lowell Mason, 1792-1872

HAMBURG
LM

Trust and Guidance

When I Survey the Wondrous Cross

This hymn by Isaac Watts is built on Galatians 6:14. It was first published in 1707. The text expresses the totality of Christ's gift to humanity upon the cross and our response to that amazing gift.

HAMBURG was originally written by Lowell Mason to accompany a metrical paraphrase of Psalm 100 by Isaac Watts in 1824. It follows an ABAC form where C is used to explore motives found in other sections. Other tunes can be used to sing this hymn including ROCKINGHAM OLD.

Trust and Guidance

Foothold

To you, O Lord, I lift my soul, let me
All the paths of God lead the lost a - long through the
In our lone - li - ness, in the world's dis - tress, to

ne - ver sink in shame. Keep your strong hand near and my
knot - ted snares of death. As you free our song and un -
you, our hope we turn. Let us spread the fire of the

hope se - cure on the foot - hold of your name. Re -
tie our bonds, you con - fide a mys - ter - y yet. O
Spi - rit's pow'r and a fier - cer cour - age learn. Re -

mem - ber, Lord, your mer - cies old for the
school us, Lord, in your heal - ing word; make us
deem us soon from af - flic - tion's rule, for we

fail - ures of youth weigh down. Show me truth - ful ways and
hum - ble, ho - ly, wise to the gen - tle grace of your
trust in you a - lone. May we bear your peace till we

fear - less days; lead me to the high - er ground.
tear - stained face in its e - v'ry grim dis - guise.
dwell at ease in you, our sur - est home.

Text: Debra Reinstra
Tune: English folk tune
Text © 2006 Debra Reinstra

KINGSFOLD
CMD

Trust and Guidance

Foothold

This hymn text was written for a hymn contest sponsored by the Brehm Center for Worship, Theology, and the Arts in honor of the fortieth anniversary of the founding of the School of Psychology at Fuller Theological Seminary. Foothold became the winning submission to the contest and was premiered at the anniversary celebration. Recalling times in her life when the insights of modern psychology combined with Christian spirituality helped her to endure and to be healed, the author turned to Psalm 25 for inspiration. She drew upon her earlier work on modern English translations of the psalms to create this psalm paraphrase. The text plays with the psalm's image of "the pit" as a frank acknowledgment of human pain. The image of foothold is a reference to God's name upon which the person in lament steps to find solid ground.

The author selected the tune KINGSFOLD with its minor harmonies and urgent rhythms as the most fitting musical setting for her words.

Trust and Guidance

Jesus Loves Me

1. Je-sus loves me, this I know, for the Bi - ble tells me so.
2. Je-sus loves me— he who died heav-en's gate to o - pen wide.
3. Je-sus loves me, this I know, as he loved so long a - go,

Lit - tle ones to him be - long; they are weak, but he is strong.
He will wash a - way my sin, let his lit - tle child come in.
tak-ing chil - dren on his knee, say-ing, "Let them come to me."

Yes, Je - sus loves me! Yes, Je - sus loves me!

Yes! Je - sus loves me! The Bi - ble tells me so.

Text: Anna Warner, 1827-1915; David R. McGuire, 1929-1971
Tune: William B. Bradbury, 1816-1868

JESUS LOVES ME
7 7 7 7 with refrain

Trust and Guidance

Jesus Loves Me

This hymn is, without doubt, the most popular of all Sunday school songs. The Sunday school movement was started in the late 18th century with the goal of teaching children who otherwise did not have access to education. Instruction included standard educational curricula as well as religious studies. Several small Sunday school hymnals were written with this education system in mind, this hymn being only one of countless, produced for the religious education of children.

William Bradbury wrote the tune for this hymn, adding the refrain. It was originally published in 1862. It is sometimes known by the name CHINA, possibly because of its popularity among children with whom Chinese missionaries worked.

Trust and Guidance

Be Thou My Vision

1. Be thou my vi - sion, O Lord of my heart;
2. Be thou my wis - dom, and thou my true word;
3. Rich - es I heed not, nor vain, emp - ty praise,
4. Light of my soul, af - ter vic - to - ry won,

naught be all else to me, save that thou art:
I ev - er with thee and thou with my, Lord.
thou mine in - her - i - tance, now and al - ways:
may I reach heav - en's joys, O heav - en's Sun!

thou my best thought by day or by night,
Thou my soul's shel - ter, thou my high tower,
thou, and thou on - ly, first in my heart,
Heart of my own heart, what - ev - er be - fall,

wak - ing or sleep - ing, thy pres - ence my light.
raise thou me heav'n - ward, O Pow'r of my pow'r.
great God of heav - en, my trea - sure thou art.
still be my vi - sion, O Rul - er of all.

Text: Irish, 8th cent.; vers. E. Hull, 1860-1935, alt.; tr. M. Byrne, 1880-1931   SLANE
Tune: Irish traditional   10 10 10 10

Trust and Guidance

Be Thou My Vision

This text originated as an ancient Irish hymn (perhaps eighth century) of unknown authorship. It was translated into English by Mary Byrne for *Erin*, Vol II, 1905. Byrne's work was versed in 12 couplets by Eleanor Hull, and included in *Poem Book of the Gael*, 1912.

SLANE, a traditional Irish melody, appeared in Patrick W. Joyce, *Old Irish Folk Music and Songs*, 1909. Its popular harmonized form appeared in Church Hymnary, 1927.

Trust and Guidance

Trust and Obey

1. When we walk with the Lord in the light of his Word, what a
2. But we nev-er can prove the de-lights of his love un-til
3. Then in fel-low-ship sweet we will sit at his feet, or we'll

glo-ry he sheds on our way! While we do his good will he a-
all on the al-tar we lay; for the fa-vor he shows and the
walk by his side in the way; what he says we will do, where he

bides with us still, and with all who will trust and o-bey.
joy he be-stows are for those who will trust and o-bey.
sends we will go— nev-er fear, on-ly trust and o-bey.

Trust and o-bey, for there's no oth-er way to be

Text: John H. Sammis, 1846-1919 (1 Jn 1:7)   TRUST AND OBEY
Tune: Daniel B. Towner, 1850-1919   6 6 9 D and refrain

Trust and Guidance

hap - py   in   Je - sus   but to   trust   and   o - bey.

Trust and Obey

During a testimony meeting held by famed 19th century evangelist Dwight L. Moody, a young man stood and spoke. While his words betrayed his lack of formal training in theological matters. However, his final words, "I'm not quite sure but I'm going to trust, and I'm going to obey," rang true with Daniel Towner. He brought these words to John Sammis, a Presbyterian minister and hymn writer, who in turned wrote this hymn.

Daniel Towner in turn wrote this hymn tune. Towner was a church musician and prolific hymn writer. He spent nearly 30 years as the music director of the Moody Bible Institute, travelling with Moody to various events and providing music for these meetings.

Trust and Guidance

My Faith Looks Up to Thee

1. My faith looks up to thee, thou Lamb of
2. May thy rich grace im-part strength to my
3. While life's dark maze I tread and griefs a-
4. When life's swift race is run, death's cold work

Cal - va - ry, Sav - ior di - vine! Now hear me
faint - ing heart, my zeal in - spire. As thou hast
round me spread, be thou my guide. Bid dark - ness
al - most done, be near to me. Blest Sav - ior,

while I pray, take all my guilt a - way.
died for me, O may my love to thee
turn to day, wipe sor - row's tears a - way,
then in love fear and dis - trust re - move.

O let me from this day be whol - ly thine!
pure, warm, and change-less be, a liv - ing fire!
nor let me ev - er stray from thee a - side.
O bear me safe a - bove, re - deemed and free!

Text: Ray Palmer, 1808-1887   OLIVET
Tune: Lowell Mason, 1792-1872   6 6 4 6 6 6 4

Trust and Guidance

My Faith Looks Up to Thee

Ray Palmer wrote this hymn in 1830, jotting it down in a notebook. Palmer had no intention that his hymn would be used publically, instead writing it for his personal devotion. It was only when Lowell Mason contacted Palmer and asked for a hymn to put in a new hymnal that this hymn was published in 1832. The original text had six stanzas; most hymnals only publish these four.

Lowell Mason wrote OLIVET for this text. It only took a few days to compose the tune. It was first published in 1833 but modified by Mason in 1839. The modified form is what we sing today. The phrases are short (all but the final phrase are only two measures) and is an easily sung tune.

Trust and Guidance

Savior, Like a Shepherd Lead Us

Sav - ior like a shep-herd lead us;   much we need your ten-der care.
We are yours; in love be-friend us,   be the guard-ian of our way;
You have promised to re - ceive us,   poor and sin - ful tho' we be;
Ear - ly let us seek your fa - vor,   ear - ly let us do your will;

In your pleas - ant pas - tures feed us,   for our use your fold pre -
keep your flock, from sin de - fend us,   seek us when we go a -
you have mer - cy to re - lieve us,   grace to cleanse, and pow'r to
bless - ed Lord and on - ly Sav - ior,   with your love our spir - its

pare. Bless - ed Je - sus, bless - ed Je - sus, you have bought us; thine we
stray. Bless - ed Je - sus, bless - ed Je - sus, hear us chil - dren when we
free. Bless - ed Je - sus, bless - ed Je - sus, ear - ly let us turn to
fill. Bless - ed Je - sus, bless - ed Je - sus, you have loved us, love us

Text: attr. Dorothy A. Thrupp, 1779-1847
Tune: William B. Bradbury, 1816-1868

BRADBURY
8 7 8 7 D

Trust and Guidance

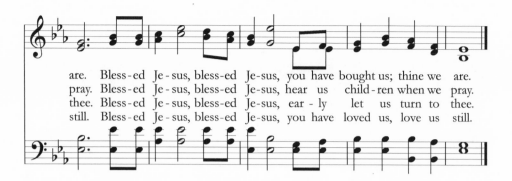

are. Bless-ed Je-sus, bless-ed Je-sus, you have bought us; thine we are.
pray. Bless-ed Je-sus, bless-ed Je-sus, hear us child-ren when we pray.
thee. Bless-ed Je-sus, bless-ed Je-sus, ear-ly let us turn to thee.
still. Bless-ed Je-sus, bless-ed Je-sus, you have loved us, love us still.

Savior, Like a Shepherd Lead Us

While widely attributed to Dorothy Thrupp, the authorship of this hymn remains a lingering question. In some early publications it was signed simply, "Lyte" while in others it was left completely anonymous. Thrupp is known to have used pseudonyms to publish her work and Lyte may have been one of them. Or, it may have been written by Henry Lyte, who wrote "Abide With Me."

William Bradbury wrote this tune and it is named after him. It uses a formal structure of AABB' (where B' indicates a variation on the B phrase) making it easy to sing and to learn.

Trust and Guidance

Gaelic Blessing

Text: Clayton J. Schmit
Tune: Irish traditional, adapted by C. J. Schmit
Text & tune © 2006 Clayton J. Schmit

THE LEAVING OF OLD LIVERPOOL
8 9 10 8 10 9 9 9

Trust and Guidance

Un-til we meet a - gain my friend, may you

til we meet a - gain, my friend, may you

rest in the palm of God's hand.

rest in the palm of God's hand.

Gaelic Blessing

This text is an adaptation of the traditional Gaelic Blessing, "May the Road Rise Up to Meet You." It has been metrically paraphrased to fit the melody. In addition, the author added three lines in order for the text to match the length and shape of the melody.

The tune, THE LEAVING OF OLD LIVERPOOL, is a traditional Irish sea chantey.

Trust and Guidance

Children of the Heavenly Father

1. Chil - dren of the heav - enly Fa - ther safe - ly
2. God his own shall tend and nour - ish; in his
3. Nei - ther life nor death shall ev - er from the
4. God has giv - en, he has tak - en, but his

in his bo - som gath - er; nest - ling bird nor star in
ho - ly courts they flour - ish. From all e - vil powers he
Lord his chil - dren sev - er; for to them his grace re -
chil - dren ne'er for - sa - ken; his the lov - ing pur - pose

heav - en such a ref - uge e're was giv - en
spares them; in his might - y arms he bears them.
veal - ing, he turns sor - row in - to heal - ing.
sole - ly to pre - serve them pure and ho - ly.

Text: Caroline V. Sandell Berg, 1832-1903   TRYGGARE KAN INGEN VARA
Tune: Swedish folk tune   LM

Trust and Guidance

Children of the Heavenly Father

This much beloved hymn is from 19th century Sweden. Lina Sandell (Sandell-Berg after her marriage) was a daughter of a Lutheran pastor and she wrote this text when she was still a teenager. She published it anonymously in 1885. The hymn reflects on God as a parent who guards humanity from all manner of evil. The third stanza is evocative of Romans 8:38-39.

The tune is a Swedish folk song, wed together since 1873. Note that the second musical phrase is a sequence of the first, raised a second. The third phrase is the highest of the hymn with the final phrase falling back, giving this hymn a melody range of exactly one octave.

Thanksgiving

Come, Ye Thankful People, Come

1. Come, you thank-ful peo - ple, come, raise the song of har-vest home;
2. All the world is God's own field, fruit un - to his praise to yield;
3. For the Lord our God shall come and shall take his har-vest home;
4. E - ven so, Lord, quick - ly come to your fi - nal har-vest home;

all is safe - ly gath-ered in ere the win - ter storms be - gin;
wheat and weeds to - geth - er sown, un - to joy or sor - row grown:
he him-self in that great day all of-fense shall take a - way,
gath - er all your peo - ple in, free from sor-row, free from sin—

God, our Mak - er, does pro-vide for our needs to be sup-plied;
first the blade and then the ear, then the full corn shall ap-pear;
give his an - gels charge at last in the fire the weeds to cast,
there, for - ev - er pu - ri - fied, in your pre - ence to a - bide;

Text: Henry Alford, 1810-1871, alt.
Tune: George J. Elvey, 1816-1893

ST. GEORGE'S WINDSOR
7 7 7 7 D

Thanksgiving

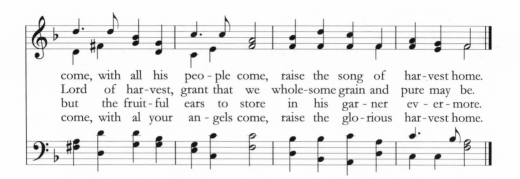

come, with all his   peo - ple come, raise the song of   har - vest home.
Lord   of har - vest, grant that we   whole-some grain and   pure may be.
but   the fruit - ful ears to store   in his gar - ner   ev - er - more.
come, with al your   an - gels come, raise the glo - rious har - vest home.

Come Ye Thankful People Come

Henry Alford wrote this hymn with traditional harvest festivals in mind.
While rich in agrarian language and imagery, much of the text is still pertinent
to modern audiences with stewardship in mind. Alford weaves several
different threads into this text including the harvest festival context and two
parables of Christ involving agrarian themes (Matthew 13:24-30, 36-43 and
Mark 4:26-29).

George Elvey worked for 47 years as the organist at St. George's, Windsor
just outside London, hence the unique name of this tune. This tune is only
one of several compositions written during his tenure there. In 1871, Elvey
was knighted by Queen Victoria. This tune is easily singable by
congregations as it consists of two eight-measure periods which share
identical rhythms.

Thanksgiving

Now Thank We All Our God

1. Now thank we all our God with heart and hands and voic-es,
2. O may this boun-teous God through all our life be near us,
3. All praise and thanks to God the Fa-ther now be giv-en,

who won-drous things has done, in whom this world re - joic-es;
with ev - er joy-ful hearts and bless-ed peace to cheer us,
the Son and Spir - it blest, who reign in high-est heav - en,

who from our moth-ers' arms has blessed us on our way
to keep us in his grace, and guide us when per - plexed,
the one e - ter - nal God, whom heaven and earth a - dore;

with count-less gifts of love, and still is ours to - day.
and free us from all ills in this world in the next.
for thus it was, is now, and shall be ev-er - more.

Text: Martin Rinkhart, 1586-1649
Tune: Johann Crüger, 1598-1662

NUN DANKET ALLE GOTT
6 7 6 7 6 6 6 6

Thanksgiving

Now Thank We All Our God

This hymn is a staple of Lutheran German hymnody. It was written more than a hundred years after the Reformation, during the Thirty Years War. It is both a suitable hymn for thanksgiving and for the facing of challenges and sorrows. Catherine Winkworth translated it into English in 1858 and since then it has been published in nearly every English hymnal.

Johann Crüger wrote NUN DANKET ALLE GOTT in 1647 to accompany this text in German. The original version is rhythmic in nature as opposed to the isometric version presented here.

Hymn and Song Appendices

How to Read a Hymn Page

There are many publishing conventions that standardize the way hymns are typically displayed in hymnals. This pictorial guide provides the essential conventions and their meanings. The numbers below correspond to numbers on the hymn page that follows.

Hymns are typically arranged in four-part harmony placed on two distinct musical staves. The top musical line on the upper staff indicates the melody of the hymn. This is sung by all people, or by sopranos when singing the four parts. The lower notes on the top staff indicate the alto part. The lower staff contains notes for the tenor (top notes) and bass (lower notes) parts. This type of arrangement is known as *homophonic* because the vertical alignment of the notes allows for each note of the melody to sound as one with the other three voices.

[1] *Title of the hymn.* This is often derived from the first line of the hymn text, as in "Amazing grace, how sweet the sound." Alternatively, a hymn may be known by an alternative name, perhaps deriving from another phrase in the hymn text. For example, the first line of one familiar hymn is "O Lord, my God," but it is better known as "How Great Thou Art."

[2] *Treble staff.* The upper staff in each system is called treble because it contains notes sung by higher voices. In accompaniment, the pianist or organist plays the notes in the treble staff with the right hand.

[3] *Treble clef.* This symbol indicates the treble staff.

[4] *Bass staff.* The lower staff in each system is called bass because it contains notes sung by lower voices. The pianist/organist plays the notes on this staff with the left hand.

[5] *Bass clef.* This symbol indicates the bass staff.

[6] *Soprano line.* In part-singing, the sopranos sing the top notes of the treble staff.

[7] *Alto line.* In part-singing, the altos sing the lower line of notes on the treble staff.

[8] *Tenor line.* In part-singing, the tenors sing the upper notes of the bass staff.

191

[9] *Bass line*. In part-singing, the basses sing the lower notes of the bass staff.

[10] *Key signature*. This area denotes the key of the hymn music using sharp (#) or flat (*b*) symbols. Changing the key of a hymn allows for it to be sung higher or lower than written. Skilled keyboardists learn to transpose to other keys, even while reading music in the given key.

[11] *Time signature*. These numbers indicate the metrical form of the melody. The top number indicates the number of musical beats that occur in each measure. The lower number indicates the kind of note that gets one beat. 3/4 means that there are three beats in each measure and that the quarter note is counted as one beat. Hymns are typically in 2/4, 3/4, or 4/4, although other meters are possible. Some hymnals omit the time signature, leaving it to the musicians to determine the tune's meter.

[12] *Measure or bar*. The measure is indicated by vertical bar lines on the staff. Each measure corresponds to the numbers in the time signature (for example, 3/4: three beats to each measure, where the quarter note gets one beat).

[13] *Pick-up beat*. The first notes of a hymn may not fit into a full measure. They are pick-up notes that lead into the first full measure of music. Where pick-ups occur, there is a corresponding short measure at the end of the piece. The time signature value of the pick-up measure and the final measure equal the value of one full measure.

[14] *Text author*. Usually near the composer's name, the name of the hymn text author is given. It may give the author's dates. In cases where the text is translated from another language, the original author is listed, followed by the name and dates of the translator.

[15] *Composer of tune*. Usually at the top or the bottom of the hymn page, an indication of the music's composer is given. It often includes the dates of the composer's life, or if living, the date of the hymn's composition. When a specific composer's name is unknown, this may also include an indication of the tune's original publication domain, for example, Southern Harmony.

[16] *Name of tune*. Hymns are known both by text names and tune names. Sometimes, the tune name is related to the text with which it is most commonly associated. For example, *Ein Feste Burg* is the tune name associated with "A Mighty Fortress"; it is the beginning of the hymn text in German. The tune name can also be related to the name of the composer or text author (Toplady, the author of "Rock of Ages"), a place (Gethsemane), a person (St. Clement), a historic association (Old Hundreth refers to the musical setting of the 100th psalm in the Geneva Psalm book), or an image from the hymn text (Solid Rock). The tune most commonly associated with "Amazing Grace" is New Britain, an Appalachian folk tune. The name probably references the new country of America as the New Britain. Contemporary hymn tune composers

[19] → Trust, Guidance

[10]   [11] [13]   [1] → **Amazing Grace**   [12]

[2] →
[3]
[20] →
[5]
[4] →
[6]
[7]
[8]
[9]

1. A - maz - ing grace — how sweet the sound — that
2. 'Twas grace that taught my heart to fear, and
3. The Lord has prom - ised good to me, his
4. Through man - y dan - gers, toils, and snares I
5. When we've been there ten thou - sand years, bright

saved a wretch like me! I once was lost but
grace my fears re-lieved; how pre - cious did that
word my hope se-cures; he will my shield and
have al - read - y come; 'tis grace hath brought me
shin - ing as the sun, we've no less days to

now am found, was blind but now I see.
grace ap - pear the hour I first be - lieved!
por - tion be as long as life en - dures.
safe thus far, and grace will lead me home.
sing God's praise than when we'd first be - gun.

[13]

[14] → Text: John Newton, 1725-1807; stanza 5, John Rees, c. 1859
[15] → Tune: W. Walker, Southern Harmony, 1835

[16] → NEW BRITAIN
[17] → CM

[18] → Public Domain

have the privilege of naming their tunes. A strong convention in publishing holds that the hymn tune name is given in capital letters on the hymn page, though not necessarily elsewhere. For example: DUKE STREET occurs on the hymn page, but is indicated as Duke Street in some indexes. The reader will note that in this hymnal, CAPS are used both on the hymn page and in the index.

[17] *Meter.* These numbers indicate both the meter of the music and the corresponding meter of the text. Each number indicates the number of syllables or pulses in a particular line of the hymn. For example, 6686 meter indicates a hymn with six syllables in the first, second, and fourth lines and eight syllables in the third line. It is important for the number of syllables in a text line to match the flow of notes in the melodic line. See the following "Selecting Alternate Tunes for a Hymn Text" to see how the meter of text and tune allow for some texts and tunes to be used interchangeably. In some cases, the meter is designated by letters with the following meanings:

> SM: Short Meter, 6686
>
> SMD: Short Meter Double, 6686 6686
>
> CM: Common Meter, 8686
>
> CMD: Common Meter Double, 8686 8686
>
> LM: Long Meter, 8888
>
> LM and alleluias: 8888 plus a refrain containing alleluias
>
> Irregular: a complex or uncommon meter

[18] *Copyright notice.* Somewhere at the bottom of the hymn page, an indication of the copyright for the tune and text are given. Hymns in the public domain may so indicate; or if copyright information is not given, it means that the hymn or tune (or both) are old enough to be included in the public domain. Copyright is held by the composer/author unless it has been sold or assigned to a publishing firm. When the copyright notice is not indicated at the bottom, center of the page, it is sometimes found with the names of the authors and composers. For example Text: ÓEdwin Willmington, 2012.

[19] *Heading.* The heading gives an indication of the orientation or theme of the hymn text. It suggests how the hymn might be used in worship or devotional practice.

[20] *Stanzas.* The term verse applies to songs of various types. The term stanza is used for the verses of hymns.

Copyright and Public Domain

The right to copy, use, sell, or create derivative works on any intellectual property is called the copyright. It belongs to the creator of a work from the moment it is created.

It is wise to indicate the copyright owner on any new work. An additional step for protecting a work is to register the copyright with the national copyright office in Washington, DC. The copyright is often assigned to a publisher when a work is published. This means that all publishing rights, along with the rights to sell or control the work, are owned by the publisher. The advantage to the creator of the work is that the publisher provides a means by which to disseminate the material and control its future use. The creator of the work is usually paid by the publisher for these rights.

A work falls into the public domain when its intellectual property rights expire. This is generally a long time from the creation of the work. It is usually tied to the date of the creator's death. For example, in the United States, the general rule is that the copyright lasts for the life of the creator plus seventy years. However, the rule is more complicated than that simple formula. For example, this rule applies to works created since the revised copyright laws in 1978. The rule is also informed by statements such as: the copyright exists for ninety-five years from the first publication date or 120 years from the work's creation, whichever is shorter. Things are further complicated by the fact that in some circumstances, heirs of the creator can file for extended copyright. Most of the hymns and songs in this hymnal are in the public domain. Others are used with permission of the copyright holders. Note that hymns in the public domain are not necessarily available to be copied without permission of the hymnal publisher: the particular artistic layout on the page of a public domain hymn is a unique artistic creation that bears its own independent copyright. As noted in the "Acknowledgments and Permissions" section at the end of this hymnal, permission is granted for individuals and institutions to freely copy material from the *Teaching Hymnal* for one time educational or worship use. Another instance where public domain hymns are not available for copying freedom occurs when the public domain hymn is set to a musical arrangement that is still protected as intellectual property.

Selecting Alternate Tunes for a Hymn Text

There is a musical joke often played with the hymn "Amazing Grace." The text can be sung to many tunes, some of which are comical. For example, it can be sung to the tune of "Gilligan's Island." On a serious note, many hymn texts can be sung to alternate tunes when a person understands how to use the indexes located in the back of most hymnals. Using the metrical index and the index of hymn tunes, hymn texts can be matched with alternate tunes. Here is how it works for "Amazing Grace."

The meter of the text is CM or 8686. By looking in the hymn tune index, you can select other tunes with matching meter. The tune McKee (associated with "In Christ, There Is No East or West") is also in Common Meter and can be used as an alternative melody for the text. One must be careful, however, to sing the hymn with the new tune to ensure that it scans properly. Scanning refers to the way that the text fits with the melody. There are times when a syllabic accent does not match a musical accent, rendering the substitution a clumsy fit. For example, "I Know that My Redeemer Lives," typically sung to Duke Street, is in Long Meter (8888). Another Long Meter hymn is "Children of the Heavenly Father," but its tune (Tryggare Kan Ingen Vara) is a lilting waltz in Long Meter. Attempting to sing "I Know that My Redeemer Lives" to the waltz places the text's syllables drastically at odds with the musical accents. The natural syllable accents are: "**I** know that **my** Re**deem**er **lives**." Set to Tryggare Kan Ingen Vara, the syllables are forced into this strange configuration: "I know **that** my Redee**mer** lives."

Hymn and Song Indexes

Sources of Hymn and Song Texts

Tune Sources

Metrical Index of Tunes

Songs without a meter are omitted from this index.

Tune Index

Songs without named tunes are omitted.

First Lines and Common Names

Common names occur in italics.

Part II: Prayers and Services of Worship

Orders for Daily Prayer

In its earliest inception, theological education was closely connected to the life of worship. Monks studying in monasteries kept regularly scheduled times for prayer that punctuated their workday (see "The Daily Office (Praying the Hours)" in the Essays and Resources section of this book). The practice of *ora et labora* (prayer and work) became a ritual habit for persons entering the monastery and has persisted to this day in the form of morning prayers (*Matins*), evening prayers (*Vespers*), and other forms of daily prayer.

Though each educational institution approaches the integration of prayer and work differently, a need still exists for students and faculty to ground their theological work in worship and prayer. The following forms provide a flexible template for daily prayers in educational institutions. The long form is a Service of the Word, appropriate as a liturgy for school chapel. The short form is more suitable for meetings and classroom devotions. Both provide the opportunity for assisting faculty and students in connecting the task of theology with its source.

Daily Prayer Long Form (Service of the Word)

Call to Worship
Prayer of the Day
Opening Hymn or Song
Psalm
Silent Prayer
Scripture Reading(s)
Interpretation of the Reading(s)
Hymn, Song, Canticle, or Creed
Prayers of Thanksgiving or Intercession
Lord's Prayer
Closing Hymn or Song
Sending

Daily Prayer Short Form (Devotions)

Call to Worship
Prayer of the Day
Scripture Reading(s)
Prayers of Thanksgiving or Intercession
Lord's Prayer
Closing Hymn or Song
Transition to Work or Study

Daily Prayer for Classes or Meetings

Call to Worship

>One: O Lord, open my lips.
>**All: And my mouth shall proclaim your praise.**

Read responsively from one of the following litanies paraphrased from the psalms.

A *(From Psalm 11)*

The Lord is in his holy temple; and seated on high, in heaven.
The eyes of God behold his creation, the gaze of God examines humankind.
>**The Lord puts the righteous and the wicked to the test,**
>**And his Spirit judges the lover of violence.**

For the Lord is righteous; God loves the good deeds of his people;
>**The Lord is in his holy temple. Come, let us worship**
>**the Lord our God.**

B *(from Psalm 16)*

Bless the Lord who guides our way;
>**Let us keep the Lord always before us.**
>**Because he is always with us, we shall not be moved.**

Therefore, let your hearts be glad and let our souls rejoice.
God does not abandon us, nor let his faithful ones fall away from him.
>**Show us, O God, the path of life.**

May we find in your presence the fullness of joy;
In your right hand, pleasures forevermore.
>**Let us praise the One who gives us life,**
>**forgives our failings, and lights our way.**

C *(from Psalm 36)*

Your steadfast love, O Lord, extends from earth to the heavens,
>**Your faithfulness reaches to the clouds.**

Your righteousness is like the mighty mountains,
>**Your judgments are like the great ocean depths;**

You protect humans and animals and all creation.
>**How precious is your steadfast love, O God!**

All people may take refuge in the shadow of your wings.
>**We gather, now, to worship you, Abiding God and Author of Justice.**

D *(from Psalm 71)*

O God, stay near your people; make haste, O God, to help us.
>**We will hope continually in you and praise you with all our breath.**

Our mouths will tell of your righteous acts,
>**Our lips will declare your countless deeds of salvation.**

We will praise the mighty deeds of the Lord God of Israel,
>**We will praise his righteousness all our days.**

Through prayer and praise we come, O God,
>**Because you are always near and ready to hear us.**

E *(from Psalm 95)*

O come, let us sing to the Lord,
>**Let us make a joyful noise to the rock of our salvation!**

Let us make a joyful noise to God with songs of praise!
>**For the Lord is a great God and a great King above all gods.**

In his hand are the depths of the earth; the heights of the mountains are also his;
>**The sea is his, for he made it.**
>**The dry land is his, for he formed it with his own hands.**

O come, let us worship and bow down, let us kneel before the Lord our Creator!
>**For he is our God, and we are the people of his pasture,**
>**And the sheep of his fold.**

Prayer of the Day
A prayer is read or extemporized by the designated person.

Scripture Reading(s)
One or more lessons are read from the Bible. They may be followed by silence for reflection, or by commentary from a leader.

Prayers of Thanksgiving or Intercession
Prayers are said by a leader or by appointed individuals. They may also be offered extemporaneously by those gathered. The bidding prayer, or another form may be used.

Lord's Prayer
The Prayer of Jesus is said by all.

> **Our Father, who art in heaven,**
> **Hallowed be thy Name.**
> **Thy kingdom come.**
> **Thy will be done, on earth as it is in heaven.**
> **Give us this day our daily bread.**
> **And forgive us our trespasses,**
> **as we forgive those who trespass against us.**
> **And lead us not into temptation,**
> **But deliver us from evil.**
> **For thine is the kingdom, and the power, and the glory,**
> **for ever and ever.**
> **Amen.**

Closing Hymn or Song

Transition to Study or Work
Daily Prayer concludes with one of the following responses.

> **A**

> The grace of God be with us all, now and always.
> > **Amen.**
> Let us bless the Lord,
> > **And praise his holy name. Amen.**

B

May the God of hope fill us with the peace of Christ, through the power
of the Holy Spirit.
> **Amen.**

C

May God keep us in his light and truth and love forever.
> **May he give us joy and peace. Amen.**

D

May we continue to grow in the grace of God and the knowledge of
Jesus Christ, our Lord.
> **May the Spirit of God give us peace. Amen.**

E *(Aaronic Blessing)*

May the Lord bless us and keep us.
> **May the face of the Lord shine upon us and be gracious to us.**
May the Lord look upon us with favor and give us peace.
> **Amen.**

Fuller Morning Prayer

This setting of Morning Prayer (composed at Fuller Seminary) follows the general pattern of services traditionally designed for use at the break of day. Following the historic Jewish custom of prayer throughout the day, admonitions in the Epistles to pray without ceasing (as in 1 Thess 5:16–17), and the practice of the early church (encouraged by church fathers such as Tertullian and Origen), the monastic practice of praying a set of seven or eight liturgies throughout the day and night became established. The terms *liturgy of the hours, praying the hours, opus Dei*, and *the daily*, or *divine office* all refer to these set modes of prayer. (See "The Daily Office (Praying the Hours)" which follows this service of Morning Prayer.) The Morning Prayer service is often called *Matins* (Latin for morning) or *Lauds* (Latin for praise, named for the traditional use of the psalms of praise, particularly 148, 149, and 150). The range of practice and form for Morning Prayer has varied greatly throughout history and around the globe. *Matins* is traditionally said (and/or sung with chants) at daybreak, reflecting on the rise of the sun as a symbol for Christ's resurrection. This service of Morning Prayer is designed for use at the start of the day as people begin their work or ministry. It incorporates a series of meditative or cyclical chants fashioned in the manner for worship made familiar by the Taizé community in France. Where indicated, the chants may be sung repeatedly, successively drawing worshippers into prayer. They are designed to be sung *a capella* (unaccompanied by instruments), though a C instrument such as a flute or violin may play along with the melody where desired. Where smaller notes are indicated in the music, they represent a harmony part that may be sung.

Invitatory *(Psalm 51:15)*
The Invitatory may be sung repeatedly as a cyclical chant. It concludes with a single voicing of the Gloria Patri.

214

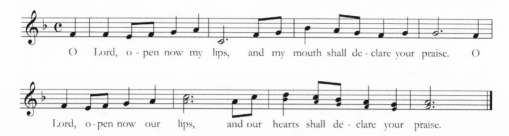

O Lord, o-pen now my lips, and my mouth shall de-clare your praise. O

Lord, o-pen now our lips, and our hearts shall de-clare your praise.

Gloria Patri *(early Greek doxology, paraphrased from the English Orthodox liturgy)*
Sung once as a conclusion to the Invitatory.

Glo-ry___ to the Fa-ther, to the Son, and the Ho-ly Spir-it. For

now and e-ter-ni-ty, for all a-ges to come. A - men

Silence

Morning Antiphon

One of the following antiphons is sung. They may be sung repeatedly as cyclical chants. Either of these antiphons can be sung as a canon (a round). The second voices begin in the third measure (at the asterisk*).

Christ the Lord is ri-sen. Come now and a-dore him. Al - le-lu - ia.

For Lent and times of pensiveness or despair:

In the womb of mor-ning, light re-pla-ces dark-ness. Mor-ning joy re-pla-ces grief.

Silence

Venite *(Psalm 95:1–7, 96:9, 13)*
Read responsively: † *designates the first group,* ‡ *designates the second group;*
all speak bold portions.

**All: O come, let us worship and bow down; let us kneel before
the Lord, our Creator.**

† O come, let us sing to the Lord.
  ‡ *Let us shout aloud to the rock of our salvation.*

† Let us come before his presence with thanksgiving.
  ‡ *Let us extol him with songs.*

† For the Lord is a great God, a great King above all gods.
  ‡ *In his hand are the deep places of the earth; the heights of*
the mountains are also his.

**All: O come, let us worship and bow down; let us kneel before
the Lord, our Creator.**

† The sea is his, for he made it.
  ‡ *His hands have formed the dry land.*

† He is our God. We are the people of his pasture, and the sheep in his care.
  ‡ *Worship the Lord in holy splendor. Tremble before him, all the earth.*

† For he comes to judge the earth.
  ‡ *He will judge the world with righteousness, and the peoples with his truth.*

**All: O come, let us worship and bow down; let us kneel before the Lord,
our Creator.**

Morning Song/Hymn
A song or hymn suitable for the morning or fitting to the scriptural texts is sung.

Scripture Reading(s)

One or more Scripture lessons are read. After each reading, the following affirmation may be said.

> One: God gives us this word to guide our day.
> **All: Thanks be to God.**

Silence

Song of Zechariah *(Luke 1:68–79, paraphrased)*

Antiphon (to be sung by all after each portion of the reading; it may be sung repeatedly after the final reading)

Bles-sed be the Lord God of Is-ra-el. Bles-sed be the Lord, our God.

> One: God has looked with kindness on his people and redeemed them.
> He has raised up a savior in the house of David;
> He has spoken to us through the mouth of his prophets of old,
> And told that we would be saved from our enemies and from the hand
> of all who hate us.

Antiphon

> One: God has shown the mercy promised to our forebears,
> and has recalled his covenant,
> the oath that he swore to our father Abraham.
> He will rescue us from the hands of our enemies,
> And we will serve in righteousness before him all our days.

Antiphon

> One: The tender mercy of our God, as the dawn from on high,
> will break upon us.
> It will give light to those who sit in darkness and in the shadow of death;
> it will guide our feet into the way of peace.

Antiphon

Prayers

The prayers begin with singing the prayer refrain. The refrain is then sung following each petition. It may be sung repeatedly at the conclusion of the prayers.

Prayer Refrain (Psalm 27:7)

Hear our prayers as we cry a - loud. Be gra - cious and an - swer us.

Collect for the Morning

The collect is said by all.

O God of Light, you have made both night and day to order our days. Thank you for the rest, however complete, brief, or troubled, that has come to us this past night. We bless you for the light that shines in the daytime, and for the light of your love that guides us through the activities and concerns of this new day. Let all we strive to do today be pleasing to you, O God, and advance your reign on earth. We pray through your Son, Jesus Christ, who is the Lord of Light. Amen

The Prayer of Jesus

The Lord's Prayer is said by all.

> **Our Father, who art in heaven,**
> **Hallowed be thy Name.**
> **Thy kingdom come.**
> **Thy will be done, on earth as it is in heaven.**
> **Give us this day our daily bread.**
> **And forgive us our trespasses, as we forgive those who trespass against us.**
> **And lead us not into temptation, but deliver us from evil.**
> **For thine is the kingdom, and the power, and the glory,**
> **for ever and ever.**
> **Amen.**

Benediction

The blessing may be sung repeatedly as a cyclical chant.

The Lord bless us and keep us in his light and love for - e - ver.

The Lord bless and keep us in his ho - ly light.

Sacramental and Occasional Services Templates

The following templates indicate the typical shape of baptismal and communion rites and liturgies for weddings and funerals. Many Christian denominations have hymnals, service books, and occasional services materials available that provide such liturgies for their congregations. These templates can be used both by churches without denominational resources and as blueprints for designing alternative liturgies for those who have denominational materials. Note that some churches (following the Baptist denominational tradition) use the term *ordinance* rather than *sacrament*. The term reflects a Zwinglian view of the Lord's Supper as a remembrance, rather than as a means of grace through which the presence of Christ is mediated. The word derives from the understanding that baptism and communion were mandated by Jesus and that he ordered his followers to baptize and to remember him through communion.

Baptismal Rites

Most churches hold two things in common in their baptismal rites. The first is the use of water as a sign of God's adoption of people into the body of Christ. The second is the use of the *baptismal formula* whereby candidates are baptized in the name of the Triune God. Some traditions baptize people of all ages, including infants, as did the early church. Others believe in and practice *believer's baptism*, whereby persons proclaim their faith as a prerequisite for baptism. Both traditions make use of the elements listed here, though free church traditions usually use fewer of them than more formal traditions.

Location and Placement of Baptism

Baptisms may take place in many locations, essentially wherever there is water and a gathering of believers. Some churches practice baptism in rivers, lakes, or oceans. Most, however, hold baptismal rites in churches or places of worship. Baptismal fonts and pools are part of the furnishings found in most sanctuaries.

Baptismal theology holds, in most churches, for baptisms to be performed in the presence of the body of Christ. It is fitting for the congregation to be gathered around and in support of the newly baptized, whether the rite occurs in the church or elsewhere. In circumstances where baptisms are performed outside the assembly of believers, the converts may be introduced to the people during a subsequent worship service. There is often an urging from nervous or shy families for baptism to be done privately. It is the minister's responsibility to teach that baptism is a public rite that properly involves the witness of the congregation. Ministers are right to encourage (if not insist) that baptisms be performed in public worship. In urgent circumstances baptisms are sometimes performed in hospitals or at the scene of accidents. It is commonly held that any baptized Christian may perform a baptism on such occasions. An ordained minister otherwise typically performs baptisms.

Within a service of worship, baptisms are often scheduled to follow the sermon. This is a fitting response to the proclamation of the Word of God. They are also performed at the beginning of worship services, and occasionally at other times during the service. Worship planners should be intentional about the placement of baptismal rites within worship.

Consideration should also be given to the scheduling of baptisms during the church year. The strongest tradition is to hold baptisms during the Easter Vigil, following a Lenten period of catechetical instruction. Another common placement for baptisms is during celebration of the Baptism of Our Lord, which usually falls on the first Sunday after the day of Epiphany (January 6).

Elements of the Rite

Denominational polity and theology will dictate the shape of a congregation's baptismal rites and the proper age for baptisms to occur. Free church traditions have simple rites, whereas churches with formal liturgy traditions have more elaborate rites with established patterns. The following elements are those found most commonly; they have roots in the practices of the early church. Free church traditions typically use fewer of these elements; formal liturgies often use them all. The two elements that appear to be nearly universal are the use of water and the baptismal formula.

Water

In Roman Catholic and many Orthodox settings, baptisms are performed with holy water, water that has been blessed in advance by a bishop or a priest. In most Protestant churches, ordinary tap water is used for baptisms. In some traditions, the rites of baptism have elements (prayers over the water) that effectively bless the water for holy use.

The amount of water used is dependent upon church polity and tradition. Most free church congregations prefer to use a pool for full immersion of the candidates. This is not inappropriate in more liturgically formal churches, though they often prefer to use a font from which water is placed or poured upon the head of the candidate. It is an interesting historical accident to note that as the church moved from the Mediterranean area from which it originated, into the northern climates of Europe, baptisms tended to move from full immersion to head washing. The colder climates made full immersion impractical during winter. Even where a limited amount of water is used in baptism, it can be generously applied to the head so as to allow the rich symbol of water to be recognized by all observers. Some churches emphasize this symbol by pouring water into the font during a prayer over the water.

Songs and Hymns

It is appropriate for songs and hymns to be sung by the congregation before, during, and/or after the baptismal rite. Selections can be made from among those specifically written with baptismal themes, as well as hymns and songs relating to faith, commitment, witness, and trust.

Presentation

Baptismal candidates are sometimes presented to the congregation by the minister or by baptismal sponsors selected as mentors from the congregation. Sponsors of adults walk beside the candidates and the newly baptized as they learn about the faith and engage in the life of the community. Sponsors for children and infants (also known as Godparents) typically agree to work alongside parents to see that the children are raised faithfully in the practice of faith. When called upon to present candidates, sponsors may say these or similar words: "I present John to receive the sacrament of Holy Baptism."

Pastoral Pronouncements or Instructions

Those presiding over baptisms sometimes make pronouncements in order to frame the event and orient the assembly toward the purpose and significance of baptism. The rite may begin with a description of the meaning of baptism with references to entrance of the baptized into the community of faith, their liberation from sin and death, the use of water as a sign of God's adoption, the power of the Holy Spirit working through baptism, and the life of obedience that follows baptism.

When young children are baptized, another pronouncement may follow the presentation. This statement is directed toward the parents and sponsors, reminding them of the significance of bringing children to faith through the sacrament. It may include a question of commitment, asking them their willingness to fulfill the obligations of bringing the children to worship and raising them in the faith. The question may be framed in these or similar words: "Do you promise to fulfill these obligations?" The parents and sponsors may respond, "We do."

Blessing or Prayer of Thanksgiving Over the Water

A blessing over the water may be offered by the presiding minister. This may be extemporized or written as a collect or other prayer form. Some traditions use a traditional prayer formula known as Martin Luther's Flood Prayer. This was not a form initiated by Luther, but adapted by him for use in baptisms as a way to recall and give thanks for God's use of water as a means of grace throughout history. It contains references to:

- God's Spirit moving over the waters at creation

- The gift of water that nourishes all living things

- The waters of the flood that condemned the wicked, but saved Noah and his family

- God's leading the Israelites out of bondage and to the Promised Land through the Red Sea

- John's baptism of Jesus

- Water as a sign of the kingdom of God and of cleansing and rebirth

- Jesus' command to baptize all nations in the name of the Triune God

and concludes with a prayer for those being baptized and a closing Trinitarian doxology.

Profession of Faith

The Apostle's Creed is a baptismal statement in use since the eighth century. It developed as a response to the three-fold question historically asked of candidates at baptism regarding their belief in the Trinity. The creed is still typically used as a part of baptismal rites. It is sometimes preceded with the question, "Do you renounce all the forces of evil, the devil, and all his empty promises?" To this the candidates, or the parents and sponsors of young children respond, "I do." They are then asked the three-fold question. The first article of the creed is said by the candidates (and/or parents and sponsors) in response to: "Do you believe in God the Father?" The second article is in response to: "Do you believe in Jesus Christ, the Son of God?" The third article responds to: "Do you believe in God the Holy Spirit?"

The Baptism

The minister then baptizes each of the candidates. Sometimes, the minister first says to the candidate, "*Name*, do you desire to be baptized?" When the candidate responds, "I do," he or she is then washed with or immersed in water.

There are two common ways to do this. The minister says, "I baptize you in the name of the Father, and of the Son, and of the Holy Spirit (or Ghost)." Alternatively, he or she may say, "You are baptized in the name of the Father, and of the Son, and of the Holy Spirit." The minister usually first declares the person's first (baptismal) name: "Mary, you are baptized . . ." The water may be applied as a single washing or immersion, with the full Trinitarian formula being proclaimed (e.g., "I baptize you in the name of the Father and of the Son and of the Holy Spirit"), or it may be a triple washing/immersion corresponding to the naming of each member of the Trinity: "You are baptized in the name of the Father (wash/immerse), and of the Son (wash/immerse) and of the Holy Spirit (wash/immerse)".

Baptismal Prayer

This is a prayer offered by the presiding minister for the invocation of the Holy Spirit upon the newly baptized. It may begin with thanksgiving for freeing believers from the power of sin through Christ's death and resurrection and through baptism. The prayer may call upon the Holy Spirit to pour the gifts of the Spirit upon the life of the newly baptized: the spirit of wisdom and understanding, the spirit of counsel and might, the spirit of knowledge and the fear of the Lord, and the spirit of joy in God's presence (see Isa 11:2–3).

Sealing

Some traditions today hold to the ancient practice of sealing the newly baptized with oil as a sign of being safeguarded from evil. The practice is also known as anointing or chrismation (*chrism* is a Greek based term for *anoint,* just as Christ is a Greek version of the Anointed One). In the oldest traditions, the anointing was known as confirmation (the baptism being confirmed by the Holy Spirit). Olive oil, or a fragrant oil, is placed upon the brow of the baptized in the shape of the cross. The action is usually accompanied by a pronouncement such as: "*Name*, you have been sealed by the Holy Spirit and marked with the cross of Christ." The baptized may respond, "Amen."

Baptismal Candle

In some churches it is common to present the newly baptized a candle to be lighted on the anniversary of one's baptism. A white candle usually represents Christ, the Light of the World.

Conclusion

Other prayers for the lives of the baptized and words of introduction to the assembly may conclude the baptismal rite.

Communion Liturgies

Celebrations of the Lord's Supper usually occur within worship services that contain the reading and proclamation of God's Word. Communion is typically located after the sermon, as a fitting response to hearing the Word.

Liturgies for the Lord's Supper vary greatly according to tradition and polity. Most churches celebrate Holy Communion regularly, though a few (such as strict Quakers) do not celebrate sacraments at all. Communion, whether celebrated quarterly, monthly, weekly, or daily, usually involves a liturgy of prayer and declaration. The declaration (almost universally used) is of the Institution Narrative, the words from Scripture that describe the Last Supper.

Free church traditions usually have a reduced communion liturgy; formal liturgical traditions have more elaborate, prescribed liturgies that include the Peace, the Offering, the Preparation of the Table, the Dialogue, the Preface, the Sanctus, the Institution Narrative, the Anamnesis, the Epiclesis, the Intercessions, the concluding Doxology, and the Agnus Dei. These are followed by the distribution of the bread and wine (or grape juice). The terms Great Thanksgiving and Eucharistic Prayer apply to the elements of the communion liturgy. Several denominations employ the custom of singing or chanting portions of the communion liturgy.

Luther, the first Reformer, taught that no single form of worship or communion liturgy was to be considered normative. Still, his German Mass (*Deutsche Messe*) followed closely the elaborate forms of the Roman Catholic Church. Later, Reformers chose to shorten communion liturgies and to make them less formalized. They also introduced the pattern of less frequent offerings of the Lord's Supper. Luther advised that communion be celebrated weekly; not so that people might commune every Sunday, but so that on the occasion when a person chose to receive the sacrament, it would be available. Today, many forms of liturgy and patterns of practice are used and deemed acceptable, varying according to tradition and denomination. In constructing communion liturgies, worship planners and presiding ministers can select from among these ritual elements.

Elements of the Rite

The Peace

The kiss of peace (see Rom 16:16; 1 Cor 16:20; 1 Thess 5:26) is a New Testament practice that became ritualized as part of the communion liturgy. Today, it is usually referred to as the sharing of peace. The peace is introduced by the presiding minister with these or similar words, "The peace of Christ be with you all." The people may respond, "And also with you." Then, the people are invited to share the peace with others. This is typically done with a verbal greeting (e.g., "The peace of Christ be with you") accompanied by a handshake, hug, or kiss.

The Offering

This action was originally the preparation and presentation of the bread and wine for communion. As early as the fourth century, the practice had expanded to include bringing forth gifts from the people for the ministry of the church. In many churches today, this action is entirely reserved for the congregation's offerings of tithes and other gifts and no longer has to do with bringing forth bread and wine for communion. The ancient practice of presenting bread and wine along with other gifts is being reintroduced in many churches today. A relevant song or hymn and/or an offertory prayer usually follow the offering.

The Preparation of the Table

If the bread and wine (grape juice) are brought forward during the offertory song or prayer, they are received by an assisting minister and placed for use on the table. If they are not brought forward during the offering, they are usually placed nearby on a credence table and brought to the table during the offering. Alternatively, the table may be set before worship begins with the elements in place all through the Gathering and Word portions of the service. The preparation of the bread and wine or juice for communion is usually handled by a select group of persons whose ministry is to serve the congregation by procuring the communion elements, sometimes baking the bread, keeping the communion vessels and cloths clean, and making the table and elements ready for the Lord's Supper. These people are sometimes referred to as the *altar guild*.

The Dialogue

This is a ritualized conversation between the presiding minister and the congregation. In this exchange the people prepare themselves for hearing the prayers of the Great Thanksgiving and for the reception of Holy Communion. The exchange, sometimes called the *sursam corda* (the Latin phrase for "lift up your hearts"), is in three parts:

> Presider: The Lord be with you.
> People: And also with you.
> Presider: Lift up your hearts.
> People: We lift them up to the Lord.
> Presider: Let us give thanks to the Lord, our God.
> People: It is right to give God thanks and praise.

The Preface

In traditions that make use of the dialogue, the preface usually follows. This is a prayer of thanksgiving to God for what he has done through Jesus Christ. It is said by the presider on behalf of the people. The preface usually reflects the season of the church year and is accordingly referred to as the *proper* preface (see *propers* in the Glossary of Liturgical Terms found near the end of this book). The purposes of the preface are to articulate reasons for giving thanks at the particular occasion and to join the praise of the assembly with that of the whole church on earth as well as the church in heaven. The preface usually concludes with words similar to these: "With the church on earth and the host of heaven, we praise God's name and join their unending hymn."

The Sanctus

The *sanctus* is the unending hymn referred to at the conclusion to the Preface. It derives from Isaiah's holy vision of heaven (Isa 6:3). *Sanctus* is the Latin word for "holy." For the full text, see "The Ordinary of the Roman Catholic Eucharistic Service (Mass)" in the "Ecumenical Texts of the Church" essay found in the Essays and Resources portion of this book. The *sanctus* is usually said or sung by the people. The presider continues with concluding words.

The Institution Narrative

In most traditions, whether a church celebrates the full communion liturgy or an abbreviated version, a declaration of the institution narrative (also called the words of institution, or *verba*) is used as a central element of the rite. The words are found in Matt 26:26–28, Mark 14:22–25, Luke 22:17–20, and 1 Cor 11:23–26. As used in the liturgy, the *verba* are commonly a pastiche of the four New Testament versions. There is no general ecumenical agreement on the form of the *verba* used in communion liturgies. Some traditions provide a congregational acclamation following the narrative.

Two things should be noted about the narrative: First, Protestant liturgical theologies, though they differ on points relating to the Lord's Supper, agree that the words of institution are not said in order to confect the body of Christ or mysteriously make communion happen. They are recited as a sacred reminder and a warrant for the church's continued celebration of Holy Communion. Second, presiding ministers should take care not to enact the words of the narrative while they are spoken. Breaking the bread (also called *fraction*) at the words, "Jesus took bread, blessed, and *broke* it," strongly implies that it is the very act of breaking the bread in imitation of Jesus that mysteriously turns the bread into the body of Christ. Ministers should avoid actions in worship leadership that give impressions contrary to the theological beliefs of the community.

The Anamnesis

This is a Greek based term that means memorial or remembrance. But it suggests more than these English words convey. *Anamnesis* suggests both memory of a past action (Jesus' death and resurrection) and commemoration of those events in the present. The Eucharistic Prayer is, in its entirety, an act of *anamnesis*. The specific portion of the communion liturgy known as the anamnesis occurs within the *verba*: "Do this in remembrance of me."

The Epiclesis

The Great Thanksgiving may continue with an invocation of the Holy Spirit (*epiclesis*) as a response to Christ's saving acts. Said by the presiding minister, it may take the form of a consecration, inviting the Spirit to allow ordinary bread and wine (or grape juice) to be understood as sacramental elements. Alternatively, the epiclesis may call on the Spirit to come upon the assembly, assisting people to engage in holy living that reflects the fruits of the Spirit.

The Intercessions

In some forms, the Eucharistic Prayer includes intercessions for the local congregation and the broader Church of Christ. The intercessions commonly pray that through communion, the church is united and/or that it is made holy and perfect in love.

The Concluding Doxology and Amen

The final words of the Great Thanksgiving typically include a doxology that draws together the themes of the prayer. It usually concludes with praise of the three persons of the Trinity. The prayer is sometimes followed by the people saying or singing the great Amen, thus signifying the assembly's consent to the words and themes of the Eucharistic Prayer. In some traditions, the bread is raised up or broken during the Amen. The purpose of breaking the bread is to prepare it for distribution. There is no purpose in breaking the bread if it is in the form of a small communion wafer. To do so is a superfluous gesture that suggests a superstitious understanding of the sacrament.

The Lord's Prayer

Whether the Great Thanksgiving or the simple institution narrative is used as the center of the communion liturgy, it is typically followed by the congregation's recital of the Prayer of Jesus.

The Agnus Dei

A historic congregational response to the Eucharistic Prayer is to say or sing the *Agnus Dei*. This is a prayer that Jesus, the Lamb of God, will have mercy on the people. (See "The Ordinary of the Roman Catholic Eucharistic Service (Mass)" in the "Ecumenical Texts of the Church" essay found in the Essays and Resources portion of this book.)

The Distribution

Following the communion liturgy, the congregation receives the bread and wine (or grape juice) in a customary manner. Some traditions serve the elements to people as they are seated in chairs or pews. Others invite people forward to stand or kneel as they receive the elements from the hands of the communion ministers. Worship planners should be aware of the customs for distribution within their churches and arrange for distribution accordingly. Note that there are other practices, including one found in some vineyard churches: The people go forward during a song to receive bread and grape juice. There is no communion liturgy, except for the act of taking of the elements to their seats where they are consumed.

The Post-Communion Prayer

At the conclusion of the distribution of communion elements, a prayer and/or song may follow. Typically, it thanks God for nourishing the church through the sacrament of Holy Communion.

Sending or Dismissal

Celebrations of Holy Communion usually conclude shortly after the distribution. Having been fed by the Word of God and nourished through the sacrament's holy food, the people are dismissed or sent from worship. For a description of the theological nature of this moment and why the term *sending* is preferable to *dismissal*, see "The Four-Fold Pattern of Worship" in the Essays and Resources section of the *Teaching Hymnal*.

Wedding Ceremonies

Services of Holy Matrimony are commonly (and historically) officiated by ordained ministers (pastors) and priests of the church. Though weddings may legally occur outside the church, when presided over by a pastor (whether in a church building or at another site) they are to be considered services of worship. Accordingly, the presiding pastor should include in his or her pre-marriage counseling a time of instruction about the nature of such a service and those things appropriate to it. The minister should not be timid about making theological judgments regarding what happens in a wedding ceremony. Even when marriage couples urge the inclusion of elements that are inappropriate to worship (such as their *favorite song*), the presiding minister should help them plan a service that is sacred and Christ centered. Occasionally, a couple will elect to have their wedding take place within a Sunday worship service. This appropriately indicates that though the ceremony is one of life's important events, it takes place within the larger context of the life of faith and the worship of God.

While marriage is typically solemnized by a ceremony, the actual legal joining in marriage occurs when an authorized person (ordained minister, licensed minister, judge, or justice of the peace) signs the marriage license. A wedding ceremony without such a legally signed document does not constitute a legal marriage. Pastors should always consult local authorities (usually the County Clerk's office within a given county) to determine how a person becomes authorized to officiate over weddings in the area. Note that some wedding licenses require additional signatures (the wedding couple and/or witnesses), while some do not.

Wedding rehearsals are often necessary to ensure an orderly ceremony. They are typically held the day or evening before the wedding. The main purpose of the rehearsal is to instruct wedding participants as to when, how, and to where they should move; where to stand or sit; and to provide for rehearsal of readings and songs. The couple, presumably having met with the minister in planning and pre-marriage counseling sessions, will already be aware of the details of the wedding.

Marriage and domestic partnership among same-sex individuals is increasingly more visible in society today. In some traditions, same-sex marriage is permitted. It is important that church leaders familiarize themselves with local civil law concerning same-sex marriage and domestic partnership as well as denominational and congregational policies. If same-sex unions are part of your denominational tradition, the rite operates within the principle that there are not separate rituals for same-sex and opposite-sex couples; rather, the rite is the same. Pronouns are changed as appropriate.

Elements of the Rite

Hymns and Songs

Wedding ceremonies may include congregational hymns and songs. Their use requires appropriate means by which to provide song texts for use by those gathered. The people may be referred to a hymnal or song texts may be projected on a screen or placed in a worship folder or bulletin. When copying song texts, it is important to follow copyright guidelines. Churches should not be in the habit of breaking laws and stealing copyrighted material. (See "Copyright and Public Domain" in the Hymns and Songs for Worship section of the *Teaching Hymnal*.) Congregational songs can be sung at various places: at the beginning of the ceremony, following readings, following the sermon, and at the end of the ceremony.

It is common for weddings to include songs sung by soloists or vocal groups. The minister should carefully work with the wedding couple to select songs that support marriage and that are worshipful in nature. Especially appropriate are the songs that make reference to scriptural passages about marriage and love. As noted above, the wedding ceremony is not the place for romantic songs or favorite popular songs. These are best reserved for wedding receptions.

Other Music

It is common for instrumental music to be played as a prelude to the service, during the procession of the bridal party, at the conclusion of the ceremony, and at other times. As with hymns and songs, care should be given to select music that is appropriate to the sacred nature of the event.

Greeting

The minister typically greets people in the name of Christ and invites their witness of and participation in the ceremony.

Prayers

Christian weddings presume that the ceremony takes place within the context of worship. This means that prayers spoken on behalf of the people by the minister are appropriate. They may occur in several places:

> Prayers at the beginning of the ceremony may thank God for the love of the wedding couple and for the favor God has shown to marriage in Scripture and through history.

> Prayers following the vows and exchange of rings may include petitions for faithful adherence to the vows made by the couple, for blessing of the marriage, for the possibility of parenthood, and for the blessing of all those who are married.

> The Lord's Prayer can be said following other prayers near the end of the ceremony. Because it is so widely known, recitation of Jesus' prayer is a fitting way to invite the participation of all gathered.

Pronouncement or Instruction

Following an opening greeting, the minister may offer words of instruction about the holy nature of marriage, its warrants in Scripture, and God's present and continuing blessing of holy matrimony.

Scripture and Other Readings

As with all services of worship, it is appropriate to read one or more lessons from the Bible, especially those that speak to marriage, human relationship, and the nature of love. It is not inappropriate to include other readings (such as poetry) so long as they are fitting for worship and supportive of the holiness of marriage.

One of the ways that wedding couples honor members of their families and friends is to ask them to serve as readers for the ceremony. The wedding rehearsal allows for a time of rehearsal for those who read. When necessary, the minister should offer suggestions to the readers so that the material is performed audibly and with clarity and meaning. Alternatively, the minister may read the lessons.

Homily or Sermon

In Christian weddings, it is most appropriate for the minister (or another qualified person) to give a brief sermon. The term *homily* sometimes refers to such a brief reflection on Scripture. Some ministers neglect to preach at weddings. They miss an opportunity to proclaim the love of God to an assembly that is typically beyond their usual audience. While it is inappropriate for the preacher to evangelize during a wedding sermon, he or she can be bold in speaking of God as the author of love and the source of sustenance for married couples and families. As with all sermons, the wedding homily should reflect appropriately upon the scriptural texts that have been read. Generally, wedding sermons should be briefer than a preacher's typical sermon. When couples of mixed religious background are married, the minister should carefully work out with the couple the Christian nature of the ceremony. Just as it is inappropriate for a Christian minister to preside over a completely secular wedding (there are other persons more suited for such occasions), it is inappropriate for a Christian minister to avoid mention of Christ or persons of the Trinity. Christian ministers are legally allowed to perform weddings because of their faith commitments and should not neglect to represent the faith responsibly.

Vows

Speaking the vows stands at the center of the marriage rite. Vows are sacred promises made in the presence of God and God's people. That they are witnessed by a community reinforces the public nature and necessity of marriage as a strong bond within society and the church. There are many versions of marriage vows from which a minister and couple may choose. They are typically crafted with an eye toward beauty of expression as well as significance of intent.

Some couples may request to write their own vows. While this is not inappropriate, the minister should instruct the couple in their import. Vows are not intended to be romantic expressions of love. They are, rather, sacred oaths that bind couples together for a lifetime. The vows should be statements that speak of the reality of life together rather than unrealistic declarations about personal feelings. Vows reflect the nature of love in action, rather than love as feeling: they should state the unequivocal commitment of persons to one another. It is advisable that vows written by the wedding couple be shown in advance to the minister who can ascertain whether they are proper or need editing before use in the service. When couples write their own vows, it is prudent to advise them not to attempt delivering them from memory at a time when they are likely to be nervous.

The minister should assist the couple in reciting their vows by asking them to repeat the words. He or she should break the vows into short phrases so that the nervous bride and groom do not become confused in their speech.

Rings

It is customary for the wedding couple to exchange wedding rings. They stand as circular, unbroken symbols; signs of love and faithfulness. The exchange of rings generally follows immediately upon the vows. Some ministers provide the congregation with a verbal instruction about the symbolism of wedding rings; some lead the couple in making promissory statements as the rings are exchanged. Though it is a strong custom in many cultures, there is no requirement that marriages need to be marked by the exchange or wearing of rings.

Pronouncement of Marriage and Charge

Following the vows and the exchange of rings, the minister may pronounce the couple as husband and wife with these or similar words: "Name and Name, by their promises before God and in the presence of this assembly have bound themselves to one another as husband and wife." This may be followed by a blessing and a charge: "Blessed be God, the Father, Son, and Holy Spirit." and "What God has joined together let no one put asunder."

Note that in some places, where same gender weddings are performed, the pronouncement may be spoken so as to correspond with the individuals involved.

Blessings

Following the pronouncement, the minister, parents, and/or others may offer a blessing for the couple.

Customs

There are many cultural traditions that find their way into marriage ceremonies. Lighting of a unity candle is common in many places. The intention is to represent the joining of two persons and two families as one. Jumping the broom is an African American custom that signifies that the newly married persons are passing from one stage of life to another. Tying a cord of unity around the couple is practiced in some cultures. In some traditions, the joining of hands forms the central symbolic ritual of marriage. These and other customs are appropriate to wedding ceremonies. They provide occasion to honor persons according to their culture and tradition. Such customs usually follow the blessings.

Holy Communion

When a wedding takes place during a Sunday morning (or other regularly scheduled) worship service, it may incorporate the Lord's Supper. The celebration of Holy Communion may also be appropriate in cases where the couple, their families, and friends are known to be people of faith and are comfortable with celebration of the sacrament. Because the Lord's Supper is a public event, it is inappropriate for a wedding couple to be served communion if it is not offered to the entire gathering. It is advisable to avoid inclusion of the sacrament in weddings where it causes an obvious division between believers and nonbelievers. If communion is to take place, it usually follows the vows and pronouncement.

Benediction

It is appropriate to conclude a marriage ceremony with a benediction. Note that this is not a closing prayer. Closing prayers are also appropriate, but the benediction is a declaration of God's blessing on the couple and those gathered.

The Presentation and the Kiss

It is customary in many places for the minster to introduce the new status of the married couple with these or similar words: "It is my pleasure to present to you Mr. and Mrs. . . ." The minister should carefully plan how to make this presentation with the following considerations in mind: Will one or both of the couple change their surnames? Do they prefer *not* to be called Mr. and Mrs.? What order shall their names be given? What are the couple's preferences in same-sex situations? The wise minister will seek agreement about how to make this pronouncement with the couple.

Following the presentation, it is customary in many cultures for the couple to kiss one another. This may be occasioned by a remark from the minister such as: "You may now kiss the bride," or "You may now kiss as husband and wife." Alternatively (and perhaps more pastorally sensitive), the couple can be instructed (during the rehearsal) to kiss one another without a verbal direction by the minister. The kiss can occur directly after the benediction, or if there is a presentation, immediately thereafter. In some cultures, it is customary for the assembly to break into applause after the Presentation. This can be a nonverbal signal for the kiss.

Funeral and Memorial Services

Christian funerals and memorial services are occasional worship events that occur frequently in the life of a congregation. The key difference between them is the presence or absence of the deceased. Because funerals have the remains of the deceased present, whether in a coffin or cremated remains in an urn, the event is usually scheduled for a few days after the death. When a funeral is followed by the interment of the body at a cemetery, an additional rite is typically employed. Alternatively, a graveside service can take the place of the church service and move directly to committal of the remains to the ground. In some cultures, it is customary to spread cremated ashes at sea or in other places. Local laws should be observed regarding the spreading of ashes near or on land.

Memorial services usually take place after the deceased has been committed for burial or the ashes are spread. They sometimes take place well after the death, allowing time for the travel of distant family and friends.

The shape of funerals and memorial services can be identical, though the presence of the deceased and the timing of a funeral often make it more intensely emotional. In designing a funeral or memorial service, it is critical for the minister to meet with the family and friends of the deceased to make decisions about a number of considerations such as: scriptural readings; selection of pallbearers; other persons to involve in the service; whether or not ancillary rites by military personnel or those representing clubs or lodges will be included; whether or not there will be a time of personal sharing, and who will speak; and so forth. This is also a time for pastoral listening and prayer.

The style of worship at a funeral or memorial service is usually solemn and formal. The great hymns of the faith are fitting expressions during such services. More contemporary songs can also provide comfort. All hymns and songs should be theologically and liturgically appropriate to the tenor of the service. Though solemn, funerals and memorial services can also be an occasion for joyful reflection on the hope of the resurrection, especially when the deceased has lived a long and fruitful Christian life.

There are many pastoral issues to deal with at the time of death. The departure of an elderly person evokes different emotions than the death of a young person or a child. Where the faith commitments of the deceased are strong and widely known, pastors can make hopeful reference to their faith. When the faith of the person is unknown, pastors need to proceed carefully, so as to serve the family without passing judgment on the deceased. In such cases, proclamation of the Gospel to the living is one of the main goals. Services following accidental deaths, suicides, and stillbirths also present pastoral care challenges. Close ministry and prayer with family members are especially needed in such situations.

Location

Funerals and memorial services usually take place in one of three settings: within a church building, at a funeral home chapel, or at a cemetery. When a funeral is followed by a cemetery committal, there is usually a formal procession of hearse and automobiles from the church to the grave. When funerals and memorial services are held at funeral home chapels, special consideration needs to be given to the availability of musical instruments and hymn or song books for congregational singing. Regardless of the location of the service, worship planners should bear in mind the presence of flower bouquets that can dominate the space. When a coffin is present, it is usually brought into the worship space and placed at the head of the central aisle. In some traditions, it is placed perpendicular to the aisle. In others, it is placed in line with the aisle with the head of the deceased toward the chancel or communion table.

At memorial services, families often desire to place photographs of the deceased and other mementos at the front of the church or chapel as a visual reminder of the one who died. This allows for people to reflect on the life of the person as well as his or her death.

Elements of the Rite

Non-Christian Ancillary Rites

Burial rites have been developed by the US military branches, as well as social and fraternal societies. These typically take place outside the place of Christian worship. Military honors are best observed at the graveside. They typically involve a bugler playing "Taps" and a ceremonial folding and presentation of the American flag. Some honors include a twenty-one gun salute, making it imperative that the event take place out of doors.

Rites provided by lodges or other fraternal organizations do not belong within a Christian church. Families often insist on these rites and it is pastorally wise to consider when and where such rites take place.

Music

It is common for instrumental music to be played as prelude and postlude to the service of worship. The planners may choose to incorporate congregational hymns and songs in the service. They are especially appropriate at the beginning and end of worship, between readings, and after the sermon. Alternatively, solo or ensemble voices may sing songs fitting to the occasion at these times. If there is Holy Communion, songs can also be sung during the Distribution.

Entrance

Ministers, funeral directors, and pallbearers, along with the bereaved, usually meet together at the entrance to the sanctuary. A procession is made to the front of the church, where the coffin is situated, as the bereaved take their seats in the front row. The procession may be accompanied by instrumental music or a congregational hymn. The minister may offer a greeting and/or a pronouncement praising God as the source of mercy, consolation, and comfort.

The Pall

The pall is a large cloth placed over the coffin during funeral services. Usually white, it is reminiscent of the white robe of baptism (as well as the white alb worn by the baptized when they lead worship). The pallbearers may ceremonially place the pall upon the coffin when it arrives at the entrance of the church. The minister may accompany this action with a pronouncement linking the baptism, death, and resurrection of Christ to the baptism, death, and resurrection of the deceased. This can be the first of many declarations in the service of the hope Christians hold in the resurrection of the dead.

Prayers

Prayers for the deceased and for the comfort of the bereaved may take place in several places during the service. It is fitting for the minister or prayer leader to mention the deceased by name. The first of the prayers may take place prior to the liturgy of the Word. It is often in the form of a collect. It may be introduced by the pastoral dialogue:

> Presider: The Lord be with you.
> People: And also with you.
> Presider: Let us pray.

Liturgy of the Word

One or more lessons from Scripture are read. They may be accompanied by recitation of a psalm, the singing of hymns, or special musical presentations. The readings should be selected to speak directly to the hope believers have in God's saving mercy. Gospel and Epistle readings that declare the forgiveness of sins and the resurrection are especially appropriate. The readings may be followed by congregational acclamations or affirmations.

The sermon follows the reading of lessons and is based upon the hope found in the texts. There is no question that a funeral or memorial service should include a sermon. In the face of grief, the bereaved require and depend upon a clear, concrete assurance that Christ conquers death. The preacher should be direct and explicit in proclaiming this hope. The funeral sermon is not a time for subtle implication or complex theological explication. Unlike most other sermon settings, it is appropriate for the preacher to particularly address the people in the front row. Persons who knew best and loved most the deceased are typically seated there. If the preacher speaks good news to them, all who attend the service will certainly overhear it.

There may be a number of responses to the sermon. A strong hymn is appropriate at this point. The Apostle's Creed may be said as a further declaration of the hope that comes through faith. Prayers also naturally follow the reading and proclamation of the Word.

In many places it is customary for an obituary to be read, recounting the story of the life of the deceased. There may also be testimonial statements made by friends, family members, and colleagues who wish to remember the departed. When personal remembrances are included in the service, the presiding minister should guide the people and be prepared to step in if grief precludes a person from finishing his or her remarks. The minister should be aware that this element of a funeral rite can become the most chaotic: people may speak too long, too many may wish to speak, aching silences can occur when no one responds to the invitation to speak, people can be overcome, etc. The wise presider will plan in advance with the family to determine who will speak and how to help them through the process.

When obituaries and testimonials of remembrance are part of a service, they should not be considered a substitute for the sermon. It is up to the preacher to make sure that the words of hope ring clearly through the service.

Holy Communion

Celebration of the Lord's Supper is another sign of hope and assurance. If the service is held in the church and if the attendees are largely known to be believers, communion may be served. As with weddings, where the celebration of the sacrament draws a clear division between believers and nonbelievers in attendance, it is prudent to omit this element of worship.

The Lord's Prayer

A congregational recital of the Prayer of Jesus is appropriate at the conclusion of other prayers. Because it is widely known, its inclusion here allows for people outside the church community to participate in the liturgy in a meaningful way. If the Lord's Supper is celebrated, the prayer is commonly said as part of that liturgy.

The Commendation

At the conclusion of the service, the ministers may offer a prayer commending the deceased to God's care. The prayer asks God to receive him or her into blessed rest in the company of the saints in heaven.

Memorial services end at this point. The people may be dismissed or invited to a reception in honor of the deceased.

The Committal

When the funeral service is followed by a committal at the cemetery, the ministers lead the procession (often in cars) with the body of the deceased. As people gather around the gravesite, scriptural sentences may be read (such as Ps 118:5, 8–9, 13, 15–17, 19–20; Job 19:25–26; Rom 14:7-8; and John 11:25–26a). When all have arrived at the place of burial, additional prayers may be said and additional lessons may be read. Especially appropriate are John 12:23–26; 1 Cor 15:51–57; and Phil 3:20-21.

As the coffin is lowered into the ground, members of the family and friends may place earth upon it. A strong Jewish tradition is not inappropriate at this point. It holds that the action of covering the coffin with dirt is a final, selfless gift presented to the deceased who cannot repay the favor. The minister may accompany the lowering of the coffin with a final commendation and/or a blessing of the departed. The commendation may contain the traditional phrase, "Earth to earth, ashes to ashes, dust to dust." The Aaronic Blessing is a fitting benediction for the departed:

The Lord bless and keep him/her.

The Lord make his face shine upon him/her and be gracious to him/her.

The Lord look upon him/her with favor and give him/her peace. Amen.

The Lord's Prayer may be said again. Another traditional phrase is often said after the committal: "Rest eternal grant him/her, O Lord; and let light perpetual shine upon him/her. Amen.

The graveside service may conclude with a blessing of the people and, where appropriate, an invitation to a reception in honor of the deceased. The minister may say, "Let us go in peace," and lead the way from the burial site.

Part III: Essays and Resources

Lessons from St. Paul on Corporate Worship

> "And let us consider how to provoke one another to love and good deeds, not neglecting to meet together, as is the habit of some, but encouraging one another, and all the more as you see the Day approaching." Heb 10:24–25

"When do you worship?" This question, akin to the corollary question, "How do you worship?" can be a telling one. This latter question can easily function as a spiritual and liturgical Rorschach Test. One can hear responses that vary from what style of music one prefers to what ecclesial or theological tradition one embraces. The first question, however, can illustrate the vagueness of the term "worship" in contemporary parlance. Worship has come to mean everything from an interior attitude to a corporate ritual. When one worships can be seen as everything from a walk along the beach to an online video of a church service. This can lead to an unhealthy lack of clarity in the spiritual discipline of gathering as the body of Christ to offer thanks and praise to God.

Let us be clear: it is possible to pray apart from the larger community. And there are many different types of prayer that we offer when we do: prayers of confession, petition, and intercession to name a few, along with prayers of adoration and thanksgiving. These latter two prayers are often described as personal or private worship. But is this *worship*?

On the one hand, even when we pray in private, secluded from others, we still pray as part of a community of faith. The clearest example of this is the instruction of our Lord when he taught us to pray, saying "Our Father . . . " We pray as part of a community of faith created by the redeeming and reconciling work of Christ.

On the other hand, it appears that there is a presupposition in the New Testament that we are expected to gather to pray when we worship, not only because it is a good or valuable thing, but because it is an essential part of being a member of the body of Christ.

We reach this conclusion by taking seriously Paul's admonitions about worship in 1 Corinthians. Though we often turn to Paul's correction of table practices in the church at Corinth in chapters 10 and 11 as instructions on worship, for those of us in traditions where we don't celebrate the Lord's Supper weekly, it seems that Paul's corrective in chapter 14 is more directly relevant. After promising at the end of chapter 12 to provide more instructions about worship when he visits Corinth again, Paul turns to the topics of spiritual gifts and unity in diversity in chapters 12 and 14, which sandwich the "love chapter," chapter 13. Paul concludes with teachings and correctives about the *synaxis* or gathering of the church for prayer.

At the conclusion of chapter 14, Paul shifts from the hierarchy of spiritual gifts to the use of spiritual gifts in Christian worship. Paul makes three significant points that help us define what worship should be. First, it is a gathering of God's people in which each person is expected to bring something to contribute to the *synaxis* (gathering, assembly) of the church. And each contribution (whether a hymn, a teaching, a prophetic word, a word in tongues) is to be offered to the building up of the body as well as to honor God. This implies that worship leadership is primarily the coordination and orchestration of the gifts and offerings of the people. Paul assumes that worship is not only corporate, but that it is essentially so. If one should come and not contribute his or her gift, or not attend at all, the building up of the community will be deficient.

Second, there is an interdependence in the gifts that people offer, resulting in the whole of the service of worship. So much so that if some gifts are absent, others may not use their gifts. In particular, Paul instructs that if someone speaks in tongues, they should only contribute it to the gathering if there is someone there to interpret, for everything is done for the glory of God and the building up of the community. If there is no one to interpret, those with a tongue to speak should speak it to God in silence, for an un-interpreted utterance will not build up the body.

Third, the service is empowered by the Spirit but is not spontaneous. Twice Paul states that worship should reflect the nature of God—that being orderly, as God is a God of peace and decency, not disorder (vv. 33, 40). To this end Paul actually prescribes a sequence with which the contributions of this gathering should take place: tongues, interpretations, prophecy, revelations; all offered for the building up of the community to the glory of God, decently and in order.

I am not advocating that we follow these instructions slavishly or literally. I would have problems applying this teaching to communities that have neither tongues nor prophecies. I would further have difficulty literally applying Paul's principal of "decently and in order" to women who are expected by Paul to be silent in these gatherings. I do believe, though, that the three principles above—that Christian worship is a corporate, interdependent gathering empowered by the Spirit in an orderly way—can help us in our worship planning, leading, and participation today.

We can summarize the application of these principles this way: when people plan worship they should do so with the question, "What sequence of actions do I want to lead the people through for the worship of God and the building up of the community?" These are not such actions as *sing* or *clap*, but instead such actions as *praise, confess, adore, give thanks*. And each of these actions should be in a logical sequence. Those leading worship services need to ask how they can resource the people so that they are able to do those actions of worship successfully, that God might be glorified and the community strengthened. And those who go to worship should go with the expectation that they will be the primary actors in the worship service. They are going to contribute their gifts to the worship of the entire community; without their contribution, their community's offering will be less than it otherwise could be.

In the end, it is not that we have discovered a new insight into worship but have been corrected by the apostolic wisdom of the Apostle Paul, which critiques the fuzziness of our definition and understanding of worship. And this wisdom is echoed in this seventeenth century hymn that presents many of these same themes:

> We gather together to ask the Lord's blessing,
> he chastens and hastens his will to make known;
> the wicked oppressing now cease from distressing:
> sing praises to his name; he forgets not his own.
>
> (From *Nederlandtsche Gedenckclanck* by Adrianus Valerius *circa* 1600;
> translated by Theodore Baker, 1894.)

So let us be committed, whenever and however we worship, to provoke one another to love and good deeds, to the glory of God and for the building up of the Body of Christ.

Todd E. Johnson

Biblical Foundations for Christian Worship

Those who plunder the depths of Holy Scripture looking for a rubric for Christian worship will be seriously disappointed. Truly, no hidden code dwells within the letters of Paul that—once properly decoded—reveals a divinely appointed order for worship. Churches that claim to "worship as the Bible tells us" are left with a few scattered references about particular church communities in particular areas whose practices may not have been done elsewhere. As contemporary liturgical scholarship has so convincingly argued, there was no "early church," only early *churches*. The extension to this argument is that there is no single way that all Christians worshiped God, but multiple ways. For example, certain communities did not baptize as a sign of initiation but instead practiced foot-washing. Some communities gathered on the Sabbath (Saturday) while others on Sunday. And so forth.

Thus, to consider the "biblical foundations of Christian worship" is not to assume biblical warrant for the particularities of our worship (i.e., how many songs should be sung in a row, should the congregation be seated or standing, what translation of Scripture should be used, etc.). Neither is it to suggest that there is one "biblical" method of worshipping God. Rather, Holy Scripture assists us in understanding the broader parameters of Christian worship. This essay seeks to outline several basic biblical, and ultimately theological themes that should play a significant role in shaping our contemporary worship schematics, no matter the denominational tradition.[1]

1. **Trinity:** The biblical witness to Jesus Christ as the perfect revelation of the invisible God (John 15:15; Col 1:15; Eph 1:9; Heb 1:1–3; etc.) as well as the empowering presence of the Holy Spirit (John 15:26; Acts 2:4; 1 Cor 12:3; Heb 2:4) forms the basic orientation of the Christian in worship. We worship God (the Father) because we now know God (by the Son) and are renewed, comforted, and inspired by God's presence in our midst (the Spirit). Hence our classic benediction, taken from 2 Cor 13:13: "The grace of the Lord Jesus Christ, the love of God, and the communion of the Holy Spirit be with you all." All too often, our worship

---

1. We admit here, with due humility, that we are not attempting to forge the "perfect" liturgy that all denominational traditions could point to and say, "That's right!" Such a task is not in the human purview. Rather, the goal is to identify themes that distinguish "Christian" worship from other religious acts of devotion. For example, regardless of your tradition, it is an inseparable doctrine of the church that God is Triune. Therefore, our worship should be effectively Trinitarian.

focuses on a single person of the Trinity to the exclusion or diminishment of the other two. However, faithful Christian worship is perpetually dependent of the work of Father (the Creator), Son (Revealer/Redeemer), and Spirit (Sustainer) and should reflect such dependence.

2. **Scripture-rooted:** A central Christian affirmation is that the Word became flesh and made its dwelling among us in the person of Jesus of Nazareth (John 1:10–14). In Jesus, Paul writes, "All the fullness of God was pleased to dwell" (Col 1:19). This act of revelation was unparalleled in salvation history. Because of this, Christians believe that the Bible—as it witnesses to the revelation of God in Christ—is the primary source of our knowledge about God. In its sacred texts, we encounter the radical movements of God throughout history, culminating in the incarnation, ministry, death, and exaltation of Jesus Christ. Thus, our worship should be dutifully informed, shaped, and patterned around the biblical witness to Jesus Christ and to the works of God in history. Because Scripture is the only reliable witness to Jesus Christ, it is the only authoritative text upon which preachers should craft sermons. And as such, it should be read publicly and joyfully throughout a service of worship.

3. **Order, not Chaos:** It is seemingly common knowledge among Christians that the Holy Spirit is primarily an agent of spontaneity, moving wherever and whenever it so chooses. This implies that for the Spirit to be present, worship ought to be similarly spontaneous and loosely structured. Some hold a grand assumption that "true" worship is always spontaneous, "heart-felt," structureless, and "open to the Spirit." Order in worship is considered a vice, something that supposedly restricts the Spirit and inevitably prompts humans toward meaningless rituals. *However compelling such an argument is, it is quite foreign to the biblical witness.* The descent of the Holy Spirit at Pentecost, for example, however sudden and powerful, was primarily a witness of the re-union of the dispersion of people at Babel and not necessarily the inauguration of a normative act in Christian worship. Those who spoke in foreign languages spoke so that all who were present could detect and celebrate the new and mighty movement of the Lord God. This was *not* utter chaos or overflowing emotional outburst. Further, Paul takes great pains in the latter chapters of 1 Corinthians to explain the need for orderliness of worship in Corinth (indicating how many people should prophecy, how it should be interpreted, the orchestration of bringing revelations, hymns, songs, prayers, etc.). Such orderliness ultimately bears witness to the theological statement that "God is not a god of disorder, but of peace" (1 Cor 14:33). He concludes his argument by noting, "So, my friends, be eager to prophecy, and do not forbid tongues, but all things should be done decently and in order" (1 Cor 14:39–40). Structuring liturgical time is not inherently restrictive of the movement of the Spirit (though when done poorly it can be), but rather it speaks to a greater truth: The

God who creates, redeems, and sustains is not a God of chaos and uncertainty, of inconsistency and unreliability, but the God of order, peace, sovereignty, and trust.

4. **Dialogue, not Monologue:** Christian worship is not simply the action of the people in thanks and praise toward God. God is not the Kierkegaardian "audience of one" watching our liturgy from the floor of the theater. But neither is Christian worship something that God alone does. Rather, worship is both. God is simultaneously the object of our worship as well as the prompter of our worship. Here the German word *Gottesdiest* "service of God" is arguably one of the best understandings of Christian worship. It is remarkable because the word can grammatically function both objectively and subjectively. Christian worship includes the human acts of articulating thanks, lament, praise, and commitment to God. In this manner the people serve God. This presumes that those involved in this dialogue are not merely worship leaders (preachers, song leaders, prayer leaders, readers, etc.), but all the people, as they are invited to respond verbally and physically throughout worship. Likewise, Christian worship includes the divine acts of revelation, consecration, and sanctification of and to the people. In this way, worship is a service of God on behalf of the people. Biblical examples of this dialogue in worship include: Exod 23:25; Isa 6:1–6; Luke 1:10–20; 24:30–32; Phil 4:6; Eph 1:9; and 1 Tim 2:1–3.

5. **The Breadth of Human Emotion:** The briefest of surveys of the prayers in the Book of Psalms demonstrates the wide range of human emotion that can be conveyed in prayer. There are psalms that express deep distress rooted in a fear of divine abandonment: "Why, O Lord, do you stand far off? Why do you hide yourself in times of trouble?" (Ps 10); "How long, O Lord? Will you forget me forever? How long will you hide your face from me?" (Ps 13). Other psalms are mournful dirges: "By the rivers of Babylon—there we sat down and there we wept when we remembered Zion. . . . How could we sing the Lord's song in a foreign land?" (Ps 137). Yet many psalms express everlasting joy in the great things God has done: "For I know that the Lord is great; our Lord is above all gods" (Ps 135); "I waited patiently for the Lord; he inclined and heard my cry" (Ps 40); "Praise is due to you, O God, in Zion; and to you shall vows be performed, O you who answer prayer! To you all flesh shall come. When deeds of iniquity overwhelm us, you forgive our transgressions" (Ps 65). Christian worship must address this tension between lament and praise, providing a healthy diet of both and allowing the breadth of human emotion to exist in the liturgy. Any given Lord's Day, congregations are comprised of members who may have recently buried a spouse, a child, or a parent, or who are reeling from all forms of depression or pain. Likewise, many in that same congregation on that same Lord's Day may be experiencing great joy due, perhaps, to the healthy birth of a child, or because

of some sense that God has intervened in their life. Biblical Christian worship is tasked with providing avenues for both kinds of people to offer their thanks, praises, and laments to God.

Joseph A. Novak

The Ecumenical Shape of Corporate Worship

Only a few months after his accession to the papacy in 1959 Pope John XXIII issued an ecclesiastical summons to all the Roman church. The Second Vatican Council, convened four years later, was tasked with "opening the windows of the church and letting in some fresh air." From 1962 until 1965, the council partnered with hundreds of theological and liturgical scholars in an attempt to reform the source, mission, and worship of the Roman Church. Protestants and Orthodox sent delegations to watch the proceedings, anxious about the decisions that would be made. The council's work was reflective of the influence of the Liturgical movement, an informal ecumenical movement begun in the late nineteenth century.

When the council was finished in 1965, several prominent documents had been written and approved. Not least among these was the document *Sancrosanctum Concilium* (Constitution on the Sacred Liturgy), written and approved in December 1963. This document set out the basic treatise that Christian worship ought to demand a fully conscious and active laity.

> [The] Church earnestly desires that all the faithful should be led to that fully conscious and active participation in liturgical celebrations which is demanded by the very nature of the liturgy. Such participation by the Christian people as a chosen race, a royal priesthood, a holy nation, a redeemed people (1 Pet. 2:9; cf. 2:4–5), is their right and duty by reason of their baptism. (*Constitution on the Sacred Liturgy*, 14)

While the Second Vatican Council itself was a watershed moment in ecclesiastical history, this document became a watershed moment for liturgical practice in both Protestant and Catholic churches. Church architecture was altered in many Roman churches, the altar was moved forward and placed within view of all the people. The priest no longer offered the Mass with his back turned to the congregation, but faced them, including them in the prayers. Many churches built in the years following the council were built with seating in-the-round, so as to encourage lay participation and concentration. New hymns were written that were more congregational in nature. Scripture was read in the common tongue and the priests were expected to preach biblically faithful homilies.

For Protestants, the promulgation of *Sancrosanctum Concilium* meant a reorganization of worship schematics to take into account a more ecumenical order. Between 1965 and 1993, virtually all of the major Protestant mainline denominations revised their worship books, in some cases publishing all-new documents, that brought an incredible unity to liturgical practice amongst Catholics and Protestants. They include:

> *Lutheran Book of Worship* (ELCA, 1978)
> *Book of Common Prayer* (Episcopal USA, 1979)
> *Covenant Book of Worship* (Evangelical Covenant, 1981)
> *United Methodist Hymnal* (UMC, 1989)
> *Book of Common Worship* (PCUSA, 1993)
> *The Worship Sourcebook* (CRC/Ecumenical, 2004)

As Protestants reorganized their worship books and published revised liturgies for church use, a consistent pattern emerged in almost all of the schematics. The published liturgies were organized around four movements: Gathering, Word, Table, and Sending (see "The Four-Fold Pattern of Worship" in this section of the *Teaching Hymnal*). Even the evangelical churches on the periphery of the Liturgical movement fit under this rubric.

This four-fold pattern, Gather-Word-Table-Sending, is the basic plot structure for most forms of Christian worship. The service begins with rites that consecrate and initiate the time for worship. First, the people are gathered from their vocations in the world and assembled as the body of Christ. This usually is enacted by the offering of hymns that call one another to worship, statements from Scripture, or the rites of confession and absolution. In evangelical churches, this portion of worship typically incorporates the singing of a set of gathering and praise songs. After being gathered and constituted, the people next listen to Scripture read and proclaimed, anticipating the revelation of God in the presence of Jesus Christ. Following the proclamation of Scripture, the people are nourished and sealed by participation in the sacraments (or ordinances, depending on one's tradition). Having been gathered and nourished, the people are then sent back out into the world in peace, charged with taking the love of God back into their respective communities of work and play.

There is some biblical warrant for the four-fold pattern as described above. The most notable is the story of the travelers on the road to Emmaus at the close of Luke's gospel. Following the resurrection of our Lord, two disciples were traveling from Jerusalem to Emmaus when they encountered the risen Christ on the road. Not knowing it was Jesus, they traveled together and engaged in holy discourse. "Then, beginning with Moses and all the prophets, [Jesus] interpreted to them the things about himself in all the Scriptures" Luke 24:27). After arriving in Emmaus, they shared a meal together at which Jesus took bread, blessed it, broke it, and gave it to them. "Then their eyes were opened," Luke reports, "and they recognized [Jesus]; and he vanished from their sight" (Luke 24:31).

Several fascinating aspects of this story stand out: First, the pattern the writer notes of "taking, blessing, breaking, and giving" of the bread is the exact same pattern that is used throughout Jesus' ministry of table fellowship. "And taking the five loaves and the two fish, he looked up to heaven, and blessed and broke them, and gave them to the disciples to eat before the crowd" (Luke 9:16; Mark 6:41; Matt 14:19). Each of these actions (taking, blessing, breaking, giving) corresponds to a basic movement in the four-fold pattern. In gathering, we are taken from the world. In the hearing of the Word we are blessed by the revelation of God and his saving presence. In the reception of the sacraments we are broken by the revealed grace of God. And in the sending, we are given to the world as ministers of Christ.

Secondly, and more importantly for us, is the way in which the encounter of the two disciples with the risen Christ is summarized and retold to the other eleven disciples. Following their encounter with Jesus, Luke reports the following:

> They said to each other, "Were not our hearts burning within us while he was talking to us on the road, while he was opening the Scriptures to us?" That same hour they got up and returned to Jerusalem; and they found the eleven and their companions gathered together. . . . Then they told what had happened on the road and how [Jesus] had been made known to them in the breaking of the bread. (Luke 24:32–33, 35)

The two disciples made a connection between the interpretation of Scripture and the revelation of Christ during the meal. This combination of Word and Meal formed a summary of many early Christian liturgies and soon the rites of entrance (Gathering) and dismissal (Sending) were appended. We gather, we listen to Scripture read and proclaimed, we sit together at table and look for the revelation of Christ in the breaking of bread, and we are sent back into the world.

An additional perspective on the relationship between Word and Meal comes from liturgical theologian J. J. von Allman, who argued that the ministry of Jesus in the gospel of Luke is patterned around early Christian liturgical practice. The first half takes place in Galilee and is concerned with Jesus' preaching and healing ministry there. The second half, roughly, takes place in Jerusalem and centers around his betrayal, death, resurrection, and ascension. Von Allman suggests that the first half corresponds with the "Word" segment of the liturgy and the second half corresponds with the "Table" segment. Jesus' ministry of teaching and healing in Galilee is the equivalent of our reading and proclamation of Scripture, whereas his ministry of death and resurrection is the equivalent of our Eucharistic practice.

While the four-fold pattern (Gathering, Word, Table, Sending) is prevalent among most churches, few Protestant churches offer weekly Eucharistic practice (Lutheran, Episcopal, and Campbellite churches are notable exceptions). Thus, many churches have elected to offer a time of response to the Word following the sermon. This may be in the form of the Offering, a congregational reading of a creed or confession, or an invitation to conversion or to discipleship. Regardless, the dominant pattern in non-Eucharistic liturgies is Gathering-Word-Response-Sending.

The four-fold pattern is discernible in virtually every Christian tradition. (For an additional perspective on its ecumenical character, see "The Four-Fold Pattern of Worship" following this essay). Many Presbyterian, Lutheran, Baptist, nondenominational, or Pentecostal-Charismatic orders of worship are organized after this fashion. While some traditions may emphasize one movement to the subordination of another, the basic structure holds. The order seems to transcend the theological differences between Protestant and Catholic churches and provides a basic starting place for corporate worship. In sum, this biblically informed pattern for public worship represents the ecumenical shape of corporate worship among Christian churches.

Joseph A. Novak

The Four-Fold Pattern of Worship

Christians have developed countless forms for worship through the ages. Many of them spring from early Jewish practice and most account for local issues of context and culture. Still, there is a general pattern that has emerged through the centuries. It is not a particular liturgy, but a way of shaping liturgy that seems to hold historic wisdom. It also derives from clear practicalities. In order for corporate worship to take place, people need to *gather* from various places to pray together in one place. Following historic Jewish practice, Christians then attend to God's *Word*. In keeping with Jesus' command to "do this in remembrance of me," Christians, at least occasionally, follow preaching with celebrations of the *sacraments*. When all is accomplished, the faithful are *sent* out into mission as their worship continues from a time of adoration to the time of action in the world. This creates a four-fold pattern that can be, and certainly is widely interpreted, as Gathering, Word, Sacraments, and Sending. However varied the practice within this framework, consideration of it allows for Christians to see that they have more in common with one another than meets the eye if they consider only the detailed design of worship within various traditions.

It must be noted that in some traditions, the *sending* is also known as the *dismissal*. This comes from the Roman Catholic Mass where the concluding Latin text is "*Ite, missa est*," "Go, it is the dismissal." This is also the origin of the word *Mass*. While it is true that people are dismissed at the conclusion of worship, the word suggests adjournment, as if worship is entirely ended, not to commence again until the following week's gathering. The word *sending* is to be preferred because it suggests the missional nature of worship that occurs in two spheres: within the church during the hour(s) of adoration and within the world, during the days of service to God's people.

The pattern described here is so practical that it could also be used to describe any number of human gatherings. For example, if someone throws a dinner party for friends, the people will 1) gather, 2) talk and discuss things of mutual interest, 3) share a meal together, and 4) be sent on their way home. Accordingly, it is not difficult to trace the shape of this pattern in various worship traditions. The following chart[1] shows, in very general ways, how the four-fold pattern relates to four broad categories of worship tradition: those known for high or formal liturgy, those who order worship

---

1. This chart is borrowed from Clayton J. Schmit, *Sent and Gathered: A Worship Manual for the Missional Church* (Grand Rapids: Baker Academic, 2010) 73.

with moderate liturgical formality, those who practice free church liturgy, and those with a highly spontaneous liturgical tradition. These four categories are represented by four groups of worship tradition, respectively: Roman Catholic and Lutheran; Presbyterian and Methodist; Baptist; and Pentecostal.

The Fourfold Pattern of Worship in Various Traditions

Roman Catholic Lutheran	Presbyterian Methodist	Baptist	Pentecostal
		Gathering	
Confession of sins and absolution Apostolic greeting Entrance song or psalm *Gloria in excelsis* (Glory to God in the highest) or song of praise *Kyrie eleison* (Lord have mercy) Prayer of the day	Call to worship (Greeting and sentences of Scripture) Prayer of the day or opening prayer Hymn, song, or psalm of praise Confession of sins and declaration of pardon Sharing the peace Song, hymn, or psalm	Welcome and prayer Call to worship or invocation Opening hymns and songs Pastoral prayers (sometimes concluding with the Lord's Prayer)	Call to worship Praise and worship through song and hymn singing (for an indeterminate length of time) Pastoral welcome and prayer (Speaking in tongues and prophetic interpretation may happen at any time)
		Word	
Old Testament reading Psalm Epistle reading Gospel acclamation Gospel reading Sermon Hymn or song of the day Nicene or Apostles' Creed Prayer and intercessions Sign of Peace	Prayer for illumination Old Testament reading Psalm for the day Epistle reading Anthem, hymn, psalm, song Gospel reading Sermon Hymn or song Affirmation of faith (Nicene or Apostles' Creed) Prayers of the people	Scripture reading Anthem Sermon and invitation to faith Hymn or song of response Offering and prayer (sometimes placed after the Scripture reading)	Scripture reading Anthem Sermon Call to commitment or recommitment Offering of tithes

Table (The Lord's Supper)

Offering of tithes and communion elements	Offering of tithes	Prayer of thanksgiving	Words of institution
Prayer over the gifts	Invitation to the Lord's Table	Words of institution	Distribution (with singing, and/or prayer and dancing)
Eucharistic Prayer: Great Thanksgiving, preface, *Sanctus* (Holy, holy, holy, Lord), acclamations, institution narrative, the Lord's Prayer, *Agnus Dei* (Lamb of God)	Eucharistic Prayer: Great Thanksgiving; Holy, holy, holy, Lord; acclamations; institution narrative; the Lord's Prayer)	Distribution Hymn or song	
Breaking of bread and distribution	Breaking of bread and distribution		
Nunc dimittus (Simeon's song) or post-communion song	Prayer after communion		

Sending

Blessing or Benediction	Hymn, song, or psalm	Benediction	Benediction
Dismissal	Charge and blessing or benediction	Parting hymn or song	Parting song or hymn
Closing hymn or song	Final hymn or song		

Principles for Worship Planning

Gatherings of Christian worship do not typically occur spontaneously. Usually, there are a number of people who prepare in advance for the gathering of the larger community. If a single individual desired to worship alone, he or she could do anything desired: pray on a beach, sing in a bedroom, meditate on a mountain. If two people agree to worship together, some level of planning needs to occur. Where will they meet? What will they do? What resources (Bible, hymnal, or prayer book) should be used, etc. Accordingly, the more people expected for worship, the greater the level of preparation that is required. In most settings, worship planning is best done by a team of people who are attuned to the needs, habits, and expectations of the assembly. The following principles for worship planning represent *best practices* that can serve worship planning teams whether they represent liturgically formal or free traditions.

1. Worship is about God. It involves the participation of many people, but the focus is on God and God's relationship to God's people.

2. Worship planning teams should understand that in addition to what God has to say in worship (through reading and proclaiming Scripture, and in the still small voice of silence), the most important voice in worship is that of the gathered people. All others speak or sing only to serve and/or enliven the voice of the congregation. This ensures that worship is designed in ways that invite (and do not stifle) congregational participation.

3. Worship is more than what happens on Sunday morning. Everything that people of faith do in life can be considered part of their worship, including their work and service in the world. The portion of life that takes place in worshipping assembly is known as public or corporate worship. Worship planners understand that what happens in the assembly is only a part of a faithful person's life of devotion.

4. Corporate worship consists of more than a set of songs that surround a sermon. It includes the sermon, the reading of Scripture, prayers, recitation of creeds or corporate statements, use of music and the arts, even silence. Worship leaders, correspondingly, are those who lead in each of these activities.

5. Worship planning teams include people who represent readers and preachers, musicians, the artists within the community, ushers and greeters, technical support staff, and so forth. Anyone with a stake in executing worship events should have a voice in worship planning.

6. Planning teams should have an understanding of the resources (technical, artistic, musical) that are available within each community. Many of these resources will come from the congregation. There is also value in inviting people from the local artistic community into worship planning and execution on some occasions.

7. Worship planning is done best by teams who have a solid awareness of their worship context. For example: What are the congregation's liturgical rhythms and seasons? What are its worship values and habits? What are the local commemorations and festivals? What are the congregation's attendance habits?

8. Given the significant place that reading and proclaiming Scripture hold in public worship, planning teams should be aware of the scriptural texts and biblical themes that will be used by readers and preachers. This allows for music, art, prayers, and other elements to be coordinated with the presentation of the Word.

9. Planning worship should take place well in advance of worship events so that coordination can take place effectively. Musicians and artists require weeks, often months, of preparation in order to present or perform their work well.

10. Execution of worship requires adequate time and opportunity for rehearsal. This naturally applies to technicians, musicians, and other performing artists. It also applies to those who read, pray, preach, usher, and so forth. All worship leaders need to practice their parts in order for worship to engage the people meaningfully and effectively.

11. Worship teams can do general planning on a quarterly or seasonal basis in order to determine broad themes and seasonal emphases.

12. A critical function of worship planning teams is to engage in regular evaluation of worship events. This allows for adjustments, improvements, and ongoing creativity. A good practice is to look both a month forward as well as a month backward. This is a good way to avoid the ruts into which worship so easily falls.

13. Worship planners should strive for creativity. Worship can be both ordinary (in the sense that the same basic and expected worship format can be used each week) and extraordinary. It reaches beyond the ordinary when fresh ideas, the arts and artists, and new arrangements, are thoughtfully employed. Worship planning teams can gather new ideas from attending worship conferences together, reading worship journals and resource books, consulting local artists, etc.

14. Extraordinary worship can stretch a congregation's awareness and appreciation of music and art forms. But, the thoughtful worship planning team will be aware

of when stretching tastes can lead to the breaking point. Freshening, rather than offending a congregation's worship tastes is the right goal. Worship planning teams work best when they know their congregation's tastes and habits as well as the appropriate stretching points.

15. Worship planners are responsible for ensuring that worship is congruent with what the congregation believes. They must know and represent both the theological commitments of the orthodox Christian faith as well as the faith commitments of the local congregation. Worship evaluation is critical for addressing issues that arise from worship elements that speak contrary to what is believed.

16. Worship planners seek to assure balance in the worship palette of the congregation. There are many things to hold in balance: involvement of various demographic groups (ethnicities, gender, and age), styles of music and art, elements that engage people cognitively as well as experientially, and so forth.

17. Planning teams should have an awareness of the power of simplicity. Religious symbols should not proliferate. For example, one main cross in the chancel communicates more effectively than a dozen crosses competing for people's attention.

18. Silence is a powerful tool for communicating in worship. Though it may confuse or annoy those not used to silence in worship, its use can be slowly and effectively introduced.

19. Worship planning teams should possess a strong awareness of the possibilities and limitations of a church's worship space. These considerations include an understanding of its acoustic space properties, sound amplification capacities, projection possibilities, versatility of congregational seating areas, and sight line limitations. Planners can solve potential problems by walking through the worship space to visually and acoustically try out ideas.

20. Introduction of new music and ideas should take place before using them in worship. As instrumental preludes or choral presentations, new melodies can be presented weeks in advance of asking a congregation to sing them. New expressions or songs can be taught during pre-service announcement periods, rather than at the time of their use in worship.

21. Worship planning teams can foster the development of artists and musicians within their communities. As public school systems cut art and music budgets across North America, churches can fill the gap by offering art and music classes. This not only enriches young peoples' lives, but prepares them for service in the church, the cultural venue where art and artists are still highly valued.

22. Worship planning teams can support artists and musicians by including adequate payment for their work in their budgets. Some artists and musicians are pleased

to volunteer their services. Others make their living through the arts and deserve fitting payment, just as do the pastors and other professional ministers.

23. Artistic excellence is maintained by worship planning teams who are aware that poor art and performance disengages worshippers. Excellence does not mean perfection. A children's choir will not perform at the same level as an adult group or a hired professional. Performers at each level should be instructed and assisted to give their *best account* through adequate rehearsal and training.

24. Planning teams should have an understanding that *performance* in worship is not the same thing as *mere performance*, a practice that draws attention to itself. Understanding performance rightly acknowledges that executing worship leadership roles (whether as a preacher, reader, prayer leader, or musician) requires rehearsal, confidence, presence, and poise. Not all professional musicians and performing artists (nor preachers, for that matter) are aware that their work in worship is to serve the people, rather than to serve their own art or career. Where necessary, training in worship's purpose can be offered by planning teams before professionals are invited to contribute to public worship, helping them to understand that singing or playing in worship is different than performing for adoring fans on a stage.

Clayton J. Schmit

Shaping the Liturgy for the Twenty-First Century: Utilizing the Ritual Process Model

Church leaders spend a lot of time discussing church attendance these days. It is a concern for many because we have watched church attendance fall over the past few decades. When we say that church *attendance* is down we primarily mean that *attendance in worship* is down. For better or worse, this is the measuring stick by which we gauge the success of our leaders, our ministries, and our evangelism. But at the heart of this issue is another one. What is it about worship that makes people stay at home? Sharp thinkers in the church have helped articulate some of these problems, ranging from a rise in individualism in our culture to the irrelevancy of the church in modern society. While many of these theories are worth studying, this is another theory—and consequently another solution—to this problem facing the church.

People are ambivalent about attending worship because they see corporate worship as an *event* rather than a *process*. What dominates is a perspective that each worship event is singular, individual, independent, and unconnected. This line of thinking, a ritual event model, sees life punctuated by individual worship events. These may be Sundays (or other days of regular worship) but increasingly we see people who attend worship only for specific events. Christmas and Easter are the most common; beyond these, many attend worship only for other special events: funerals, baptisms, weddings, perhaps confirmation in traditions in which this is an important event. Over and against this way of looking at worship is another model, a ritual process model. In this model, each individual worship service is connected to another. Each gathering of believers flows from another gathering and flows to another gathering. In this model, a believer who attends worship just once should experience a pressing need to attend again because the process of worship is not complete—the process is never complete.

Another way to see the difference in these two models is through a comparison to the way television shows are structured. A situational comedy, or sitcom, is often designed so that even if you missed the previous show, you can watch this week's show without missing anything important. Mostly for a sitcom, a plot arch occurs over a single show. Next week, there will be a new plot with new problems and new resolutions to those problems. Different from the sitcom is the drama. Week by week, the drama builds a single through-plot, often in addition to the plot of each episode. This larger through-plot brings people back to watch every week. Writers of dramas are masterful at the cliffhanger, designed specifically to bring people back. A whole season of a drama may account for one larger overarching plot.

When we compare the ritual event model and the ritual process model to the sitcom and the drama, we can see some similarities. The ritual event model views worship as individual events, unconnected, allowing an individual to float in and out of weekly worship at will. This model is like the sitcom because there is little drawing a person back into worship next week. On the other side of the table is the ritual process model, which draws people to worship weekly because of the interconnectivity of each individual worship service. This model compares to the way dramas are written, constructed in a way to bring people back week by week. This is a vast oversimplification but might help us understand why many are ambivalent about attending worship.[1]

Church leaders for centuries have known the value of the ritual process model and have employed it throughout history. Within the very culture of the church, across denominational traditions, are several ways in which individual worship services are connected to one another. While there are many, we are going to focus on four for the remainder of this essay: lectionary cycles, sermon series, liturgical seasons, and rituals that lead to other rituals.

Lectionary Cycles

Worship traditions that use a lectionary will find texts appointed for certain days that flow from previously used texts and draw people back in the following weeks. These patterns can be hard to discern. Typically, only someone who is looking ahead a month or more will be able to see these patterns, but they exist. This fact, that patterns in the lectionary may be hard to distinguish, should not discourage us to use them to our advantage but rather speak more on the need of diligence on the part of worship planners when it comes to worship planning.

A good example of the way in which the lectionary utilizes the ritual process model is in the "bread of life" cycle of the lectionary. Occurring in year "B" of the Revised Common Lectionary, five Sundays in a row cover nearly the entire sixth chapter of the Gospel according to John. This chapter deals with the feeding of the five thousand and Jesus' declaration, "I am the bread of life." Many preachers over the years have fallen into the trap of exhausting sermon material on the first of these Sundays having not looked forward in the lectionary to see what was to follow. Many others, however, have utilized this lectionary pattern to enrich worship services week by week.

---

1. This comparison might suggest that worship constructed in line with the ritual process model should be done in a way that missing a single worship service would be a detriment in attending any subsequent services. Consider the fact, however, that even the densest dramas start with a "previously on . . ." segment, allowing viewers who missed previous episodes to catch up and be ready for this new show. Likewise, we should construct worship services with a balance of both, allowing people who missed previous worship services to jump back in, while simultaneously drawing people back to next week's worship service by looking forward to it.

The drama of the sixth chapter of John builds over the course of the chapter. With this in mind, preachers and worship planners can capitalize on the five Sundays to draw people back week by week. For example, there are a lot of hymns that utilize bread of life imagery. A good worship planner would not use them all up on the first Sunday. Instead, consider selecting a single hymn that would be sung on all five Sundays with these other hymns supplementing as needed. A good preacher would not use up all his or her good points that first week. Instead, sermons might be crafted in a way to draw people back the following week, perhaps crafting a little cliffhanger.

Sermon Series

In many ways, the suggestions above concerning preaching on the "bread of life" texts from John are recommending taking those weeks and making a sermon series out of them. A sermon series is a group of sermons organized around a common theme. Weekly, a new sermon in the series is preached which, at the end of the series, results in a comprehensive picture of a subject. A sermon series can be of nearly any length, though reason dictates some restrictions. The great advantage of a sermon series is that a preacher can get more into a sermon series than he or she could in a single sermon on a subject.

Crafting a sermon series takes dedication and there are a number of pitfalls. One danger of a sermon series is turning the sessions into biblically based self-help sessions. Sermons principally declare the good news of the crucified and risen Lord. Cutting short this prerogative diminishes the message of the Gospel and actually changes the nature of the church.[2] Instead, a sermon series should, as all sermons must, ask and answer the question, "What does God have to say?" or "What is God doing about x?" What many preachers know is that the Bible has a large range of things to say about many subjects and using one text to address concerns with the complexity of poverty, justice, money, and countless others is not sufficient. Utilizing several texts over several weeks can both paint a more comprehensive picture of what God is doing in the world when it comes to these complex issues, as well as draw people back to worship using the ritual process model. Knowing that the sermon preached today is part of a series may help draw people back for next week's message, allowing people to build their own more comprehensive view of these complex issues.

Seasons

In traditions that have seasonal cycles, these seasons can have their own larger overarching "plots" that lead to and from key celebrations. For example, Advent is a season that leads up to Christmas; likewise Lent is a period of preparation for Easter. Following these celebrations, seasons also extend the celebration taking place: the twelve

---

2. Cf. Kenda Creasy Dean, *Almost Christian: What the Faith of Our Teenagers Is Telling the American Church*, New York (Oxford University Press, 2010) for more about the way this "self-help" pseudo-Christianity has been damaging the church.

days of Christmas and the season of Epiphany prolong the celebrations of the birth of Christ beyond Christmas Eve, and the fifty days of Easter lengthen the joy of the resurrection. Good worship planners will take advantage of these themes to craft worship services that reflect the movement of the season toward or from a significant celebration.

One of the best examples of the ritual process model at work in worship is in the services of the Paschal Triduum. The Paschal Triduum consists of the three days prior to Easter: the evening of Maundy Thursday, Good Friday, and the Easter Vigil on Saturday evening. The Triduum spans three days but is understood as a single worship service. It is for this reason that there is no blessing or dismissal at the end of the liturgies for Maundy Thursday or Good Friday. This is often misunderstood as a sign of somber mourning following the grave drama of the liturgy of these days. In reality, the blessing and dismissal for these services are omitted because the service is not at a close but continues forward, all the way to the Vigil of Easter. In a way, this is the quintessential cliffhanger of the liturgical year: seeking resolution to the drama of Maundy Thursday, a worshipper must return again for the completion of the service over the next two days.

Rituals that Lead to Other Rituals

A final good example of opportunities for worship planners to employ the ritual process model is found in the occasional rituals of the church. These rituals are called "occasional" not because they rarely happen (though for many this may indeed be the case) but because they reflect a unique occasion in the life of the community that is cause for worship, prayer, or celebration. Common occasional services are those surrounding birth, death, baptism, marriage, and coming of age. One will notice that there is a close connection between the occasional services and life events.

Most of the time when we think of these kinds of services, we often think of a single worship event: a baptism, a wedding, a funeral. However, the church has long lifted up the ritual process model when approaching these life events.

Christian marriage may include a rite where, publicly in front of the congregation, the couple declares their intent to wed. In turn the assembly promises to pray for the couple as the wedding draws closer. This ritual may take place months ahead of the wedding. Following the wedding, at each anniversary, many traditions have prayers and blessings celebrating the couple's life together at important milestones.

Another area where we might apply the ritual process model is baptism. The early church had an elaborate process consisting of several rituals. Efforts over the past fifty years to reclaim this tradition have resulted in programs that combine ritual with education, like Welcome to Christ (Lutheran) and The Rite of Christian Initiation of Adults (Roman Catholic). Both have elaborate and colorful rituals to accompany individuals as they become more in touch with their Christian discipleship and prepare for baptism.[3]

Weddings and baptisms are two examples of the potential of ritual process, but there are countless others. Many worship resources have separate publications dedicated to occasional rituals that can be consulted for a more comprehensive worshipping life in community.

A Rich Tapestry of Ritual

Each of these examples shows the possibility of moving communities into deeper worshipping lives. Yet, the effects of utilizing the ritual process model are best seen when using these all together, creating a comprehensive vision for the worship patterns of any given community. We can see the way seasonal cycles and lectionary texts interplay with one another to result in a sermon series. We can see the way in which individual life events play out in a community through worship. Together, these make a tapestry of ritual that enriches the entire church. The ritual process model has realms of application beyond these examples too. Ultimately, it is a tool that the church has held in stewardship and worship leaders are entrusted to utilize.

C. E. Weber

---

3. Cf. C. E. Weber, *Not By Mere Water: Ritual Process in Baptism and its Restoration in Lutheran Ritual*, Kindle edition for more information about the ritual process model in baptism.

Scripture Reading in Worship

The art of bringing printed material to life through public reading is known as oral interpretation of literature. The skills of oral interpreters include techniques relating to textual study and interpretation, embodiment, and articulation (what some call emphasis, or vocalics).

The public reading of Scripture in worship depends on these techniques in order to bring the Bible to life in the hearing of God's people. Some will argue that a reading should not be enlivened with technique or dramatic effect. They maintain that a reading should be spoken evenly and without human interpretation. The assumption is that God will allow each person to interpret for him or herself the meaning of the text when it is intelligibly articulated. It is a fact, however, that every reading of a text *is* an interpretation of it. To read the text in a clear but flat manner is not to allow it to speak for itself with clarity and urgency. An evenly toned, unenthusiastic reading of a text simply indicates that the reader does not find the text interesting. The listener receives the unmistakable impression that God's Word is not a lively, vital word for today. Because reading Scripture is a principal means of proclaiming the Word of the Living God, it both *deserves* our best interpretive and performance skills, and it *requires* their use so that the Word will be heard and understood clearly by the worship assembly.

Study and Interpretation of the Text

In order to interpret a text in a meaningful way, the biblical reader needs to study it and come to an understanding of its meaning. Some texts are straightforward and take little research. The meaning of a psalm or a story might be self-evident. Other Scripture readings can be complex and require greater investigation. Historical passages or theological material from the epistles, for example, may require considerable study. Those who possess skills in exegesis and use of biblical languages can undertake a thorough investigation of a text in preparation for public reading. Others can consult Bible commentaries in order to gain a sense of the background and meaning of a text. Generally, the reader will need to investigate these kinds of things:

- What comes before and after the assigned reading (also known as the pericope)? How does this reading relate to its literary placement?

266

- Who is the author of the material and what circumstances gave rise to it being written?

- What are the overall themes the biblical author addresses in the book and how does this pericope relate to them?

- What are the elements that need to be looked up (place names, people, events, related passages, etc.) in order for the reader to understand the material of the assigned reading?

- To whom was the reading originally addressed?

- What is the tone of the material? Does the tone change?

- What is the direction of communication (is the textual voice spoken as if to a church community? To the nations? To God? etc.)? Does the direction of speech change (as from a word of prayer to a call for praise) as occurs regularly in the psalms?

Introducing a Scripture Reading: Some readings require an introduction in order for listeners to understand who is speaking and what is being discussed. Selections from the writings of Paul, for example, usually require a brief explanation before they are read. Other readings, such as psalms and stories about Jesus, may need little or no introduction. When they are appropriate, readers should take care to craft introductions that are clear and brief. Generally, one or two sentences are sufficient to provide a meaningful background for the hearing of a lesson. Introductions should not interpret the material, but set the stage for an interpretive reading.

Embodying the Reading

Effective reading of a text in worship presupposes that the material has been carefully prepared for clear and meaningful interpretation. But it also allows for the realization that the material has not been committed to memory. For memorized enactments of a text, much more use of the body and physical movement is expected. Textual recitations may require generous gestures, use of the entire body for emphasis, even walking about the stage or chancel. Those who *read* biblical texts are not expected to move from behind a lectern or to wander about during the lesson's presentation. Consequently, they need only be concerned about the following aspects of embodiment: breath control, vocal production, and the use of eyes, face, and hands.

Breath control: The reader should generally stand erect either holding the Bible or placing it on a lectern. Good posture is essential for gaining breath support.

Breath is drawn when the abdominal muscles relax outward. The voice gains air support when the abdominal muscles press inward to create a flow of air through the lungs, past the vocal chords (folds), and out the mouth. The articulation of abdominal muscles is the key to "breathing through the diaphragm." The diaphragm, a horizontal muscle that lies beneath the lungs, is difficult to manipulate on its own. But, it comes into play in breathing when the abdominal muscles are employed. Relaxing the abdominal muscles outward drops the diaphragm and allows the lungs to expand with air. Pressing inward with the abdominal muscles raises the diaphragm against the lungs, pushing air outward in a controlled manner. Filling the lungs with ample breath allows for the voice to speak with the volume and tone that the reading requires. Those reading in worship are cautioned against overusing the air supply to produce a breathy sound. This occurs when a more-than-necessary amount of air passes over the vocal folds. Good breath control provides for economical use of air to produce the desired volume and tone.

While erect posture is generally called for in reading Scripture, there are times when the tone or mood of the reading calls for another posture. For example, in reading a lament psalm, one might choose to bend forward slightly and stoop the shoulders as in a posture of despair. Regardless of stance, attention to breath control is the key to vocal production.

Breathing exercises: The simplest exercise for establishing good breathing habits is for a reader to lie flat on his or her back. Gravity forces the body into the best posture (spine straight, shoulders back, lungs poised). In this position, breathe deeply and note how the abdominal muscles rise while inhaling and drop when exhaling. Now, stand erect and try to duplicate that posture while breathing deeply. As an exercise to develop good control, take a deep breath and read a section of Scripture for as long as your breath lasts. Try to increase the length of time you can speak on a single breath.

Vocal Production: Fueled by the breath, the voice creates vowel sounds that are separated and articulated by consonants. The Scripture reader should remember that the sound of the voice carries principally on the vowel sounds (a few voiced consonants also carry sound: l, m, n, r, v, ng, w, y, and z). Vowel sounds carry best when they are allowed to resonate within the throat and vocal chamber. The initial sound emitted by the vocal chords is small and inarticulate. Its strength and quality come through the way the sound is shaped and amplified while traveling through the body and especially through the mouth and nasal cavities. A closed, diminished vocal cavity creates a small, pinched sound. An open, relaxed vocal chamber creates a round tone that is pleasant and appropriate to most public speech. It is this tone that can be projected best in places where there is no electronic amplification of the voice.

Vocal exercises: 1) Take a deep breath and hum for as long as you can. Use only as much air as needed to make the sound. 2) Repeat the phrase, "mah, may, mee, moh, moo," at different volumes. Elongate the vowels and consonants to create a smooth, unbroken phrase. 3) Speak the following phrase rapidly, with emphasis on the consonants:

"Quickly, the cat captured the rat." Note how the tempo and energy of a crisp, quick reading match the tone of the phrase and help express the visual image.

Voice and Interpretation: Oral interpretation of Scripture requires that the reader return the written word to life through the natural, lively use of the voice. In normal speech, we sound lively because we naturally know how to pace our words, vary our pitch, and cast tones that articulate our intended meanings. The Scripture reader needs to work with a text until he or she knows how to incorporate the natural skills of vocal inflection, pause, pace, and use of tone to capture a lively and meaningful interpretation of the text. This is achieved in practice through trial and error as the reader assesses different ways of articulating each sentence, thought, or phrase. Once interpretive decisions are made, the reader should find a means by which to create visual cues to guide the oral presentation of a text. Whether actually making marks in one's Bible, or printing the text on a page that can be cued for performance, it is important both to experiment with phrasing and emphasis, and to mark the text as a performance script.

To summarize, in using the voice, the following issues should be kept in mind:

- Vowel sounds should be round and full; they carry the words.

- Emphasis can be achieved in a word when a vowel sound is elongated and allowed to resonate.

- All formal public speech, and especially the Word of God, requires that words be fully formed and articulated. Say, for example, "going to" instead of "gonna," or "let me," instead of "lemme."

- Stressing consonants in a phrase allows for a percussive effect that indicates action, tension, or energy.

- Pitch and tone should vary in public reading in the same way that it does in ordinary conversation. These elements should be practiced with every reading so as to capture what is necessary for meaningful interpretation. Though we typically know to do this in ordinary conversation, we often place the stress on the wrong words or syllables when we read in public. A common mistake, for example, is to place emphasis on prepositions. This is uncommon in ordinary speech and is reserved for times when the speaker intends to emphasize place or time. (The dog is *in* the house, not outside.)

- Pitch and tone should not fall into predictable patterns, which create an undesirable sing-song effect.

- The reader should become familiar with proper use of electronic amplification systems when they are available. When such tools are unavailable, the speaker can learn to project his or her voice and speak distinctly enough for all to hear. The speaker should remember to enunciate, articulate, and exaggerate speech when projecting to a large room. Saying these three words crisply is a common technique for practicing clear expression. Say: "Enunciate! Articulate! Exaggerate!" and repeat as necessary to limber the mouth and tongue for clear speech.

Use of Eyes: Because the reader of a text does not have it committed to memory, he or she is not expected to maintain constant eye contact with the audience. (As one critic remarked, looking constantly at one's audience is not eye contact, it is staring.) Nor should the reader feel the need to keep frequent eye contact with all parts of the audience. This creates a bobbing head effect that does not add significance to the reading. The reader can more effectively use the eyes in three ways: 1) The eyes can be used to look down at the written material, both to see the printed words and to observe those visual interpretive cues added during practice. 2) The eyes can be cast in the direction of the audience. While many readers look up and down frequently, as if eye contact with the audience were an unwritten regulation in oral interpretation, it can be done sparingly, but thoughtfully and meaningfully. There are two purposes accomplished by looking at the audience during a reading. The first is to gauge audience response to the reading. One may determine the need to speak more slowly, loudly, or distinctly, depending on audience reaction. The second purpose is to use a strong look at the audience to add emphasis to a phrase or sentence. For example, one might choose to look up at those places in the text where visual contact with the listeners would highlight certain words: "I do not know him!" or "As for me and my house, we will serve the Lord." Speaking these lines while looking at the audience lifts them in a visible way from the page and raises awareness of their significance. In such cases, the words and phrases need to be rehearsed so they can be delivered without a clumsy, mid-phrase glance back at the printed material. 3) The eyes can be cast off into space as if to suggest an idea or object for reflection. It may be the suggestion of an imagined person or object. Example: the reader looks to the side and speaks as if to someone standing nearby while rendering Pilate's question to Jesus, "Are you the king of the Jews?" A casted glance can also indicate a distant place or idea: "I lift my eyes to the hills." When listeners see the speaker make a near or distant glance, into their minds comes an image of the person, object, or place the speaker is imagining.

Use of Gesture: We typically think of hands when we speak of gesture. But facial gesture is more important in reading Scripture than hand gesture. While adjusting one's posture can help create a gesture of mood, most of the visual mood of a reading is captured by the look on the reader's face. Because it is visible from a long distance, the face provides a strong clue to meaning in oral communication. It can match and reinforce the vocal tone of the reading as its appearance shifts according to the reader's interpretation of the moods in the text. In preparation for public readings, readers can use a mirror to practice the facial gestures of delight, anger, doubt, despair, gratitude, and so forth. Once these become part of the speaker's facial and gestural vocabulary, they can be employed to add visual emphasis to a reading.

The use of hand gestures in reading a text is generally to be discouraged. While not strictly wrong, it is unnecessary and often distracting in a reading. In cases where a text is enacted from memory, there is a strong expectation for the use of hand gestures and body movement. Such expectations do not apply when a text is read. In fact, they may simply look silly, as when people gesture without lifting their eyes from the Bible text. When the audience sees the hands spread emphatically while they can see only the top of the reader's head, they sense a natural incongruity of action.

A good use of the hands during a reading is to hold the Bible. This gives a strong signal that the word spoken is, indeed, "The Word of the Lord." Even if a reader types and prints a large print version of the text and marks it with performance cues, it is a thoughtful gesture to place that page discreetly in the Bible during the reading. One may argue that doing so is somewhat deceptive. On the contrary, giving the listener a visual indication that the text comes from Holy Scripture is a symbolic reinforcement of the authority of the reader's speech.

Articulation of the Reading

In addition to the attention given to the careful articulation of words in a reading, the reader needs to consider other aspects of oral interpretation that make for interpretive phrasing. They include the use of pause, emphasis, pace, inflection, and volume.

Pause: The use of pause in reading and public address achieves two primary effects (a third is indicated below): it gives the listener time to process what has been said, and it allows the listener to prepare for that which follows. Inexperienced speakers and readers often use pause too infrequently and too briefly. A long pause is needed when the scene or mood changes in a reading. Carefully placed pauses give room for meaning to occur in the mind of the listener.

In placement of pauses, the reader has a guide in the text's punctuation. Beware, however, because punctuation can be a faulty guide for oral interpretation. The original biblical languages did not use punctuation to guide the readers of ancient texts. Such markings are common in literature today; they are added to provide visual clues to meaning as a text is read silently. The reader needs to know, however, that these markings function differently for silent reading than for reading aloud. Commas, for example, are needed in written material for the eye to sort out phrases, lists of objects, and grammatical effects. A common mistake, however, is for an oral reader to use all commas as pause markings. This usually makes for a choppy delivery. Readers should practice reading aloud so as to determine how to separate ideas, images, and phrases according to sense units. Here are a few pointers about where to pause:

Pause in those places that separate images, not between them. Example: "The large, yellow dog sat on the porch, / chewing on the remnants of a t-bone steak." Give a brief pause only after "porch." This separates the image of the dog sitting, and the image of the dog eating.

- Do not pause during the reading of lists. The commas are there to separate the objects, but do not need to be vocalized: "Don't forget to bring home milk, eggs, bread, and cheese from the store." (No pauses are necessary in this sentence.)

- Do not pause when introducing quotations with words like "saying" or "said." Pausing between these words and the quotation that follows places an emphasis on them that is not warranted. When done correctly, these words become subsumed in the quotation and disappear when there is no pause after them. Example: "He broke bread and gave it to them/ saying, "Take and eat.""

- Pauses are usually brief within sentences. Large pauses are necessary when something complex has been articulated or when the scene or topic changes.

Emphasis: Within each phrase, the reader needs to determine which words to emphasize. This is usually done by adding volume and stress to a word within a phrase. Exercise in emphasis: Speak the following sentence eight times. Note the change in meaning as you volubly emphasize a different word each time. "I don't want that dog in my house."

"I don't want that dog in my house."
(Meaning: she may want the dog in here, but I don't.)

"I don't want that dog in my house."
(Meaning: you may have thought I did, but I don't.)

"I don't want that dog in my house."
(Meaning: I may need him, but I don't want him.)

And so forth.

Another way to achieve emphasis is by the third use of pause. In addition to the uses described above, pauses also add emphasis when they are placed before key words or images. When used in this way, pauses shade meaning by indicating an attitude or by casting a certain kind of impression, like doubt or inquisitiveness. For example, note how the meaning shifts in this exercise. Say, "His name was William." Now say it with a slight pause before the name: "His name was / William." It sounds as if one needs to recall the name. Now, say it with a long pause: "His name was / / William." It now sounds as if there is something interesting or odd about William. The pause adds color to the sentence, a shade of meaning that your interpretation of the text may call for, but that the words alone do not supply.

Pace: The pace of a reading needs to be appropriate to the material. Scenes of action, for example, are best delivered quickly, with emphasis on short words and percussive consonants. Pastoral material is better delivered at a slow pace with pauses for reflection.

For those who tend to speak too quickly, the overall pace of a reading can be regulated by the careful articulation of the syllables in each word. Readings also sound hurried when words are slurred or rushed together. Note, for example, the difference in articulation if one says: "She'll be comin' 'round the mount'n when she comes," and "She will be coming around the mountain when she comes." The second rendition will automatically be spoken more slowly and distinctly, and will be more easily understood, especially at a distance.

Use of Inflection: The natural use of the human voice involves a high degree of pitch fluctuation. Few people speak in a flat or monotone delivery during ordinary conversation. Flat delivery should especially be avoided in public reading of Scripture. It signals to the listeners that the reading is uninteresting and unimportant. Readers should practice bringing the natural range of their vocal musicality into their readings. To practice this, take note of the range of pitch used when you hear yourself recount an exciting event. "Wow, you should have seen my daughter's basketball game yesterday. It went into overtime and her team won by a three point shot at the final buzzer." Such a line can hardly be delivered meaningfully without bold fluctuations in pitch.

Volume: While readers always need to speak audibly, variations in volume can add meaning or emphasis to words and phrases in a reading. A strong effect can be achieved when a person suddenly speaks in a volume that is different from the average level used in a reading. For example, a shout is emphatic when it comes as a surprise. Likewise, a sudden whisper can often be more effective than a loud tone. For practice, note the effect when a reader, speaking loudly, says, "I do not know the man!" and then, suddenly soft, says, "And immediately the cock crowed a second time."

Conclusion

Reading the Bible aloud is one of the most common elements of Christian worship. There are those who do it with grace and meaning, and those who do it inarticulately. For some reason, we seem to think that any person who can read at all has the skill or experience to do adequate oral interpretation of literature. Remember, however, that we conclude our Scripture readings with the phrase, "The Word of the Lord." If we believe this statement to be true of the text we have read, then care needs to be given as to its adequate preparation. We also need to call on people with gifts for interpretation and embodiment to do this work and to teach the art to others. We can be on the lookout in our parishes and congregations for people who are particularly gifted in such things. They might include those with theater experience or people who work in radio and television communication. Often, the best readers are teachers of young children who regularly read to their audiences with animation and energy. They can teach the rest of us to do this, as well. The living Word of the Lord is among the greatest gifts of Christian faith and hearing it uttered in worship is among the church's most effective means of grace. May the Word of God come alive and its meaning be richly articulated whenever it is read in our houses of public worship.

Clayton J. Schmit

Forms and Practices of Public Prayer

Principles for Leading in Public Prayer

During services of corporate worship, prayers are said in a variety of ways. Sometimes all people read a composed prayer or psalm together. Sometimes the people are asked to offer extemporaneous prayers. At times an appointed prayer leader will speak aloud a prayer on the people's behalf. This is usually the case in the traditional Prayer of the Church (also known as the Pastoral Prayer). When a leader speaks to God on behalf of all people, he or she is wise to attend to a number of basic principles:

1. Because corporate prayer is intended to voice public concerns, the language used by the prayer leader should indicate a corporate voice. For example, use "we," instead of "I."

2. Prayer leaders should seek fresh means by which to make address to God. Well-worn phrases such as "Dear Heavenly Father," "Loving God," "Great Creator," and "Father God," are not inappropriate means of address. Still, any language that is over-used begins to lose its power for revealing insight and capturing the imagination. Certainly, there are favorite names we might use for addressing God. Jesus, we know, used "Abba" (the Aramaic word for "Father") and taught us to do the same. Nonetheless, there are times in public worship where our understanding of the nature of God can be broadened or strengthened through the use of fresh metaphors and imagery. Often, clues to creative names for God can come from the appointed Scripture readings for the day, for example, "Seeker of the Lost," or "Author of Love."

3. The direction of communication in public prayer is *from* the assembled worshippers (whether spoken by all people together or by a single appointed leader on the people's behalf) *toward* God. Remember, prayers are not spoken by leaders *to* the people. While this seems obvious, it is a principle often violated by well-meaning prayer leaders.

4. Prayer writers and leaders should refrain from making announcements within prayers (for example, "we pray for Joanne, who is in room 315 in the hospital). It is better to give the announcement to the people before beginning the prayer.

Then the direction of the prayer does not alternate from speaking to God in the petition and speaking to the people in making the announcement.

5. Prayer leaders should also avoid "preaching" to the people under the guise of a prayer. Let the prayers be genuine statements to God on behalf of the assembly.

6. Prayers, when led by an individual, are intended to draw the hearts and imaginations of the gathered people into assent. For this reason, prayers conclude with "Amen," which is a corporate affirmation of the prayer. Leaders should avoid speaking prayers or petitions that do not draw full assent from the worshippers. People should not have to "vote on the petitions"[1] as they are offered.

7. Imagery for prayer can be drawn from scriptural passages or preaching themes in order to emphasize the connection between various acts of worship. For example, a prayer following a sermon on the Beatitudes might begin with the address, "Fount of Blessing."

8. Prayers on behalf of God's people are intentionally bold. We dare to call upon God's name for guidance, nourishment, encouragement, and so forth, simply because God promises to hear our prayers and to respond to us as a parent does for children. Accordingly, prayers are not enriched by the uttering of qualifications: "Lord, we *just* pray for. . . ." The word *just* suggests that we are tentative about our desire to approach God with our cares. Or, it hints that we do not desire to take up much of God's time or power. We just ask this much, and nothing more. The point is made well by William Willimon who once put it this way: "Lord, we are not asking for much, *just* that you raise the dead!"

Clayton J. Schmit

The Collect

The collect (pronounced **cah**-lect) is an organized short form of prayer that was in use as early as the fifth century in the Western church. It has usually been associated with themes relating to Sundays in the church year, and to feast days. Medieval missals (service books) provided collects for every Sunday and for commemorative days. The Lutheran reformers adapted the Latin collects for their services in the German language; the Church of England also adopted their use for the 1549 *Book of Common Prayer* (*BCP*).

The person most noted for the use and development of the collect prayer form in English is Thomas Cranmer, architect of the *BCP*. Many of his collects are still in use today in Anglican and Episcopalian churches worldwide.

---

1. We are indebted to Michael Aune, who coined this phrase.

The collect is a prayer that is intended to gather or "collect" prayerful thoughts around a liturgical theme. It also gathers the hearts and minds of worshippers around the theme and draws them into prayer by means of its carefully crafted language and thoughtful sentiments. It consists of five parts, as demonstrated by this prayer from a sixth century Italian rite that was included in Cranmer's *BCP*:

1) *Address* to God:
Almighty God,

2) *Theological Statement* about God:
which dost see that we have no power of ourselves to help ourselves;

3) *Petition(s)*, making specific requests to God:
keep thou us both outwardly in our bodies, and inwardly in our souls;

4) Statement indicating the *Purpose* of the petitions, usually beginning with the words "that" or "so that":
that we may be defended from all adversities which may happen to the body, and from all evil thoughts which may assault and hurt the soul;

5) *Conclusion*, often doxological, that indicates through whom the prayer is made:
through Jesus Christ, our Lord.

These five parts have been made easy to remember and utilize by a shorthand system developed by Karen Westerfield Tucker: You, Who, Do, That, Through.

Though the language of the collects in *BCP* and other service books often seems lofty, stilted, formal, or archaic, the collect form is applicable to any language tone or vernacular. In fact, the collect form is not dissimilar to ordinary language use. Consider, for example, this comment: "Susan, you are so good at math. Can you please help me with my assignment so that I can learn to understand this difficult equation?" That is, essentially, a collect.

In modern language, the collect form offers a fitting framework for prayers of worship and devotion. Here are two examples of how the collect can work in contemporary settings.

A prayer for a meal at a church function might sound like this:
> *You:* God of All Creation,
> *Who:* You have made a bountiful planet and given us plenty of food to feed the peoples and the creatures of the earth.
> *Do:* We ask your blessing on our meal today and we pray that even as you feed us, you share your gifts with all peoples, especially the poor in our city,

That: so that everyone can know of your gracious love and receive a share of your life-giving generosity.

Through: We pray in Jesus' name. Amen.

Striking another tone, here is an example fitting for an outdoor youth meeting:

Great God, you blow our minds with the beauty of your creation. Help us to hear the wonderful sounds of nature and see the work of your hands as we work and play together. Be with us in our meeting today so that we get to know you and our friends in deeper ways. In Jesus' name, Amen.

While any style of language can be used to craft a collect, some principles for preparing public prayer are wisely observed. See "Principles for Leading in Public Prayer" above.

Sample Collects in Various Language Styles

The following are examples of collects reflecting a variety of traditions or settings. While they may be used as they are, they are offered here especially as examples of the kinds of collects that can be newly composed by prayer leaders for every occasion.

Traditional liturgical collect

Everlasting and Almighty God, you have gathered your people together to worship and adore you. We ask you to bless us with your presence and fill this place with the fragrance of your grace, so that we may come to know the depth and breadth of your abiding desire for us. We pray in the name of the One who loves us with an everlasting love, Jesus Christ our Savior and Lord. Amen.

Charismatic church collect

Glorious Spirit, you fill us with power and grace. Come fill this place with your burning presence; fill our hearts with your tongues of fire, and your house with a mighty wind, so that all who are here may experience a spiritual awakening and be set anew on pathways of justice and love. We ask this in the mighty and powerful name of Jesus, a name that is above all other names, and at whose name every knee shall bow in heaven and on earth. Amen.

Collect at the close of worship

> God of Heaven, you who have been with us during this hour of worship; we ask that you continue your presence with us as we leave this holy service, so that we may be your hands and feet, your voices and witnesses to the world we encounter throughout the week. We pray this in name of him who walks before us, beside us, among us, and with us; Jesus Christ, our risen Lord. Amen.

College/seminary chapel collect

> God of all power and knowledge, you have blessed this (university, college, seminary, school) and sustained it through its faithful years of service. We ask that you look with grace upon our students, staff, and faculty as they seek to discern your ways and follow your word; that we might learn to serve you faithfully all our days. In the strong name of Jesus Christ we pray. Amen

Litanies

The word litany comes from the Greek, "lite," which means prayer or supplication. This form of prayer offers a series of supplications or petitions that the congregation lays before God in an antiphonal manner. Litanies are usually led by One (or Leader); the response is typically said by All (or Congregation).

Kyrie eleison: this, one of the simplest historical litanies, is from early Greek and Latin liturgies; Kyrie eleison is Latin for "Lord have mercy."

> One: Lord have mercy.
> **All: Lord have mercy.**
> One: Christ have mercy.
> **All: Christ have mercy.**
> One: Lord have mercy.
> **All: Lord have mercy.**

Psalm 136 is an example of a biblical litany

> One: Give thanks to the Lord, for he is good.
> **All: His love endures forever.**

> One: Give thanks to the God of gods.
> **All: His love endures forever.**

One: Give thanks to the Lord of lords:
All: His love endures forever.

One: to him who alone does great wonders,
All: His love endures forever.

One: who by his understanding made the heavens,
All: His love endures forever.

One: who spread out the earth upon the waters,
All: His love endures forever.

One: who made the great lights—
All: His love endures forever.

One: the sun to govern the day,
All: His love endures forever.

One: the moon and stars to govern the night;
All: His love endures forever.

One: to him who struck down the firstborn of Egypt
All: His love endures forever.

One: and brought Israel out from among them
All: His love endures forever.

One: with a mighty hand and outstretched arm;
All: His love endures forever.

One: to him who divided the Red Sea asunder
All: His love endures forever.

One: and brought Israel through the midst of it,
All: His love endures forever.

One: to him who led his people through the desert,
All: His love endures forever.

One: who struck down great kings,
All: His love endures forever.

One: to the One who remembered us in our low estate
All: His love endures forever.

One: and freed us from our enemies,
All: His love endures forever.

One: and who gives food to every creature.
All: His love endures forever.

One: Give thanks to the God of heaven.
All: His love endures forever.

Litany for opening convocation at school

One: O Lord, as we begin this school year, we look to you for guidance and strength.
All: Lord, grant us your peace.

One: We seek to be faithful to your word and to your precepts in our teaching and learning.
All: Lord, grant us your peace.

One: As we struggle with class work, papers, readings, tests, and grading,
All: Lord, grant us your peace.

One: When the end of the term comes and finals begin,
All: Lord, grant us your peace.

One: When correspondence from home makes us yearn for familiar times and familiar places,
All: Lord, grant us your peace.

One: Whatever may come our way during the weeks of this quarter (semester),
All: Lord, grant us your peace.

One: Bless, O Lord, this new beginning; may it set us on a course that prepares us for lives of ministry and service.
All: Amen.

Litany following a school tragedy/loss

> One: Listen to our prayer.
> **All: Lord, have mercy upon us.**
>
> One: Let our cry come before you.
> **All: Lord, have mercy upon us.**
>
> One: Be with us now in our time of isolation.
> **All: Lord, have mercy upon us.**
>
> One: Let your light shine on our darkness.
> **All: Lord, have mercy upon us.**
>
> One: Bring peace to our anxiety.
> **All: Lord, have mercy upon us.**
>
> One: Give us hope in the face of hopelessness.
> **All: Lord, have mercy upon us.**
>
> One: Pluck the thorn of fear from our hearts.
> **All: Lord, have mercy upon us.**
>
> One: Show us the way forward when we see none.
> **All: Lord, have mercy upon us**

Litany for Thanksgiving chapel or Trinity Sunday chapel

> One: Give thanks to the Lord for he is good.
> **All: God's mercies are new every morning; his faithfulness is great.**
>
> One: Give thanks to the one who lived, died, rose from the dead,
> and is coming again.
> **All: God's mercies are new every morning; his faithfulness is great.**
>
> One: Give thanks to the Father who created the heavens and the earth.
> **All: God's mercies are new every morning; his faithfulness is great.**
>
> One: Give thanks to the Lamb who was slain but is alive forevermore.
> **All: God's mercies are new every morning; his faithfulness is great.**

One: Give thanks to the Spirit who makes us one.
All: God's mercies are new every morning; his faithfulness is great.

One: Give thanks with a grateful heart.
All: God's mercies are new every morning; his faithfulness is great.

One: Give thanks to the Lord of the Harvest for he has provided all things.
All: God's mercies are new every morning; his faithfulness is great.

The Bidding Prayer

A bidding prayer is one in which the prayer leader calls for the congregation to pray. Each bid (or prayer request) is followed by silence. Worshippers respond to the bids by praying silently, or by offering petitions aloud.

Bidding prayer for the classroom

- Pray this morning that the material presented in class will be clear, focused, and useful in preparing you for all God desires to do in your life.

- Pray for the professor that she will respond to the prompting of the Spirit and the needs of the class.

- Pray for the persons sitting on your right, that they will receive from this class something that will impact how they think, act, live, or work.

- Pray for the persons sitting on your left that they will be sensitive to the needs of others and sensitive to the prompting of the Holy Spirit during this class.

- Pray for your own lives. Pray that those things that normally distract you during class will be removed and that you will be focused and discerning as you engage the day's material.

- Finally, pray for the world beyond this classroom. Pray that you will be opened toward ministries of love and mercy as a result of being here today.

Bidding prayer prior to a major test, midterm, or final examination

- Pray that you will focus and that the peace of God will replace your anxiety.

- Pray that your mind will be alert and that you will trust in the preparation you have made for your exam.

- Pray that you will be able to write clearly from the knowledge you have acquired and that you will resist the temptation to write about knowledge you do not possess.

- Pray that you will finish the test in sufficient time to review your answers and correct mistakes.

Bidding prayer for local and world peace

- I ask your prayers for an end to all warfare in the world.
- I ask your prayers for a ceasing of human trafficking and abuse of children in the world.
- I ask your prayers for civil discourse in our nation.
- I ask your prayers for those who go without food and shelter in our community.
- I ask your prayers that we may live the commitment to be agents of love and peace wherever in God's vast world God may lead us.

Prayers Based on the Psalms

"Praying Scripture" is a form of prayer that follows a biblical text and uses its form to shape extemporized prayers. Here is an example from the psalms.

Praying Psalm 51:1–8, 10

Have mercy on me, God, according to your loving kindness.
According to the multitude of your tender mercies, blot out my transgressions.

> *We know that you are a merciful God. We trust in your grace every day. We have sinned against you and still you show us your love. You see all things and yet have taken our sins and removed them to a distance unknown. We are unworthy of your love.*

Wash me thoroughly from my iniquity. Cleanse me from my sin.

> *We have spent too much of our lives wallowing in the knowledge and the consequences of our sin. It has bogged us down, taken us along dry paths, and left us in a wilderness of despair. We are tired of carrying this burden. Take it from us, O Lord. Wash us, for we are in need of your cleansing power. We want to know the beauty of your holiness and the joy of being released from our sins.*

For I know my transgressions. My sin is constantly before me.

> *Though you have blotted out our transgressions, O Lord, we are always aware of them. We see them in our dreams and in our waking hours. There is nowhere we can go that sin does not follow. Wash us, Lord, and relieve us of the burden of carrying our sins.*

Against you, and you only, have I sinned, and done that which is evil in your sight; that you may be proved right when you speak, and justified when you judge.

We have tried to justify our sin by lying to ourselves. We have not only hurt one another, we have failed you, O God. Forgive us for our stubborn hearts and our failure to yield to your will. You are justified in punishing us, O God, but we pray that you bring forgiveness in place of the wrath we deserve.

Behold, I was brought forth in iniquity. In sin my mother conceived me.

This condition of sin has followed us all our lives. From the moment we were cast out of warmth and darkness into the bold light of the world, we began to rebel against you, O God. Adam is our father, Eve is our mother; and the serpent is an all too familiar companion. But you alone are our Savior.

Behold, you desire truth in the inward parts. You teach me wisdom in the inmost place.

We can no longer deceive ourselves with claims of goodness. We come to you naked, willing to be truthful about our lives. Look inside us, O God, and see the innermost chambers of our hearts. Everything is open to you. Show us your way.

Purify me with hyssop, and I will be clean. Wash me, and I will be whiter than snow.

Only you can make us clean, O God. You have cleansed the leper and made the unclean pure. Purge from our lives anything that displeases you. We are tired of bearing sin's great smudge. Let us gleam in the brightness of your love.

Let me hear joy and gladness, that the bones which you have broken may rejoice.

Under the crushing weight of our sin, we have become broken, disjointed. But our joy returns and our body swells with wholeness at the sound of your word. We praise you, O God, for the healing you have worked in us. Cries of joy replace our weeping. Our night turns to day at the coming of your grace.

Create in me a clean heart, O God. Renew a right spirit within me.

O God, you have lifted us up out of the desperation we have created. And you have created within us new minds, and a renewed commitment to love you and serve you. Set now our spirits aright. Let us be your people and live according to your will. Let us proclaim your name in wonder to all who see that we are changed. We praise you, O God, for you have restored your people and set us again on the lofty ledge of honor because you elect to see us even as you see your Son, Jesus Christ. We give thanks in his name. Amen.

Prayers from Christian Tradition

The Prayer of Jesus, Traditional (also known as The Lord's Prayer)

> Our Father, who art in heaven,
>   hallowed be thy name,
>   thy kingdom come,

thy will be done,
> on earth as it is in heaven.

Give us this day our daily bread;

and forgive us our trespasses (debts),
> as we forgive those who trespass against us;
>> (as we forgive our debtors;)

and lead us not into temptation,
> but deliver us from evil.

For thine is the kingdom,
> and the power, and the glory,
>> for ever and ever. Amen.

Prayer attributed to St. Francis of Assisi

Lord, make me an instrument of your peace.
Where there is hatred let me sow love,
where there is injury, pardon;
where there is doubt, faith;
where there is despair, hope;
where there is darkness, light;
where there is sadness, joy.

O Divine Master, grant that I not so much seek
to be consoled, as to console;
to be understood, as to understand;
to be loved, as to love.

For it is in giving that we receive,
it is in pardoning that we are pardoned,
it is in dying, that we are born to eternal life.
Amen.

Prayer attributed to St. Ignatius

Teach us, good Lord,
To serve thee as thou deservest,
To give and not to count the cost,
To fight and not to heed the wounds,
To toil and not to seek for rest,
To labor and not to ask for any reward,
Save that of knowing that we do thy will.
Amen.

Prayer of Sir Francis Drake

This prayer, attributed to the great explorer, is said to have been written as Drake embarked on his journey to the west coast of South America. It is a fitting prayer for New Year's Day, new starts, new school terms, and for modern day adventures and enterprises.

>   Disturb us, Lord,
>   when we are too pleased with ourselves,
>   when our dreams have come true
>   because we dreamed too little,
>   when we arrived safely
>   because we sailed too close to the shore.
>
>   Disturb us, Lord,
>   when with the abundance of things we possess
>   we have lost our thirst
>   for the waters of life;
>   having fallen in love with life,
>   we have ceased to dream of eternity;
>   and in our efforts to build a new earth,
>   we have allowed our vision
>   of the new heaven to dim.
>
>   Disturb us, Lord, to dare more boldly,
>   to venture on wilder seas
>   where storms will show your mastery;
>   where losing sight of land,
>   we shall find the stars.
>
>   We ask you to push back
>   the horizons of our hopes;
>   and to push back the future
>   in strength, courage, hope, and love.
>
>   This we ask in the name of our Captain,
>   who is Jesus Christ.
>   Amen.

The Serenity Prayer attributed to Reinhold Niebuhr

> God grant me the serenity
> to accept the things I cannot change,
> courage to change the things I can,
> and wisdom to know the difference.
> Living one day at a time;
> enjoying one moment at a time;
> accepting hardships as the pathway to peace;
> taking, as he did, this sinful world
> as it is, not as I would have it;
> trusting that he will make all things right
> if I surrender to his will;
> that I may be reasonably happy in this life
> and supremely happy with him
> forever in the next.
> Amen.

Prayer attributed to Desiderius Erasmus

> O Lord Jesus Christ,
> You have said that you are the way, the truth, and the life.
> Suffer us not to stray from you who are the way,
> nor to distrust you who are the Truth,
> nor to rest in anything other than you, who are the Life.

Prayer attributed to John Henry Newman

> Give me, O my Lord,
> that purity of conscience
> which alone can receive your inspirations.
> My ears are dull, so that I cannot hear your voice.
> My eyes are dim, so that I cannot see the signs of your presence.
> You alone can quicken my hearing and purge my sight,
> and cleanse and renew my heart.
> Teach me to sit at your feet and to hear your word.
> Amen.

Prayer attributed to Maria Ware

> Lord, hear;
> Lord, forgive;
> Lord, do.
> Hear what we speak not;
> forgive what we speak amiss;
> do what we leave undone;
> that not according to our words, or our deeds,
> but according to your mercy and truth,
> all may work for your glory,
> and the good of your kingdom,
> through Jesus Christ. Amen.

Prayer attributed to St. Augustine of Hippo

> O loving God,
> to turn away from you is to fall,
> to turn toward you is to rise,
> and to stand before you is to abide forever.
> Grant us, dear God,
> in all our duties, your help;
> in all our uncertainties, your guidance;
> in all our dangers, your protection;
> and in all our sorrows, your peace;
> through Jesus Christ our Lord.
> Amen.

The Daily Office (Praying the Hours)[1]

The daily office, also known as the divine office, *opus Dei*, or the monastic hours, is a tradition with roots in the Old Testament (from Dan 6:11, "who got upon his knees three times a day," and Ps 55:17, "evening and morning and noon I utter my complaint and moan, and he will hear my voice") and from the admonitions of Paul in his letters to pray without ceasing (1 Thess 5:17, Eph 6:18, Phil 1:4). The established pattern of these fixed times of prayer comes from the Rule of St. Benedict, written in the sixth century by Benedict of Nursia (480–543 CE). The rule was written for the monks at the monastery Benedict founded in Monte Cassino, Italy. In the rule, Benedict called for daily prayers to occur eight times during the day. These fixed times of prayer have become the standard pattern for cloistered life, whether the order is Benedictine, Dominican, Franciscan, or another. In some communities today, the eight times of prayer are reduced to six or fewer, thus limiting the interruptions of sleep and work. Nonetheless, strict adherence to pausing during the day and rising during the night to praise God is the norm for praying the divine office. While there are variations in the way that the hours are named and scheduled, there is a pattern that is most commonly followed:

- *Vespers.* As in Jewish practice, the monastic day begins at sundown. From the Latin for evening, Vespers is prayed as the new day begins. Its traditional focus is on Christ as the light of the world.

- *Compline* is prayed before bedtime. The simple life of monastic communities makes it possible for its members to retire around 9 p.m. The purpose of Compline is both to prepare one for sleep and to reflect on our final sleep in death.

- *Vigils* is the night office, requiring people to rise from sleep at midnight. Some may find it convenient to remain awake until the vigil has been kept. This is the time for earnest wakefulness, where we learn to trust God in the darkness.

- *Lauds* is the early morning time of praise. It may fall anywhere from 3 a.m. to just before sunrise. It is a time of prayer for the coming of the sun and with it, the possibilities of the dawning day. *Matins* (from the Latin word for morning) is a term

1. This essay is adapted from *Praying the Hours in Ordinary Life* (Cascade Books, 2010) by Lauralee Farrer and Clayton J. Schmit.

sometimes associated with this time of day and is often used as a synonym for Lauds. In some practices, Matins is a separate time of prayer that precedes Lauds.

- *Prime* is prayed at the beginning of the workday, about 6 or 7 a.m. The worker is fully awake, ready to set his or her sights on the tasks ahead. Traditionally, Prime is a meditation on Creation. It also reflects upon the appearance of Jesus before Caiaphas in the Passion narrative, an event that took place before dawn. (Matt 26:57–68)

- *Terce*, the third hour. The workday is well underway. Yet the worker pauses to remember that there is a purpose greater than the task at hand; it is an awareness of God. The traditional meditation of Terce is on the Holy Spirit, who appeared at this hour on the day of Pentecost. (Acts 2:1–15)

- *Sext*, mid-day, the sixth hour of the workday. The success of the day's work hangs in balance. The pause to pray reflects upon the awareness that half of the day is spent. It is a metaphor for mid-life, when we remember our youthful exuberance and we pray for remaining strength. Because this was the time of day during which Jesus hung upon the cross (Mark 15:33), Sext is a time to reflect upon his anguish, even as we meditate upon the crosses with which we are burdened.

- *None* occurs at mid-afternoon. The workday is nearly spent, as is the energy of the worker. Even so was the vigor of Christ who died at this hour. (Mark 15:34–38)

Using Choirs and Musical Ensembles in Worship

The use of choirs and musical ensembles in worship is a Christian tradition that follows the Hebrew practice described in the Old Testament. The Book of Psalms is a collection of worship songs that were designed to be sung by choirs and accompanied by instruments: "Praise him with timbrel and dance: praise him with stringed instruments and pipe (Ps 150:4).

While many churches today continue the use of choirs, usually accompanied by pianos and organs, others are using lead singers accompanied by instrumental ensembles or bands. Today's timbrel and strings are typically drums and guitars. Some churches have the capacity to involve both types of ensemble in their worship leadership. Scripture does not privilege vocal, instrumental, or acoustic music. It only, and repeatedly, tells believers to sing, play, and dance in praise to God. The following notes provide guidance for pastors, musicians, and congregations as they seek to employ musical ensembles to assist people in their praise.

First Principles

1. Musical groups in public worship have, as their first and principle duty, the responsibility to assist people with their prayer and praise. By singing with people and providing accompaniment, they exist to engage (and not to overshadow) the voice of the congregation. Their goal is to enable and inspire people to praise God with a voice and will beyond their ken. All other purposes are secondary to this primary function.

2. Secondarily, choirs and other ensembles may perform music for the congregation in order to: proclaim Scripture in song, praise God or pray on behalf of the people with music that is beyond the ability of congregational voices, and provide musical accompaniment for liturgical movement or action.

3. Choir and ensemble leaders have the responsibility to teach their groups that their purpose is to serve the congregation, to serve God, and to present (or perform) music with humility.

4. Excellence in musical leadership is to be sought, not for the sake of impressing God or people, but for the sake of clearly, confidently, and effectively leading God's people in praise and prayer.

5. The *best account* standard allows for each type of group (regardless of age or level of skill) to seek excellence through careful preparation and rehearsal. For example, a children's choir, an amateur adult ensemble, and musical professionals will perform at different levels. Yet each can strive to give their best account, so as to serve effectively.

General Notes

1. Choirs and ensembles provide an opportunity for those within the church community to use their musical gifts.

2. Choirs and ensembles teach music to the congregation. Teaching should occur in advance of the time the congregation is expected to sing. Teaching within the moment of worship interrupts the flow and energy of the service.

3. Musicians communicate not only through their voices and instruments, but also through their bodies. Facial expression and movement are part of the way they engage people in praise.

4. A congregation's ensembles can provide a community within a community. In some places the choir/instrumental ensemble becomes a small group, providing fellowship, care, and prayer for its members. In others, ensemble rehearsals provide opportunity for leaders to offer discipleship to members of the groups.

5. Musical rehearsals can be times of worship. There can be praise in a musician's heart, even while learning and rehearsing music. Setting the stage with opening prayer or devotions can give a holy orientation to the entire event.

6. A congregation's music ministry program can provide artistic training for people of all ages, teaching them musical skills and training them in the servant nature of liturgical performance.

7. Leaders of musical ensembles should be part of a congregation's worship planning team, helping to assure that artistic considerations coordinate with other elements of worship, such as preaching and celebration of sacraments.

8. Musical ensembles within a congregation can be used for special occasions and occasional services such as funerals and weddings.

9. A church's ensembles can represent the church beyond its walls, taking the mission of the church into the community and to the world. This can occur by offering performances within a community, engaging in choir/mission tours, and making musical recordings that represent the voice and mission of the congregation.

10. Making music is fun. Rehearsals can become a burden when learning too much music or pushing too quickly. Strive for maintaining the joy of making music together in rehearsals and allowing for music's healing powers to restore weary musicians who are usually gathered at the end of a day's work.

Tips for Assembling a Music Ensemble or Worship Band

1. Assess your community's gifts. Know who the musicians are and draw upon them confidently. Do not overlook young people. Often, the greatest musical accomplishments of a person's life occur during the last year of high school, after years of lessons and practice. Many musical talents are sadly set aside for life, once a person enters adulthood.

2. Establish a liturgical and acoustic vision for what you hope the ensemble will be.

3. Know and be prepared to teach the group's liturgical function. Assess regularly whether the attitude and purpose of the group are properly oriented.

4. Recruit players and singers personally, seeking the skill level and the vocal and instrumental balance that matches your artistic vision. Auditioning musicians will reveal both their level of skill and the attitude of their performance. Do not hesitate to ask people to participate: singers love to sing; instrumentalists love to play.

5. Seek humble persons who will serve together without competition. Sometimes the best musicians will be inappropriate for your group until they learn to submit to the will and purpose of the group.

6. Seek musicians that have the spiritual commitments appropriate to your vision for the use of the group.

7. Find or make musical arrangements that allow for flexibility and variety. Not all instruments need to play at all times. Allow the arrangements to carry the desired mood of a piece, or to match the liturgical moment.

8. Plan some instrumental rehearsals separate from rehearsals with vocalists. Bring the groups together when all know their parts and can begin to blend the sounds into a final form.

9. Schedule rehearsals during the week, rather than immediately before or after a worship service. The period before worship is both for prayer and preparation of the heart, as well as a time for final run-throughs. It is not the time for learning and rehearsing music.

10. Remind singers and band members that to use electronic amplification is to be privileged over the people who gather for worship. This means that they can easily overpower the main voice in worship, that of the congregation. Strive for

a use of amplification that encourages participation. If the band cannot hear the people singing, they are probably using their equipment too loudly.

Edwin M. Willmington, Jennifer Hill, Clayton J. Schmit

Hymn and Song Selection:
Singing the Faithful to Life

What is it about a hymn or a spiritual song that gives it the power to evoke an instinctive, truly primal response? What is it about a hymn or song that can release our tears in the way that mere speech cannot? What is it that can bring new confidence to the depressed and quiet hope to the sorrowing? What is it in the music that can bring courage greater than any fear? What is it about a hymn or song that stays with us through the dark night and into the next day, and will not let our hearts go? What is it about a song that lays claim to us so deeply that it sings us into life again, and again, and yet again?

More than most things in this life, that which is given to us through the human voice has the power to cut through all the façades that we use to protect ourselves and to reach the buried places within our weary hearts. For it is in these bone-deep places where we learn the truth about how deeply God loves us, and how we have no life apart from him.

In singing we come to know why God gave humankind its voice. In singing praise to the Most High and Holy God we are surprised, overwhelmed, and sometimes even overcome to find his voice sounding in ours, his love beating in our very bodies. The church, with her ritual roots in the Psalter of synagogue and temple, was born in the voice of song, and throughout most of ecclesiastical history she has intuited the need to be joined in that auditory miraculous realm wherein we trust in the God whom we cannot see.

In this historical moment in which we have instant access to the music of the ages, the question before us is, how are we to choose our hymns and songs for worship, so that all these gracious gifts of God might be sounded in their divine goodness in the assembly that is gathered in the Triune name?

Think of a congregational song as a unity of text and music within a larger unity of an order of service. A liturgy is not just one disconnected thing after another, but a singular event from Prelude and Invocation to Benediction and Postlude. A hymn or song within that ritual context relates to what comes before its sounding, as well as what comes after it. Those who plan a liturgy have to pay attention to season and appointed texts (if a lectionary is followed). Several other layers of context should also be attended to, or you risk losing the potential for a growth in faith whose depth will sustain, endure, and fulfill in such a way that it cannot be contained, spilling over into all aspects of a believer's life. Tempo, meter, tonality/modality, harmonic structure, rhythm, the lyric line and range of the melody, and musical forms, as well as particular musical genres, need to be paid attention to, for in their particularity these sounds are the means by which the gathered assembly is sung into life, the true life of community (*koinonia*) that God intends for all God's children.

Put aside all false notions that worship can be divided into categories of traditional and contemporary, for within each of these labels there are myriad genres of hymnody and song. Put aside those labels, and start asking questions about the shape and character of a sound. Is the pace so frenzied that it leaves you breathless? Do not start a service there or everything else will be anti-climactic. Does that hymn move like a dirge? Even if the hymn text clearly states the appointed preaching text, the musical mood created may be a mismatch for the proclamation that leads to eternal life. Tune and text read each other equally, and for a hymn or song to be the vehicle that it is intended to be liturgically, that equality of gravitas, solemnity, reverence, joy or even playfulness—that match is the key. If the tune brings out the spirit of the text and if the text brings out the heart and beauty of the tune, then there is a fitting match. Even if the same biblical text can be sung to metrical psalmody or light rock, rap or Gregorian chant, the appropriation of the text by the community will vary both through the cultural associations of those distinct genres of sound, and even more pointedly through the particularities of the musical elements that make up those genres. Indeed, one genre might serve as a more fitting performative exegesis of the text than another simply in its harmonic pace, or rhythmic constancy, or melodic contour. The work of the Holy Spirit through the biblical writers is being continued as we sing in a holy communion, for the hymnody of each generation leads us into an appropriation of the primary salvific events, now made known as the assembly is gathered in the power and love of that same Holy Spirit.

Take, for example, the variety of musical pairings with Ps 23 and its theological themes. In the course of a three-year cycle, Ps 23 comes up in the lectionary during Lent, Easter, and on an ordinary Sunday in the season of Pentecost. In the Marty Haugen setting of Ps 23, "Shepherd Me, O God," (SHEPHERD ME), the construction of the melody with its limited vocal range of the refrain (a major 6th), the gentle rocking of the harmonic changes utilizing the Aeolian and Dorian modes that pulse with the assurance of a sure hand on a baby's cradle, the simple movement between refrain and verse: these specific musical characteristics create a quiet and reflective mood more suited for Lent than for the alleluias of the Fourth Sunday of Easter. Here "The King of Love, My Shepherd Is," (ST. COLUMBA) in a bright major key, or Dorothy Thrup's early nineteenth century text, "Savior Like a Shepherd Lead Us," set to a tune with the bounce and verve of BEACH SPRING (or even to the more popular setting of BRADBURY) would connect to the overflowing joy of a season in which the early church forbade the assembly to kneel, for so great was their delight in the resurrection. The metrical textual setting of Ps 23 from the *Edinburg Psalter* paired with BROTHER JAMES' AIR appears to be more "neutral" on the surface, but it is not. It does not call attention to itself musically, as is common for such metrical settings. But far from neutral, it is exegeting the text of the psalm in a manner that provides stability to the ongoing interpretation of the text (think of the life of the church that is the focus of Ordinary Time) through its repeated rhythms, its *aab* form, the gravitational pull of its steady and limited harmonic vocabulary, and its opening tonic arpeggio that is modified yet recognizable for its final cadence, a cadence that drives the assembly into always wanting another verse. While some of these hymns are simply metrical settings of the psalter and other texts are more thematic, and still others, both a retelling and a reflection, ("thy rod and staff my comfort still, thy *cross* before to guide me") each one is musically leading us to a different place in the expressive life of faith, for each one is bringing forth different layers of meaning from within the Scriptures. Or we could more aptly say, in each song, where text and music are one entity, the Holy Scripture *does* something new with us through the doxological, performative exegesis of the singing assembly. Making musical selections should not happen from a quick glance at the biblical index in the hymnal, for the same words simply do not guarantee the fittingness of a hymn. These decisions should be made after repeated musical soundings that come in conversation with repeated readings of the biblical texts.

And if you have come to that place of light, then the next set of musical questions appears: If three of the congregational songs you choose for a Sunday are in an auditorily definable genre, like the SACRED HARP hymns with their pentatonic scales and open harmonies, a fourth hymn riddled with the chromaticism of a Victorian Part-song may break the mood and destroy the flow. While you may not want all the hymns to sound alike, there needs to be some sort of musical continuity, just as there is in a through-composed liturgy, for all the songs are part of the same liturgical event. So then, if you've found those hymn or song texts that relate to the biblical text and/or season, then ask yourself what is the mood, what is the pace, how are the dissonances resolved, how vocally extravagant is the melody, is unison texture preferable to four part, etc.? While the goal in some ways is simply to take folks by surprise, it will not be accomplished in a musically disjointed, jarring way, but in a breathtaking way, i.e., a way in which their breath is taken away and they find that they're still singing because the Holy Spirit is breathing for them. They find themselves singing a familiar song, but all of a sudden they hear it anew because of its organic connection to the full liturgical context. It is good to remember and experience that even one liturgical event is actually an event within a greater event, the continuum of sacred time from the world's creation to its redemption. A congregation singing together within worship is one more way that God orders all time as his own.

By balancing songs that are new to the community with hymns that are already part of its godly heritage, you can gently expand the congregation's musical repertoire within a context of some familiarity and give them an opportunity to experience the goodness of God to carry his holiness in their voices through the week. Part of the reason that songs work in worship is that there is a cadence at the end of each verse or chorus, and singing a strong cadence is a powerfully satisfying communal experience. Singing more than one solid cadence in a liturgical event creates an anticipation of such satisfaction that it subtly drives the assembly forward, telling them that there is far more goodness to come. They will want to come back next week to do it again, for the comfort, for the strength, for the release of their anguish, and simply for the holy and joyous pleasure of a heart tuned to sing God's praise. What they experience on Sunday will set the shape for the week to come, for having been sung into life again, the God who has given them voice will have also given them the faith to live out God's love, until, in the cycle of liturgical time, they meet again.

Amy C. Schifrin

On the Use of a Lectionary (FAQs)

What Is a Lectionary?

The term *lectionary* broadly refers to a prescribed order of Scripture readings, called *lessons* or *lections*. The order of lections is used by individuals or congregations for private devotion or corporate worship. Contemporary lectionaries typically include four assigned readings: an Old Testament lesson, a Psalm, a New Testament lesson taken from the Epistles, and a Gospel lesson. These lessons correspond to the particular liturgical season in which the church is situated (Advent, Christmas, Lent, Easter, etc), and their content establishes a foundation for the various liturgical actions and rituals that take place during each Lord's Day service.

When Were Lectionaries First Used?

The collection and prescription of Scriptural passages for use in Lord's Day services was a practice undertaken early in the life of the Christian Church. By the middle of the fourth century, multiple lectionaries were compiled in various languages that are presently utilized by biblical scholars to assist their work in textual criticism of the Greek New Testament. Eventually, the Western lectionaries were standardized in Latin and the Eastern lectionaries in Greek. These lectionaries provide us with a helpful compilation of canonical passages that were used in weekly Lord's Day worship by early churches.

What Is the Revised Common Lectionary?

During the Vatican II liturgical renewal of Roman Catholic Church, several mainline Protestant church leaders, together with Catholic and Orthodox contributors, formed a commission to establish a *common* lectionary that would be pertinent and available to all Christian churches that desired to follow a prescribed pattern in their public reading of Scripture. In 1963, this commission developed the Common Lectionary, which was later revised to its current form in 1992. The resulting lectionary is called the Revised Common Lectionary (RCL). The RCL is a three-year cycle of weekly Scripture readings for use in public worship. The RCL was assembled by a committee known as the Consultation on Common Texts (www.commontexts.org) in 1992 and is used throughout the world by certain church traditions.

The RCL is designed to support the church year, the ancient liturgical pattern that tells the story of Christ for half the year (Advent-Ascension) and the subsequent story of the church for the other half (Pentecost-Christ the King). In general, the theme of the Gospel readings for each Sunday reflects the theme of the particular liturgical season in which it falls.

Typical to ancient lectionaries, the RCL includes four readings for each week. These readings are comprised of a reading from the Old Testament, a Psalm, a reading from the Epistles, and a reading from one of the Gospels. During the season of Easter, the Old Testament reading is replaced with a reading from Acts. We noted above that the RCL is a three-year cycle. Each of the three years is assigned a specific synoptic Gospel from which the Gospel readings are drawn. The following chart gives the RCL Year, the Gospel assigned to it, and the calendar years in which it takes place.

Year A	**Matthew**	Begins at Advent, in the fall of:	2016, 2019, 2022, 2025, 2028, 2031
Year B	**Mark**		2017, 2020, 2023, 2026, 2029, 2032
Year C	**Luke**		2018, 2021, 2024, 2027, 2030, 2033

While it may appear that John's Gospel is not found in the lectionary, a wide array of Johannine readings are woven into the lectionary in each year's cycle, and many readings from John are prescribed for various feasts and festivals throughout the church year in every year.

Who Uses the Revised Common Lectionary?

The following list indicates churches that have representation on the Consultation for Common Texts. There are countless other churches who regularly, or occasionally, utilize the lectionary in their public worship.

> The Anglican Church of Canada
> Christian Church (Disciples of Christ)
> Christian Reformed Church in North America
> Church of the Brethren
> Episcopal Church
> Evangelical Lutheran Church in America
> Evangelical Lutheran Church in Canada
> Free Methodist Church in Canada
> Lutheran Church - Missouri Synod
> Mennonite Church
> Polish National Catholic Church

Presbyterian Church (U.S.A.)

Presbyterian Church in Canada

Reformed Church in America

Unitarian Universalist Christian Fellowship

United Church of Canada

United Church of Christ

United Methodist Church

Wisconsin Evangelical Lutheran Synod

How Is the RCL Used by Churches Today?

In churches that subscribe to its use, the RCL establishes which passages of Scripture are to be read for each Sunday. Churches that use the RCL can effectively plan their worship months in advance. It is a welcome resource for congregations that desire to generate creative, artistic, and musical expressions in worship that relate to worship and preaching themes. The use of music and arts in worship requires sufficient advance planning so as to give artists time to create and rehearse their work. Utilization of the RCL gives space and time for artistic and thematic considerations.

From the assigned lessons in the RCL, a designated preacher will typically preach a sermon oriented around one particular lesson (often the Gospel lesson) or she or he will preach a sermon that demonstrates the unity of the texts in light of the current liturgical season. *Lectionary preaching* is a helpful method for sermon text selection because it allows preachers to consider a wide range of sermon texts from all portions of the Bible.

Is the Entire Bible Contained in the RCL?

No, there are portions of Scripture that are not included in the RCL. Many of the excluded texts are those that are difficult to make use of in worship. For example, portions of Ps 139 ("O, that you would kill the wicked, O God. . . .") seem ill-fitted for public worship.

Can I Use a Lectionary for Private Devotional Worship?

Yes, the RCL can be so used. However, the commission that assembled the RCL, sensing the benefits of such usage, has established a daily lectionary that is recommended for private devotional use. The daily lectionary is a two-year cycle that is patterned after the RCL—each day of the week is assigned four lessons that correspond to the liturgical season—and is an excellent resource for family worship, private devotional exercises, and for mid-week public worship.

Where Can I Access the Daily and Sunday Lectionaries?

The Sunday lectionary is publicly available on numerous websites; for example, the website for the Divinity School at Vanderbilt University (lectionary.library.vanderbilt. edu). The Daily Lectionary is available on the Presbyterian Church (U.S.A.) website (http://gamc.pcusa.org/gamc/).

The Academic Calendar and Lectionary found in this section of the *Teaching Hymnal* is generally derived from the Revised Common Lectionary, though it contains many adjustments in order to accommodate academic calendars and purposes.

Joseph A. Novak

The Academic Calendar and Lectionary

In designing a common lectionary for use in academic institutions of theological education, equal attention must be given to the academic calendar and the church calendar. Several problems exist in determining the *liturgical time* of contemporary educational institutions. The first consideration is the nature of the academic calendar. Breaks in school terms result in student bodies being absent from school during key festivals, such as Christmas and Easter. This not only changes the time of a school's celebration of such events, it also affects other portions of the church calendar. For example, the usual four-week Advent cycle culminating in the celebration of Christmas cannot be fully commemorated. Worship planners at each school have to make a critical decision about how to celebrate both Advent *and* Christmas. What often happens is that Advent is skipped altogether, or Advent and Christmas are put together in one service. This appears to dilute the preparatory nature of the Advent season, treating it rather as a short, obligatory introduction to Christmas. Similar problems present themselves during other terms. For example, since the date of Easter determines the beginning of Lent, a late Easter means that Epiphany (the season after Christmas) may in fact occupy an entire winter term.

A second problem is that many institutions have their own festivals that are celebrated annually. Festivals of dedication are often celebrated in the fall, at the beginning of the school year. Similarly, the school calendar often culminates with a baccalaureate or commissioning service in the spring or early summer. Interspersed throughout the year are particular celebrations, lecture series, and worship events that vary from school to school.

A third problem is the functional absence of a sense of liturgical time in many school communities. All churches (with rare exceptions) follow a liturgical calendar to at least a minimal degree: celebrating Christmas and Easter, if nothing else. Similarly, most seminaries have a desire to celebrate major festivals in school worship. Yet, for many nondenominational or evangelical seminaries, the idea of a common liturgical calendar to which the entire institution submits itself is a foreign concept. Some evangelical institutions are not affiliated with ecclesial bodies that identify with the full liturgical seasons.

In light of these problems, the following calendar and lectionary has been designed to construct a basic sense of liturgical time for an academic institution. It takes into account that some schools are on a quarterly, or trimester basis; some are on a semester basis, and some have a short term in January, often known as the J term. The calendar seeks to accommodate some of the unique, local festivals often found in school worship schedules. For example, the Festival of Beginnings celebration at Fuller Theological Seminary occurs each year during the first week of classes and marks the first All-Seminary Chapel service of the new school year. The purpose in this revised calendar and lectionary is to honor both the church's sense of time and a school's academic rhythm. To impose the usual church calendar on an occasion like the Festival of Beginnings (the fifteenth week after Pentecost, for example) would fail to support and encourage the unique celebrations that define the ritual identity of a seminary or educational institution.

The context in which the following annual structure takes root will largely determine which of the festivals below are to be celebrated. The goal of presenting a revised academic church year is to assist the deans or directors of school chapels in planning services of worship that expose students to the fullness of liturgical rhythms. Use of the following model allows for effective worship planning for an entire school year, providing pertinent Scripture selections that correspond with the revised academic calendar. Note that the lectionary presented here is similar, but not identical to the Revised Common Lectionary used in churches throughout the world (See "On the Use of a Lectionary (FAQs)" in this section of the *Teaching Hymnal*).

Joseph A. Novak, Clayton J. Schmit

How to Use the Academic Calendar and Lectionary

For schools that choose to use the Academic Calendar and Lectionary, the following explanations will provide instruction for use of the resource according to the particularities of each school's schedule.

This resource attempts to provide text appointments for both the church year (adjusted as necessary, for the academic calendar) and festivals and events that fall within a typical school year (such as breaks and special commemorations). Since academic schedules vary according to the length of terms (quarter/trimester terms and semester terms), beginning and ending dates, dates for winter and spring breaks, and so forth, there is flexibility built into the following calendar. There are options for how many weeks of a given church season a school may choose to celebrate, as well as church and school Festivals and Commemorations that may be substituted for regular calendar selections.

The academic lectionary follows the typical three-year cycle (See "On the Use of a Lectionary (FAQs)" in this section of the *Teaching Hymnal*). The chart below gives the years for which each series is appointed to begin. Note that the church year begins in Advent, four weeks before Christmas. Thus Year C begins in the late fall of 2012, 2015, and so forth. For the academic lectionary, this means that when school begins in the fall, worship planning would follow the current year's cycle, but at the celebration of Advent, worship planning would switch to the next cycle. For example, in the fall of 2012 the current cycle would be Year B. At the beginning of Advent celebrations, the school would switch to Year C.

Year A	Matthew	Begins at Advent, in the fall of:	2016, 2019, 2022, 2025, 2028, 2031
Year B	Mark		2017, 2020, 2023, 2026, 2029, 2032
Year C	Luke		2018, 2021, 2024, 2027, 2030, 2033

Note also that the appointed texts in this lectionary relate to the previous Sunday's texts in the Revised Common Lectionary. Because schools typically hold chapel services midweek rather than on Sundays, the texts for the preceding Sunday can be used during the week. For example, the texts for Easter Sunday are appointed for use during the week following Easter (provided the school is not on an Easter break).

If school chapel services occur more than once a week, one of the four texts in each lectionary set can be used as the text for each day. For example, services on: Monday might use the Old Testament Lesson; Tuesday, the Psalm; Wednesday, the Epistle Lesson; and Thursday, the Gospel Lesson. Naturally, each school will need to use the resource to fit its needs and determine which texts to use on which days.

Use of the Academic Calendar and Lectionary for the Fall Term

The fall calendar will apply whether a school follows quarter or semester term schedules. From the Approximate Date column, select texts appointed for the time nearest the school start date. Select also the cycle (Year A, B, or C) that matches the common church year cycle. Follow the cycle for the first weeks of the term. Where appropriate, substitute cycle texts with those assigned for Festivals and Commemorations where they best apply to the local academic calendar. For example, Fall Convocation texts can be substituted for the cycle texts at the beginning of the term, or when appropriate. Other commemorations, such as the Feast of St. Luke, can be substituted for cycle texts where the worship planning team desires to commemorate this festival. Note that the Feast of St. Luke (and its appointed texts) has often been used to provide a Service of Healing, because the Gospel writer was known to be a physician.

As the term moves into November, several decisions will need to be made. Will school chapel commemorate Thanksgiving? If so, texts are provided. When will the season of Advent begin for chapel services? If following the common church year, Advent begins four weeks before Christmas. As noted above, the academic calendar does not usually allow for a full celebration of Advent and Christmas. Local use requires that planners determine how many weeks of Advent to celebrate, when to schedule Christmas celebrations (presumably during the final week of school before Christmas), and whether to commemorate (as the common church calendar does) Christ the King the week before Advent celebrations begin. Texts are provided that will accommodate any number of arrangements. As noted above, when Advent celebrations begin, the cycle changes. For example, if school begins during cycle A, it moves to cycle B at Advent.

Use of the Academic Calendar and Lectionary for the Winter and Spring Term(s)

The same general rules as indicated above govern the use of the Academic Calendar and Lectionary use in the winter and spring. Worship planners should follow the cycle texts (A, B, or C) for the season of Epiphany (also known as Ordinary Time) during the weeks of January and into February. Rather than starting at the beginning of the winter chart, choose from the weeks of Epiphany the week closest to the start of school in the new year. For example, if the term begins on January 14, use texts for the second week after Epiphany. This applies, regardless of the term type (quarter, J term, or semester).

Because the date of Easter is variable—and correspondingly, the dates of Ash Wednesday and Lent—there are sufficient Epiphany texts to cover Ordinary Time when Lent occurs late. When it occurs less than eight weeks after Epiphany (eight weeks after Epiphany is Lent's latest calendrical possibility), worship planners can switch from the Ordinary Time texts within a cycle to the Ash Wednesday and Lenten texts whenever Lent begins. As always, worship planners may substitute texts from Festivals and Commemorations for the Ordinary Time texts whenever desired.

In the week preceding Easter, planners have many choices to make. Will there be a commemoration of the Passion? Will it include Palm Sunday texts that reflect Jesus' triumphal entry into Jerusalem? Will chapels commemorate all the days of Holy Week, or only selected days? Will there be an Easter Vigil on Holy Saturday? Texts for all of these occasions are provided. It is up to local planners to select which texts fit the need. If an Easter break precedes Easter, it may be that none of the Holy Week texts will be used.

Following Easter, use the texts appointed for the Great Fifty Days. Baccalaureate and Commencement texts are provided as substitutes for the cycle texts at the end of the spring term (presumably the final week of school). If the term lasts into the season of Pentecost (also known as Ordinary Time), enough texts are provided to last well into June. There are no texts provided in this calendar and lectionary for chapels during the summer months.

Fall Calendar and Lectionary for an Educational Institution

Ordinary Time through Christmas			Festivals and Commemorations	
Approx. Date	A	B	C	Approx. Date
Last week of Aug.	Jeremiah 15:15–21 Psalm 26:1–8 Romans 12:9–21 Matthew 16:21–28	Joshua 24:1–2a, 14–18 Psalm 34:15–22 \ Ephesians 6:10–20 John 6:56–69	Jeremiah 2:4–13 Psalm 81:1, 10–16 Hebrews 13:1–8, 15–16 Luke 14:1, 7–14	First or second week of school

Fall Convocation (Festivals and Commemorations, Last week of Aug.)

Genesis 1:1–2:4a

Psalm 101

1 Timothy 4:6–16

John 1:1–4

Ordinary Time through Christmas			Festivals and Commemorations	
Approx. Date	A	B	C	Approx. Date
Sept. week 1	Ezekiel 33:7–11 Psalm 119:33–40 Romans 13:8–14 Matthew 18:15–20	Deuteronomy 4:1–2, 6–9 Psalm 15 James 1:17–27 Mark 7:1–8, 14–15, 21–23	Jeremiah 18:1–11 Psalm 139:1–6, 13–18 Philemon 1–21 Luke 14:25–33	

Dedication of Teachers and Theologians

Proverbs 3:13–20

Psalm 119:89–104

1 Corinthians 2:6–16

Matthew 13:44–53

Ordinary Time through Christmas			Festivals and Commemorations	
Approx. Date	A	B	C	Approx. Date
Sept. week 2	Genesis 50:15–21 Psalm 103:1–13 Romans 14:1–12 Matthew 18:21–35	Isaiah 35:4–7a Psalm 146 James 2:1–17 Mark 7:24–37	Jeremiah 4:11–12, 22–28 Psalm 14 1 Timothy 1:12–17 Luke 15:1–10	Sept. 21

Feast of St. Matthew (Sept. 21)

Ezekiel 2:8–3:11

Psalm 119:33–40

Ephesians 2:4–10

Matthew 9:9–13

Ordinary Time through Christmas			Festivals and Commemorations	
Approx. Date	A	B	C	Approx. Date
Sept. week 3	Jonah 3:10–4:11 Psalm 145:1–8 Philippians 1:21–30 Matthew 20:1–16	Isaiah 50:4–9a Psalm 116:1–9 James 3:1–12 Mark 8:27–38	Jeremiah 8:18–9:1 Psalm 79:1–9 1 Timothy 2:1–7 Luke 16:1–13	Oct.18

Feast of St. Luke (Oct. 18)

Isaiah 43:8–13

Psalm 124

2 Timothy 4:5–11

Luke 1:1–4; 24:44–53

Ordinary Time through Christmas			Festivals and Commemorations	
Approx. Date	A	B	C	Approx. Date
Sept. week 4	Ezekiel 18:1–4, 25–32 Psalm 25:1–9 Philippians 2:1–13 Matthew 21:23–32	Jeremiah 11:18–20 Psalm 54 James 3:13—4:3, 7–8a Mark 9:30–37	Jeremiah 32:1–3a, 6–15 Psalm 91:1–6, 14–16 1 Timothy 6:6–19 Luke 16:19–31	

	Ordinary Time through Christmas			Festivals and Commemorations	
Approx. Date	**A**	**B**	**C**	**Approx. Date**	
Oct. week 1	Isaiah 5:1–7 Psalm 80:7–15 Philippians 3:4b–14 Matthew 21:33–46	Numbers 11:4–6, 10–16, 24–29 Psalm 19:7–14 James 5:13–20 Mark 9:38–50	Lamentations 1:1–6 Psalm 37:1–9 2 Timothy 1:1–14 Luke 17:5–10		
Oct. week 2	Isaiah 25:1–9 Psalm 23 Philippians 4:1–9 Matthew 22:1–14	Genesis 2:18–24 Psalm 8 Hebrews 1:1–4; 2:5–12 Mark 10:2–16	Jeremiah 29:1, 4–7 Psalm 66:1–12 2 Timothy 2:8–15 Luke 17:11–19		
Oct. week 3	Isaiah 45:1–7 Psalm 96:1–13 1 Thessalonians 1:1–10 Matthew 22:15–22	Amos 5:6–7, 10–15 Psalm 90:12–17 Hebrews 4:12–16 Mark 10:17–31	Jeremiah 31:27–34 Psalm 119:97–104 2 Timothy 3:14–4:5 Luke 18:1–8		
Oct. week 4	Leviticus 19:1–2, 15–18 Psalm 1 1 Thessalonians 2:1–8 Matthew 22:34–46	Isaiah 53:4–12 Psalm 91:9–16 Hebrews 5:1–10 Mark 10:35–45	Joel 2:23–32 Psalm 65 2 Timothy 4:6–8, 16–18 Luke 18:9–14	Oct. 31	**Reformation Day** Jeremiah 31:31–34 Psalm 46 Romans 3:19–28 John 8:31–38
Nov. week 1	Amos 5:18–24 Psalm 70 1 Thessalonians 4:13–18 Matthew 25:1–13	Deuteronomy 6:1–9 Psalm 119:1–8 Hebrews 9:11–14 Mark 12:28–34	Habakkuk 1:1–4; 2:1–4 Psalm 119:137–144 2 Thessalonians 1:1–4, 11–12 Luke 19:1–10	Nov. 1	**All Saints Day** Revelation 7:9–17 Psalm 34:1–10, 22 1 John 3:1–3 Matthew 5:1–12

Ordinary Time through Christmas			Festivals and Commemorations
Approx. Date	**A**	**B**	**C**	**Approx. Date**

Approx. Date	**A**	**B**	**C**
Nov. week 2	Zephaniah 1:7, 12–18 Psalm 90:1–12 1 Thessalonians 5:1–11 Matthew 25:14–30	1 Kings 17:8–16 Psalm 146 Hebrews 9:24–28 Mark 12:38–44	Haggai 1:15b–2:9 Psalm 145:1–5, 17–21 2 Thessalonians 2:1–5, 13–17 Luke 20:27–38

Christ the King
Commemorate last week before Advent celebrations.

			Festivals and Commemorations
Ezekiel 34:11–16, 20–24 Psalm 95:1–7a Ephesians 1:15–23 Matthew 25:31–46	Daniel 7:9–10, 13–14 Psalm 93 Revelation 1:4b–8 John 18:33–37	Jeremiah 23:1–6 Psalm 46 Colossians 1:11–20 Luke 23:33–43	**Thanksgiving** Deuteronomy 8:7–18 Psalm 65 2 Corinthians 9:6–15 Luke 17:11–19

Weeks of Advent
Select from one to four weeks of Advent celebration.

First Week	**First Week**	**First Week**
Isaiah 2:1–5 Psalm 122 Romans 13:11–14 Matthew 24:36–44	Isaiah 64:1–9 Psalm 80:1–7, 17–19 1 Corinthians 1:3–9 Mark 13:24–37	Jeremiah 33:14–16 Psalm 25:1–10 1 Thessalonians 3:9–13 Luke 21:25–36
Second Week	**Second Week**	**Second Week**
Isaiah 11:1–10 Psalm 72:1–7, 18–19 Romans 15:4–13 Matthew 3:1–12	Isaiah 40:1–11 Psalm 85:1–2, 8–13 2 Peter 3:8–15a Mark 1:1–8	Malachi 3:1–4 Psalm 126 Philippians 1:3–1 Luke 3:1–6

	Ordinary Time through Christmas			Festivals and Commemorations	
Approx. Date	A	B	C	Approx. Date	

Third Week / Third Week / Third Week

	Third Week	Third Week	Third Week		
	Isaiah 35:1–10	Isaiah 61:1–4, 8–11	Zephaniah 3:14–20		
	Psalm 146:5–10	Psalm 126 or Luke 1:46b–55	Isaiah 12:2–6		
	or Luke 1:46b–55	1 Thessalonians 5:16–24	Philippians 4:4–7		
	James 5:7–10		Luke 3:7–18		
	Matthew 11:2–11	John 1:6–8, 19–28			

Fourth Week / Fourth Week / Fourth Week

	Fourth Week	Fourth Week	Fourth Week		
	Isaiah 7:10–16	2 Samuel 7:1–11, 16	Micah 5:2–5a		
	Psalm 80:1–7, 17–19	Psalm 89:1–4, 19–26	Psalm 80:1–7		
	Romans 1:1–7	Romans 16:25–27	Hebrews 10:5–10		
	Matthew 1:18–25	Luke 1:26–38	Luke 1:39–55		

The Nativity of our Lord
Celebrate Christmas during last week of classes

Dec. 25	Isaiah 9:2–7	Isaiah 62:6–12	Isaiah 52:7–10	Dec. 27	**Feast of St. John**
	Psalm 96	Psalm 97	Psalm 98		Genesis 1:1–5, 26–31
	Titus 2:11–14	Titus 3:4–7	Hebrews 1:1–4, 5–12		Psalm 116:12–19
	Luke 2:1–20	Luke 2:1–20	John 1:1–14		1 John 1:1–2:2
					John 21:20–25

Winter and Spring Calendar and Lectionary for an Educational Institution

Epiphany (Ordinary Time) Depending on date of Easter, Ash Wednesday, and Lent, select up to eight weeks of Ordinary Time.			Festivals and Commemorations	
Approx. Date	**A**	**B**	**C**	**Approx. Date**	

Jan. week 2 **Baptism of Jesus**	Isaiah 42:1–9 Psalm 29 Acts 10:34–43 Matthew 3:13–17	Genesis 1:1–5 Psalm 29 Acts 19:1–7 Mark 1:4–11	Isaiah 43:1–7 Psalm 29 Acts 8:14–17 Luke 3:15–17, 21–22	Jan. 6	**The Epiphany of our Lord** Isaiah 60:1–6 Psalm 72:1–7, 10–14 Ephesians 3:1–12 Matthew 2:1–12
Jan. week 3	Isaiah 49:1–7 Psalm 40:1–11 1 Corinthians 1:1–9 John 1:29–42	1 Samuel 3:1–20 Psalm 139:1–6, 13–18 1 Corinthians 6:12–20 John 1:43–5	Isaiah 62:1–5 Psalm 36:5–10 1 Corinthians 12:1–11 John 2:1–11		
Jan. week 4	Isaiah 9:1–4 Psalm 27:1, 4–9 1 Corinthians 1:10–18 Matthew 4:12–23	Jonah 3:1–5, 10 Psalm 62:5–12 1 Corinthians 7:29–31 Mark 1:14–20	Nehemiah 8:1–3, 5–6, 8–10 Psalm 19 1 Corinthians 12:12–31a Luke 4:14–21	Jan. 25	**Conversion of Paul** Acts 9:1–22 Psalm 67 Galatians 1:11–24 Luke 21:10–19
Feb. week 1	Micah 6:1–8 Psalm 15 1 Corinthians 1:18–31 Matthew 5:1–12	Deuteronomy 18:15–20 Psalm 111 1 Corinthians 8:1–13 Mark 1:21–28	Jeremiah 1:4–10 Psalm 71:1–6 1 Corinthians 13:1–13 Luke 4:21–30		
Feb. week 2	Isaiah 58:1–12 Psalm 112:1–10 1 Corinthians 2:1–16 Matthew 5:13–20	Isaiah 40:21–31 Psalm 147:1–11, 20c 1 Corinthians 9:16–23 Mark 1:29–39	Isaiah 6:1–13 Psalm 138 1 Corinthians 15:1–11 Luke 5:1–11		

	Epiphany (Ordinary Time) Depending on date of Easter, Ash Wednesday, and Lent, select up to eight weeks of Ordinary Time.			Festivals and Commemorations
Approx. Date	A	B	C	Approx. Date
Feb. week 3	Deuteronomy 30:15–20 Psalm 119:1–8 1 Corinthians 3:1–9 Matthew 5:21–37	2 Kings 5:1–14 Psalm 30 1 Corinthians 9:24–27 Mark 1:40–45	Jeremiah 17:5–8 Psalm 1 1 Corinthians 15:12, 16–20 Luke 6:17–26	
Feb. week 4	Leviticus 19:1–2, 9–18 Psalm 119:33–40 1 Corinthians 3:10–11, 16–23 Matthew 5:38–48	Isaiah 43:18–25 Psalm 41 2 Corinthians 1:18–22 Mark 1:1–12	Genesis 45:3–8a, 15 Psalm 103:1–13 1 Corinthians 15:35–38a, 42–50 Luke 6:27–38	
Mar. week 1	Isaiah 49:8–16a Psalm 131 1 Corinthians 4:1–5 Matthew 6:24–34	Hosea 2:14–20 Psalm 103:1–13 2 Corinthians 3:1b–6 Mark 2:18–22	Jeremiah 7:1–15 Psalm 92 1 Corinthians 15:51–58 Luke 6:39–49	

Transfiguration of Our Lord
Commemorate the week before Ash Wednesday.

Exodus 24:12–18 Psalm 2 2 Peter 1:16–21 Matthew 17:1–9	2 Kings 2:1–12 Psalm 50:1–6 2 Corinthians 4:3–6 Mark 9:2–9	2 Kings 2:1–12 Psalm 50:1–6 2 Corinthians 4:3–6 Mark 9:2–9

Lent Depending on school calendar and the relationship of Easter to spring break, select up to five weeks of Lenten commemoration.			Festivals and Commemorations	
Approx. Date	A	B	C	Approx. Date
Dependant on date of Easter	**First Week** Genesis 2:15–17; 3:1–7 Psalm 32 Romans 5:12–19 Matthew 4:1–11	**First Week** Genesis 9:8–17 Psalm 25:1–10 1 Peter 3:18–22 Mark 1:9–15	**First Week** Deuteronomy 26:1–11 Psalm 91 Romans 10:8b–13 Luke 4:1–13		**Ash Wednesday** Joel 2:1–2, 12–17 Psalm 51:1–17 2 Corinthians 5:20b–6:10 Matthew 6:1–6, 16–21
	Second Week Genesis 12:1–4a Psalm 121 Romans 4:1–5, 13–17 John 3:1–17	**Second Week** Genesis 17:1–7, 15–16 Psalm 22:23–31 Romans 4:13–25 Mark 8:31–38	**Second Week** Genesis 15:1–12, 17–18 Psalm 27 Philippians 3:17–4:1 Luke 13:31–35		
	Third Week Exodus 17:1–7 Psalm 95 Romans 5:1–11 John 4:5–42	**Third Week** Exodus 20:1–17 Psalm 19 I Corinthians 1:18–25 John 2:13–22	**Third Week** Isaiah 55:1–9 Psalm 63:1–8 1 Corinthians 10:1–13 Luke 13:1–9	Mar. 25	**The Annunciation of our Lord** Isaiah 7:10–14 Psalm 45 Hebrews 10:4–10 Luke 1:26–38
	Fourth Week 1 Samuel 16:1–13 Psalm 23 Ephesians 5:8–14 John 9:1–41	**Fourth Week** Numbers 21:4–9 Psalm 107:1–3, 17–22 Ephesians 2:1–10 John 3:14–21	**Fourth Week** Joshua 5:9–12 Psalm 32 2 Corinthians 5:16–21 Luke 15:1–3, 11b–32		

Lent Depending on school calendar and the relationship of Easter to spring break, select up to five weeks of Lenten commemoration.			Festivals and Commemorations	
Approx. Date	A	B	C	Approx. Date	

	A	B	C		
	Fifth Week	**Fifth Week**	**Fifth Week**		
	Ezekiel 37:1–14	Jeremiah 31:31–34	Isaiah 43:16–21		
	Psalm 130	Psalm 51:1–12	Psalm 126		
	Romans 8:6–11	Hebrews 5:5–10	Philippians 3:4b–14		
	John 11:1–45	John 12:20–33	John 12:1–8		

Passion Week
Commemorate the week before Easter.

	A	B	C		
	Isaiah 50:4–9a	Isaiah 50:4–9a	Isaiah 50:4–9a	**Passion Sunday**	**Procession with Palms**
	Psalm 31:9–16	Psalm 31:9–16	Psalm 31:9–16		Matthew 21:1–11,
	Philippians 2:5–11	Philippians 2:5–11	Philippians 2:5–11		Mark 11:1–11, or
	Matthew 26:14—27:66	Mark 14:1—15:47	Luke 22:14—23:56		John 12:12–16
				Monday of Holy Week	Isaiah 42:1–9
					Psalm 36:5–11
					Hebrews 9:11–15
					John 12:1–11
				Tuesday of Holy Week	Isaiah 49:1–7
					Psalm 71:1–14
					1 Corinthians 1:18–31
					John 12:20–36
				Wednesday of Holy Week	Isaiah 50:4–9a
					Psalm 70
					Hebrews 12:1–3
					John 13:21–32

Lent Depending on school calendar and the relationship of Easter to spring break, select up to five weeks of Lenten commemoration.			Festivals and Commemorations	
Approx. Date	A	B	C	Approx. Date	
				Maundy Thursday	Exodus 12:1–14
					Psalm 116:1–2, 12–19
					1 Corinthians 11:23–26
					John 13:1–17, 31b–35
				Good Friday	Isaiah 52:13–53:12
					Psalm 22
					Hebrews 10:16–25
					John 18:1–19:42

Holy Saturday: Easter Vigil

There are traditionally twelve lessons recounting the history of God's love, each followed by a psalm or other reading as a response. There are also an Epistle and a Gospel lesson appointed for the Vigil.

1) Genesis 1:1–2:4a; Psalm 136:1–9, 23–26; 2) Genesis 7:1–5, 11–18; 8:6–18; 9:8–13; Psalm 46; 3) Genesis 22:1–18; Psalm 16; 4) Exodus 14:10–31; 15:20–21; 15:1b–13, 17–18; 5) Isaiah 55:1–11; 12:2–6; 6) Proverbs 8:1–8, 19–21; 9:4b–6; Psalm 19; 7) Ezekiel 36:24–28; Psalms 42, 43; 8) Ezekiel 37:1–14; Psalm 143; 9) Zephaniah 3:14–20; Psalm 98; 10) Jonah 1:1—2:1; Jonah 2:2–9; 11) Isaiah 61:1–4, 9–11; Deuteronomy 32:1–4, 7, 36a, 43a; 12) Daniel 3:1–29; 3:35–65; **Epistle)** Romans 6:3–11; **Gospel)** John 20:1–18

	Easter Season (The Great Fifty Days) through Pentecost				Festivals and Commemorations
Approx. Date	**A**	**B**	**C**	**Approx. Date**	
Depen-dant on date of Easter	**First Week** Acts 10:34–43 Psalm 118:1–2, 14–24 Colossians 3:1–4 Matthew 28:1–10 or John 20:1–18	**First Week** Acts 10:34–43 Psalm 118:1–2, 14–24 1 Corinthians 15:1–11 Mark 16:1–8 or John 20:1–18	**First Week** Acts 10:34–43 Psalm 118:1–2, 14–24 1 Corinthians 15:19–26 Luke 24:1–12 or John 20:1–18	April 25	**Feast of St. Mark** Isaiah 52:7–10 Psalm 57 2 Timothy 4:6–11, 18 Mark 1:1–15
	Second Week Acts 2:14a, 22–32 Psalm 16 1 Peter 1:3–9 John 20:19–31	**Second Week** Acts 4:32–35 Psalm 133 1 John 1:1—2:2 John 20:19–31	**Second Week** Acts 5:27–32 Psalm 118:14–29 Revelation 1:4–8 John 20:19–31		
	Third Week Acts 2:14a, 36–41 Psalm 116:1–4, 12–19 1 Peter 1:17–23 Luke 24:13–35	**Third Week** Acts 3:12–19 Psalm 4 1 John 3:1–7 Luke 24:36b–48	**Third Week** Acts 9:1–20 Psalm 30 Revelation 5:11–14 John 21:1–19		
	Fourth Week Acts 2:42–47 Psalm 23 1 Peter 2:19–25 John 10:1–10	**Fourth Week** Acts 4:5–12 Psalm 23 1 John 3:16–24 John 10:11–18	**Fourth Week** Acts 9:36–43 Psalm 23 Revelation 7:9–17 John 10:22–30		
	Fifth Week Acts 7:55–60 Psalm 31:1–5, 15–16 1 Peter 2:2–10 John 14:1–14	**Fifth Week** Acts 8:26–40 Psalm 22:25–31 1 John 4:7–21 John 15:1–8	**Fifth Week** Acts 11:1–18 Psalm 148 Revelation 21:1–6 John 13:31–35	Final week of school or at time of gradua-tion	**Spring Commence-ment or Baccalau-reate Service** Isaiah 35 Psalm 121 Revelation 21:1–8 Matthew 28:16–20

Approx. Date	Easter Season (The Great Fifty Days) through Pentecost			Approx. Date	Festivals and Commemorations
	A	B	C		
	Sixth Week	**Sixth Week**	**Sixth Week**		
	Acts 17:22–31	Acts 10:44–48	Acts 16:9–15		
	Psalm 66:8–20	Psalm 98	Psalm 67		
	1 Peter 3:13–22	1 John 5:1–6	Revelation 21:10, 22–22:5		
	John 14:15–21	John 15:9–17	John 14:23–29		
	Seventh Week	**Seventh Week**	**Seventh Week**	Forty days after Easter	**Ascension of Our Lord**
	Acts 1:6–14	Acts 1:15–17, 21–26	Acts 16:16–34		Acts 1:1–11
	Psalm 68:1–10, 32–35	Psalm 1	Psalm 97		Psalm 47
	1 Peter 4:12–14; 5:6–11	1 John 5:9–13	Revelation 22:12–14, 16–17, 20–21		Ephesians 1:15–23
	John 17:1–11	John 17:6–19	John 17:20–26		Luke 24:44–53

The Day of Pentecost

Approx. Date	A	B	C
Commemorate the week following the Day of Pentecost	Acts 2:1–21	Acts 2:1–21	Acts 2:1–21
	Psalm 104:24–34, 35b	Psalm 104:24–34, 35b	Psalm 104:24–34, 35b
	1 Corinthians 12:3b–13	Romans 8:22–27	Romans 8:14–17
	John 20:19–23	John 15:26–27; 16:4b–15	John 14:8–27

Holy Trinity

Approx. Date	A	B	C
The week following the Pentecost commemoration.	Genesis 1:1—2:4a	Isaiah 6:1–8	Proverbs 8:1–4, 22–31
	Psalm 8	Psalm 29	Psalm 8
	2 Corinthians 13:11–13	Romans 8:12–17	Romans 5:1–5
	Matthew 28:16–20	John 3:1–17	John 16:12–15

| | Easter Season (The Great Fifty Days) through Pentecost | | | Festivals and Commemorations |
Approx. Date	A	B	C	Approx. Date
Weeks following Pentecost, until end of school	**Second Week** Jeremiah 28:5–9 Psalm 89:1–4, 15–18 Romans 6:12–23 Matthew 10:40–42	**Second Week** Genesis 3:8–15 Psalm 130 2 Corinthians 4:13—5:1 Mark 3:20–35	**Second Week** 1 Kings 8:22–23, 41–43 Psalm 96:1–9 Galatians 1:1–12 Luke 7:1–10	
	Third Week Zechariah 9:9–12 Psalm 145:8–14 Romans 7:15–25a Matthew 11:16–19, 25–30	**Third Week** Ezekiel 17:22–24 Psalm 92:1–4, 12–15 2 Corinthians 5:6–17 Mark 4:26–34	**Third Week** 1 Kings 17:17–24 Psalm 30 Galatians 1:11–24 Luke 7:11–17	
	Fourth Week Isaiah 55:10–13 Psalm 65 Romans 8:1–11 Matthew 13:1–9, 18–23	**Fourth Week** Job 38:1–11 Psalm 107:1–3, 23–32 2 Corinthians 6:1–13 Mark 4:35–41	**Fourth Week** 2 Samuel 11:26–12:10; 12:13–15 Psalm 32 Galatians 2:15–21 Luke 7:36–8:3	

Ecumenical Texts of the Church

One way the Christian Church has demonstrated its unity in Christ is to include certain written texts in its worship of God. The following texts have been prayed, chanted, sung, whispered and proclaimed by the church for hundreds of years. Some of these texts are directly from Scripture, others come from the theological councils of the church in their war against heresy, and still others are penned by anonymous sources in anonymous places. We have included them in this volume because we share the belief that their inclusion in public worship can do no less than edify the church in the understanding of our historical predecessors who stand in that great cloud of witnesses (Heb 12:1). Let the musician who owns this volume endeavor to compose new music for these texts. Let the preacher who reads these texts remember that these texts were read and proclaimed often by great preachers such as Augustine, Luther, and Calvin. Let the artist consider new ways of bringing to light the brilliance of Christ that shines in the *Te Deum* and the creeds. Let the dramaturge find new ways of conveying the relentless hope of Simeon's song, the *Nunc Dimittis*. And let us all renew our common faith in the words of these ecumenical texts. The text forms that follow are the versions adapted by the Liturgical Consultation (see notice below) and are used with permission.

The Lord's Prayer

> Our Father in heaven,
>> hallowed be your name,
>> your kingdom come,
>> your will be done, on earth as in heaven.
> Give us today our daily bread.
> Forgive us our sins
>> as we forgive those who sin against us.
> Save us from the time of trial
>> and deliver us from evil.
> For the kingdom, the power, and the glory are yours
>> now and for ever. Amen.

The Lord's Prayer lies at the heart of Christian devotion, and it is laden with rich personal and traditional associations. Change in its wording, therefore, prompts all kinds of reactions. But change common in the history of this prayer, and today no single, invariable version is in common use throughout the English-speaking world. Comparison of the text of Matt 6:9–13 in the King James (Authorized) Version of the Bible with the version in *The Book of Common Prayer* of 1662 at once reveals differences. Such variations remind us that between our traditional versions and the Greek texts of the prayer, as recorded in the New Testament, stand earlier English, and even earlier Latin, renderings. To retranslate the Lord's Prayer for a new situation is no new undertaking. It should also be emphasized that in the task of producing translations the church has never been in the position of working from one "original" text. The Greek texts of the prayer as preserved in the Gospels are themselves translations from Aramaic or Hebrew, and the texts that appear in Matthew and Luke do not agree.

The above translation of the Greek text is based mainly on that in St. Matthew's Gospel, since that version has always been the basis of the church's liturgical tradition. Its acceptance has been growing steadily but is still far from universal. Many Christians are deeply attached to more traditional versions. Some churches await a greater measure of agreement before they can consider adopting any modern version.

The Apostles' Creed

> I believe in God, the Father almighty,
>> creator of heaven and earth.
> I believe in Jesus Christ, God's only Son, our Lord,
>> who was conceived by the Holy Spirit,
>> born of the Virgin Mary,
>> suffered under Pontius Pilate,
>> was crucified, died, and was buried;
>> he descended to the dead.
>> On the third day he rose again;
>> he ascended into heaven,
>> he is seated at the right hand of the Father,
>> and he will come to judge the living and the dead.
> I believe in the Holy Spirit,
>> the holy catholic church,
>> the communion of saints,
>> the forgiveness of sins,
>> the resurrection of the body,
>> and the life everlasting. Amen.

The Apostles' Creed in its present form dates back to a Latin text of the eighth century, but it clearly incorporates far older material. In origin, this creed appears to have developed from a three-fold questioning at baptism, probably based on the Lord's command in Matt 28:19. The candidates were asked successively whether they believed in the Father, in the Son, and in the Holy Spirit. To each question the candidate, standing in the water, replied "I believe" and was three times immersed, once after each answer. At least as early as the fourth century, the candidates were also taught a fuller profession of faith in the three Persons of the Holy Trinity. This took varying forms in different places. In Rome the local form developed into what became known as "The Apostles' Creed"—not because the Apostles wrote it, but because it was taken to represent the authentic apostolic tradition.

The primary association of the Apostles' Creed with a personal profession of faith at baptism explains the singular pronoun "I" at the beginning. Because this creed is also used in such corporate services as Morning and Evening Prayer, and sometimes in place of the Nicene Creed at the Eucharist, the Liturgical Consultation has included a final "Amen" and approves of the substitution, where desired, of the first-person plural at the beginning of each paragraph; e.g., "We believe in God, the Father almighty." "Creator" also has the advantage of suggesting that God did not make the universe out of preexisting material but is the origin of all things.

Sursum Corda (Lift Up Your Hearts)

> Leader: The Lord be with you.
> **People: And also with you.**
> Leader: Lift up your hearts.
> **People: We lift them up to the Lord.**
> Leader: Let us give thanks to the Lord our God.
> **People: It is right to give our thanks and praise.**

In certain Eucharistic liturgies, this dialogue between the president (liturgical presider) and the congregation is found as early as the third century in the West (Hippolytus, ca. 215, and Cyprian, ca. 252) and the fourth century in the East (Cyril of Jerusalem, ca. 350). Its universality shows that it developed from a dialogue at Jewish ritual meals where the grace or thanksgiving after the main meal was introduced by the presider, saying, "Let us give thanks to the Lord our God" and the gathered company giving their assent. In the Eucharist the dialogue leads into the Great Thanksgiving, which traditionally begins with a preface culminating in the Sanctus. Some early liturgies amplify the simple dialogue or substitute "minds" or "hearts and minds" for "hearts."

Gloria Patri (Glory to the Father)

> Glory to the Father
> > and to the Son
> > and to the Holy Spirit;
> > as it was in the beginning,
> > is now,
> > and will be forever. Amen.

This ascription of praise to the Holy Trinity is no doubt derived from Jewish doxologies, similar to that at the end of the Lord's Prayer and those found in other Christian doxologies such as Rom 16:27, Phil 4:20, and Rev 5:13. Its use at the end of Psalms is at least as old as the fourth century, and metrical paraphrases are found attached to hymns in the early medieval offices as well as in more modern hymnody.

Te Deum Laudamus (We Praise You, O God)

> We praise you, O God,
> > we acclaim you as Lord;
> > all creation worships you,
> > the Father everlasting.
> > To you all angels, all the powers of heaven,
> > the cherubim and seraphim, sing in endless praise:
> Holy, holy, holy Lord, God of power and might,
> > heaven and earth are full of your glory.
> The glorious company of apostles praise you.
> The noble fellowship of prophets praise you.
> The white-robed army of martyrs praise you.
> Throughout the world the holy Church acclaims you:
> > Father, of majesty unbounded,
> > your true and only Son, worthy of all praise,
> > the Holy Spirit, advocate and guide.
> You, Christ, are the king of glory,
> > the eternal Son of the Father.
> When you took our flesh to set us free
> > you humbly chose the Virgin's womb.
> You overcame the sting of death
> > and opened the kingdom of heaven to all believers.
> You are seated at God's right hand in glory.
> We believe that you will come to be our judge.
> Come then, Lord, and help your people,

> bought with the price of your own blood,
> and bring us with your saints
> to glory everlasting.

This Latin hymn to the Father and the Son, traditionally (but probably wrongly) attributed to St. Ambrose in the late fourth century, is thought by some scholars to have been composed by Bishop Niceta of Remesiana. The Te Deum is particularly associated with the Office of Readings in the Roman Catholic Church and Morning Prayer in other traditions. It has often been given special musical settings for independent use on occasions of great rejoicing.

The Te Deum contains a series of acclamations that are highly stylized in their original Latin form. An attempt to produce a literal translation, maintaining the Latin word order, would result in something that would sound unidiomatic and odd. Where the Latin structure could be followed profitably, this has been attempted by the Liturgical Consultation.

Benedictus: Song of Zechariah (Luke 1:68–79)

> Blessed be the Lord, the God of Israel,
> > who has come to his people and set them free.
> The Lord has raised up for us a mighty Savior,
> > born of the house of his servant David.
> Through the holy prophets, God promised of old
> > to save us from our enemies,
> > from the hands of all who hate us,
> > to show mercy to our forebears,
> > and to remember his holy covenant.
> This was the oath God swore to our father Abraham:
> > to set us free from the hands of our enemies,
> > free to worship him without fear,
> > holy and righteous before him,
> > all the days of our life.
> And you, child, shall be called the prophet of the Most High,
> > for you will go before the Lord to prepare the way,
> > to give his people knowledge of salvation
> > by the forgiveness of their sins.
> In the tender compassion of our God
> > the dawn from on high shall break upon us,
> > to shine on those who dwell in darkness and the shadow of death,
> > and to guide our feet into the way of peace.

Alternate Version (2nd Person Singular)

Blessed are you, Lord, the God of Israel,
For you have come to your people and set them free.
You have raised up for us a mighty Savior,
    born of the house of your servant David.
Through the holy prophets, you promised of old
    to save us from our enemies,
    from the hands of all who hate us,
    to show mercy to our forebears,
    and to remember your holy covenant.
This was the oath you swore to our father Abraham:
    to set us free from the hands of our enemies,
    free to worship you without fear,
    holy and righteous before you,
    all the days of our life.
And you, child, shall be called the prophet of the Most High,
    for you will go before the Lord to prepare the way,
    to give God's people knowledge of salvation
    by the forgiveness of their sins.
In the tender compassion of our God
    the dawn from on high shall break upon us,
    to shine on those who dwell in darkness and the shadow of death,
    and to guide our feet into the way of peace.

This song, based on phrases from the Septuagint (the Greek version of the Old Testament, widely used in the first century), is placed by St. Luke in the mouth of Zechariah at the birth of his son, John the Baptist. The first part is addressed to God in thanksgiving for the fulfillment of the hopes for the Messiah; the second part (from line 15) is addressed to the child who is to be the Lord's forerunner. In the Eastern church the canticle forms part of the morning Office but is often omitted. In the West it became part of the Office of Lauds and is now used in the Morning Prayer of many traditions.

In Hebrew prayer God is praised indirectly in the third-person as well as by direct address. The third- and second-persons may alternate, as for instance in the Song of Hannah (1 Sam 2) and frequently in the psalms. There is also ancient liturgical precedent for converting an original third-person address to the second-person, as in the Sanctus where the original "his glory" has long been rendered as "your glory." In contemporary English, direct address is more natural.

In the Benedictus and the Magnificat the third-person of the original generates a number of masculine pronouns—considerably more in English than in Greek or

Latin. The Liturgical Consultation has therefore offered alternative versions, in which the third-person is replaced by the second-person.

Magnificat: Song of Mary (Luke 1:46–55)

> My soul proclaims the greatness of the Lord,
> > my spirit rejoices in God my Savior,
> > who has looked with favor on his lowly servant.
> From this day all generations will call me blessed:
> > the Almighty has done great things for me,
> > and holy is his name.
> > God has mercy on those who fear him,
> > from generation to generation.
> The Lord has shown strength with his arm
> > and scattered the proud in their conceit,
> > casting down the mighty from their thrones
> > and lifting up the lowly.
> God has filled the hungry with good things
> > and sent the rich away empty.
> He has come to the aid of his servant Israel,
> > to remember the promise of mercy,
> > the promise made to our forebears,
> > to Abraham and his children for ever.

Alternate Version (2nd Person Singular)

> My soul proclaims the greatness of the Lord,
> > my spirit rejoices in God my Savior,
> > for you, Lord, have looked with favor on your lowly servant.
> From this day all generations will call me blessed:
> > You, the Almighty have done great things for me,
> > and holy is your name.
> > You have mercy on those who fear you,
> > from generation to generation.
> You have shown strength with your arm
> > and scattered the proud in their conceit,
> > casting down the mighty from their thrones
> > and lifting up the lowly.
> You have filled the hungry with good things
> > and sent the rich away empty.
> You have come to the aid of your servant Israel,

to remember the promise of mercy,
the promise made to our forebears,
to Abraham and his children for ever.

This song of praise, attributed by St. Luke to Mary when her cousin Elizabeth had greeted her as the Lord's mother, has been associated in the West with Vespers and Evening Prayer at least since the time of St. Benedict (sixth century). In the East it is sung in the morning Office before, or more commonly in place of, the Benedictus. The Magnificat has often been provided with antiphons to be sung before and after it, and many special musical settings have been composed for it. Its resemblance to the Song of Hannah (1 Sam 2) has often been noted.

The reasons for providing an alternative version in the second-person are the same as those given in the notes to the Benedictus. As with that canticle, masculine pronouns have been used in the first version only if they have a counterpart in the Greek. This has sometimes meant expressing the subject of a verb, which is understood but not expressed in the original Greek, by "God" or "the Lord."

Nunc Dimittis: Song of Simeon (Luke 2:29–32)

Now, Lord, you let your servant go in peace:
    your word has been fulfilled.
My own eyes have seen the salvation
    which you have prepared in the sight of every people:
    a light to reveal you to the nations
    and the glory of your people Israel.

Simeon's song of joyful release has been part of the church's daily offering of prayer since the fourth century (see *Apostolic Constitutions* 7.48). Its images of peace and light make it particularly appropriate for the evening. In the East it is used at Vespers. In the West it is generally associated with Compline or Night Prayer and in some traditions with Evening Prayer.

It also has a history of use after the Eucharist. In the Liturgy of St. Chrysostom it is part of the devotions prescribed after receiving holy communion, and it has had a similar use in Lutheran and Reformed worship.

The Aaronic Blessing

The Lord bless you and keep you.
The Lord make his face to shine on you,
  and be gracious to you.
The Lord lift up his face toward you,
  and give you peace.

This blessing comes from Num 6:24. In speaking to Moses, God provides him the words of this blessing. Moses is to give them to his brother Aaron, saying, "This is how you should bless the children of Israel." The blessing is often used as a benediction at the conclusion to services of worship.

The Ordinary of the Roman Catholic Eucharistic Service (Mass)

The following five texts represent the Ordinary of the Mass, the parts ordinarily sung or said at each Eucharistic celebration. They are supplemented at each Mass by the Propers, those additional texts, songs, and prayers that befit the day of celebration. These texts are from ecumenical translations used across a wide range of traditions; currently Roman Catholic churches use a slightly altered version.

Kyrie Eleison (Lord, Have Mercy)

> Kyrie eleison, Lord, have mercy,
> Christe eleison, Christ, have mercy,
> Kyrie eleison. Lord, have mercy.

The Greek phrase *Kyrie eleison* appears in early Greek Liturgies and as part of the Latin rite from the fifth century. It was used as a response to the petitions of a litany, as it still is in Eastern liturgies. There is no agreement on the origin of the form printed above.

By the end of the eighth century what were originally responses had developed into a nine-fold acclamation addressed to Christ: *Kyrie eleison* three times, *Christe eleison* three times, *Kyrie eleison* three times. In later times this pattern was sometimes given a Trinitarian interpretation that was not part of the original. Sometimes additional phrases were added, a development known as "farcing" the Kyrie.

The nine-fold pattern remained in the Latin rite until 1969, when it was reduced to a six-fold pattern. Some liturgies of Reformation churches connected the Kyrie with the confession of sins, a practice also accepted in the 1969 Roman Catholic *Ordo Missae*. Recently, some churches have restored the litany framework by using *Kyrie eleison* or an English variant ("Lord, in your mercy, hear our prayer") as a response to the Prayers of the Faithful. As well as its place near the beginning of the Eucharist, the Kyrie is found in the monastic Office, and in various forms of Morning and Evening Prayer.

It is suggested that it sometimes be used, especially in the Eucharist, in its Latin (Greek derived) version, thus preserving a link with early Greek liturgies similar to that preserved with Hebrew worship in the retention of such forms as Amen, Hallelujah, and Hosanna.

Gloria in Excelsis

Glory to God in the highest,
    and peace to God's people on earth.
Lord God, heavenly King,
    almighty God and Father,
    we worship you, we give you thanks,
    we praise you for your glory.
Lord Jesus Christ, only Son of the Father,
    Lord God, Lamb of God,
    you take away the sin of the world:
    have mercy on us
    you are seated at the right hand of the Father:
    receive our prayer.
For you alone are the Holy One,
    you alone are the Lord,
    you alone are the Most High,
    Jesus Christ,
    with the Holy Spirit,
in the glory of God the Father. Amen.

The author and source of this Greek "Christian psalm" are unknown. Since the fourth century it has been associated in the East with morning prayers. In Rome it found its way into the Eucharistic liturgy only gradually, at first on special occasions such as Easter and Christmas (to which it is particularly appropriate). By the twelfth century a custom had grown of adding it on other Sundays as well, but not in Advent and Lent. Its purpose was to introduce the Liturgy of the Word. In 1552, for Anglican worship, Archbishop Cranmer transferred it, as an act of thanksgiving for holy communion, to just before the final blessing of the congregation. In recent years it has been generally restored to its earlier place.

It consists of a series of acclamations, a doxological and hymnodic form characteristic of the ancient Greek liturgies. Since it is not a dogmatic text like the creeds, a modern version may adapt its pattern to hymn structures that are more readily understood in English, without any basic modification of its substance and spirit. An analysis of the structure of the hymn shows that it consists of an opening antiphon based on Luke 2:14, followed by three stanzas of acclamation: the first addressed to God the Father, the second and third to God the Son.

Credo, or Nicene-Constantinopolitan Creed

We believe in one God,
> the Father, the Almighty,
> maker of heaven and earth,
> of all that is, seen and unseen.

We believe in one Lord, Jesus Christ,
> the only Son of God,
> eternally begotten of the Father,
> God from God, Light from Light,
> true God from true God,
> begotten, not made,
> of one Being with the Father;
> through him all things were made.
> For us and for our salvation
> he came down from heaven,
> was incarnate of the Holy Spirit and the Virgin Mary
> and became truly human.
> For our sake he was crucified under Pontius Pilate;
> he suffered death and was buried.
> On the third day he rose again
> in accordance with the Scriptures;
> he ascended into heaven
> and is seated at the right hand of the Father.
> He will come again in glory to judge the living and the dead,
> and his kingdom will have no end.

We believe in the Holy Spirit, the Lord, the giver of life,
> who proceeds from the Father [and the Son],
> who with the Father and the Son is worshiped and glorified,
> who has spoken through the prophets.
> We believe in one holy catholic and apostolic Church.
> We acknowledge one baptism for the forgiveness of sins.
> We look for the resurrection of the dead,
> and the life of the world to come. Amen.

The Credo, or the creed called "Nicene" or the Creed of Nicaea and Constantinople, is first known in its present form from the Council of Chalcedon (451), where it was accepted as the Creed of the Council of Constantinople (381). That council is recorded simply as having confirmed the Nicene faith with a few additions to the third article. The Council of Nicaea (325) framed its own statement of orthodox belief, stressing that the Son is of the same essential Being (*homoousios*) as the Father, against the

Arian heretics who allotted the Son a lower rank. The original Nicene statement differs considerably from the one recognized at Chalcedon. The latter, from which this version derives, appears to be based on an earlier baptismal creed possibly from Jerusalem or Antioch, and, in addition to the essential clauses from Nicaea, it incorporated material to combat later heresies.

Representing the statement of an ecumenical council, the Nicene Creed was naturally framed in the first-person plural, "we believe." This plural use is not only original, but is also appropriate in corporate worship. The reference is to the faith of the whole church, of all times and places, and not only to that of the local congregation. This is in contrast to the Apostles' Creed, which began as a personal profession of faith. The liturgical use of the singular "I believe" is, of course, a legitimate variation found both in the East and in the West. It may date back to the widespread use of this creed for baptismal profession before its incorporation into the Eucharistic liturgy. Its use in the Eucharist apparently began in Antioch in the late fifth century as a way of ensuring the orthodox belief of the communicants and later spread in the West, but was not introduced in Rome until 1014.

Sanctus and Benedictus

> Holy, holy, holy Lord, God of power and might,
>   heaven and earth are full of your glory.
> Hosanna in the highest.

> Blessed is the one who comes in the name of the Lord.
> Hosanna in the highest.

Recent scholarship suggests that the Sanctus or angelic hymn first entered the Eucharistic prayer in the East. The earliest references are from East Syria, Cappadocia, and Jerusalem. It spread rapidly in both the East and the West. Its use no doubt arose from the thought that the worshippers who had lifted their hearts to the Lord were sharing in the worship of heaven.

The Sanctus (lines 1–3) sometimes appears without the Benedictus (lines 4–5) as in the Egyptian Liturgy of Serapion (fourth century) and *The Book of Common Prayer* of 1552 and 1662. Some liturgies have used the Benedictus but not in immediate conjunction with the Sanctus. A space has therefore been left between the two texts.

These texts are acclamations of praise based upon Scripture, but not exactly conforming to the texts of Isa 6:3 or Mark 11:9–10 respectively. At an early stage in the church's liturgical use the reference to "heaven" was added in line 2. Some early liturgies expand the text in other ways.

Agnus Dei (Lamb of God)

Jesus, Lamb of God.
> have mercy on us.
Jesus, bearer of our sins,
> have mercy on us.
Jesus, redeemer of the world,
> grant us peace.

Agnus Dei (Alternate Version)

Lamb of God, you take away the sin of the world,
> have mercy on us.
Lamb of God, you take away the sin of the world,
> have mercy on us
Lamb of God, you take away the sin of the world,
> grant us peace.

The Agnus Dei is an anthem in litany form traditionally sung or said to accompany the breaking of the consecrated bread at the Eucharist. In a varied form it occurs within the Gloria in Excelsis. It appears, for example, in *The Book of Common Prayer* of 1552 and 1662, not for use at Holy Communion but rather as a prayer within the litany.

Since its introduction in the seventh century into the Western liturgy the Agnus Dei has undergone a number of variations in Latin and vernacular forms. At first the petition *miserere nobis* ("have mercy on us") was unchanged at each repetition, but in the tenth and eleventh centuries it became common to substitute in the last line *dona nobis pacem* ("grant us peace"). This was also varied at requiems to "grant them rest" and "grant them rest eternal." The medieval period gave rise to other variations on the anthem. Sometimes phrases were added to bring out the meaning more clearly. In the Reformation liturgies of England and Germany, *pacem* in line 6 was rendered "thy peace" both to keep two syllables for musical reasons and under the influence of such texts as John 14:27. The German form also sought clarity by prefixing the name "Christ" to each of lines 1, 3, and 5.

"Lamb of God," though full of meaning for those familiar with the biblical background in such passages as John 1:29, Isa 53:7, and Rev 5:6ff, does not reveal its richness at first sight. The first form above reveals some aspects of the meaning more clearly and immediately. The name "Jesus" has been prefixed to the title "Lamb of God" at the beginning of line 1. The name rather than the title is then used at the beginning of lines 3 and 5. Instead of the three-times-repeated relative clause *qui tollis peccata mundi* ("who take away the sins of the world") a phrase is used in each of lines 3 and 5 to bring out the dual meaning of these words. The verb *tollis*, like the corresponding Greek verb *aireis* in John 1:29, means both "take away" and "bear" or "lift up."

The alternative, more traditional, version is especially suitable when the Agnus Dei is treated as the accompaniment to a sometimes-lengthy breaking of bread. "Lamb of God, you take away the sin of the world, have mercy on us" may be repeated as many times as necessary.

Copyright Notice:

Joseph A. Novak

Glossary of Liturgical Terms

Italicization of words used in the following definitions indicates that the word is also to be found in this glossary.

A

Ablutions

The ritual act of cleansing the *chalice* after *communion*. This is typically performed in Roman Catholic worship and seldom in Protestant churches.

Absolution

A statement of assurance of divine forgiveness imparted by an *ordained* minister to those who repent. It usually follows a private or corporate statement of repentance. In churches with a high theology of *ordination*, the absolution represents the authoritative word of God. In churches with a low theology of *ordination*, pastors do not presume to speak for God, but assure one another with a strong word of *pardon*.

Acclamations

A congregational response, usually before and/or after the reading of the Gospel, in the form of a joyful statement or song. Usually, it contains *alleluias*, except during the season of *Lent*.

Acolyte

An attendant who helps during worship. Often a child or youth, the acolyte assists with lighting candles, carrying *communion* materials, and other tasks during the *liturgy*. Acolytes typically wear *albs*.

Advent

The *liturgical* season that begins the *church year*. It starts four Sundays before *Christmas*. Themes associated with Advent include preparing and giving thanks for the birth of Christ and his presence among us, as well as acknowledging Christ's resurrection and his expected return.

Affirmation of Baptism

A public ritual celebrating and bringing to remembrance the baptism of God's people. A rite of baptismal affirmation is sometimes used for 1) the rite of *confirmation* of young believers, and 2) receiving baptized people into a congregational membership.

Agnus Dei

Latin for "Lamb of God." The term refers to a sung portion of the *ordinaries* of the Roman Catholic *Mass*. As in the Catholic liturgy, the Lamb of God is sung as part of the *communion liturgy* in some Protestant (Anglican, Episcopal, Lutheran, and others) churches. (See p. 332.)

Alb

A loose fitting, white, ankle length, *liturgical* robe. It is typically worn by pastors, preachers, and worship leaders in churches with formal *liturgies*. The robe is often secured at the waist with a rope or *cincture*. *Ordained* ministers typically wear *stoles* over their albs. Because the alb is suggestive of the white robe associated with baptism, the alb can fittingly be worn by any baptized person assisting in worship.

Alleluia

From Hebrew, alleluia (and hallelujah) is an exclamation of praise to God. Untranslated in most languages, it is a universal word of praise. During the season of *Lent*, the singing of alleluia is usually omitted in worship.

Altar

Altar refers to a platform upon which ritual sacrifices are made. Old Testament faith is associated with the building and use of altars. For Christians, whose ultimate sacrifice is Christ, the term is usually associated with the *communion table*. In Protestant theology, the term *table* is more appropriate.

Ambo

A podium from which to read Scripture or preach. It can also be known as a *pulpit* or a *lectern*.

Amen

A Hebrew term meaning "let it be so." It is used in worship as a form of assent, and at the conclusions of prayers, sermons, and declarations of faith.

Anamnesis

A term most commonly associated with *communion*, it derives from Greek and refers to remembrance. Amnamnesis is an active form of memory that connects worshipers with past biblical actions. In particular, it is the portion of the *Eucharistic Prayer* that represents the life, *passion*, death, resurrection, and *ascension* of Christ.

Anaphora

A word of Greek derivation meaning to "lift up," this is the scholarly term for the *Eucharistic Prayer*.

Anthem

A musical piece, usually a choral work, performed during worship.

Antiphon

Usually relating to the singing of the psalms, the antiphon is a portion of the text sung as a refrain by the congregation. It is sung in response to the parts sung by the *choir* or *cantor*.

Ascension of Our Lord, The

A festive day on the *church calendar*. It is celebrated on the fortieth day of the *Easter Season*, commemorating Christ's ascension into heaven.

Ashes

These are used on *Ash Wednesday* as a symbol of purification and atonement. They are ritually placed on the forehead, often in the shape of a cross. Some churches burn the palms used in worship on the previous *Palm Sunday* and use the ashes from the palms on *Ash Wednesday*.

Ash Wednesday

The first day of the season of *Lent*. It follows Shrove Tuesday, a day that looks forward to the shriving, or repentance, of the Lenten season. In some traditions, the day before Ash Wednesday is known as Mardi Gras, a final day of carefree celebration before *Lent*. See *ashes*.

Assembly

Those who gather for worship. Also known as the body of Christ.

Assisting Ministers

Those who assist in worship including *acolytes*, greeters, ushers, readers, or *lectors*, *communion* servers, etc.

B

Banner Bearer

An *acolyte* who carries a festive *banner* into worship.

Banners

Decorated fabrics attached to processional poles. Banners represent worship themes or the seasons of the *church year*.

Baptismal Candle

A candle given to the newly baptized as a reminder of joining the body of Christ. Some people light their candle on the yearly anniversary of their baptisms.

Baptismal Font or Pool

The font is a piece of furniture that holds water for baptisms. Baptismal pools are used in churches where full immersion baptism is practiced.

Baptismal Garment

A white robe or garment worn by those who are baptized. The reference is to putting on the purity of Christ, and to the white robes given to martyrs in Rev 6:11. The *alb* and the *funeral pall* are also white, reflective of the baptismal garment.

Baptismal Oil

Fragrant oil, or olive oil placed on the forehead of the newly baptized as a sign of God's blessing. The process is called anointing. See *chrism*.

Baptistery

The place where baptisms are performed. The term often refers to the place where full immersion baptisms take place.

Benedicamus

A moment in worship when the leader exclaims, "Let us Bless the Lord," and the congregation responds, "Thanks be to God." The term comes from the Latin for blessing.

Benediction

The blessing given to the congregation as they are being sent out of the place of worship. The benediction is pronounced from the leader to the people. It is not, as commonly assumed, a prayer at the conclusion of worship.

Benedictus

The term comes from Latin, meaning "blessed." It refers to 1) a Latin based *canticle* from Luke 1:68–79, or 2) part of the *ordinaries* of the Roman Catholic Mass. The canticle text begins, "Blessed be the Lord God." The Mass portion begins, "Blessed is he who comes in the name of the Lord." (See p. 331.)

Berakah

A Hebrew term for blessing. Many Jewish and Christian prayers begin with a standard berakah formula: "Blessed are you, O Lord, our God."

Bidding Prayer

See section on Prayer in this book (pp. 283–284).

Blessing

An authoritative statement of God's favor given in public worship, or privately by a pastor or elder. See *benediction*.

Blessings

God's benevolence shown on particular people, places, and things.

Bookbearer

The *acolyte* who holds the Bible while it is being read in worship or carried in a *liturgical* procession.

Bowing

A gesture used to represent humility, reverence, or respect.

Breaking of the Bread

Also known as the *fraction*, this refers to the physical act of breaking the bread loaf used in the *communion*.

C

Cantata

A musical form, usually based on Scripture. It is most commonly comprised of choruses, solos, duets, and instrumental elements.

Canticle

A scriptural text that is set to music for congregational singing. Canticles come from other portions of Scripture than the psalms.

Cantor

The classic term for a song leader in worship. Jewish synagogues often have cantors, as do many churches. In historic times, the cantor was a person who not only led music, but had significant other duties in congregational life. For example, J. S. Bach, as the cantor of Leipzig, was in charge of the local school, composing music for worship, and teaching and playing the organ.

Cassock

A long, loose-fitting garment worn by clergy and choir members. It is usually black, purple, or red and covered with a white top garment called a surplice. Today, its use has largely been replaced by the *alb*.

Catechesis

The term applied to a period of Christian education, especially in advance of baptism or *confirmation*.

Catechumen

A person involved in *catechesis*, or training prior to baptism or *confirmation*.

Cathedral

The term applied to a church building that is attached to or associated with the ministry of a bishop in the Roman Catholic or Episcopal Church. Cathedrals are usually located centrally within a diocese (district) and are typically the largest church building in the district.

Catholic

In its original sense, catholic means of interest or use to all (universal). When capitalized, Catholic can refer to the Roman Catholic Church.

Censer

See *thurible*.

Chalice

From the Latin, for "cup," this is the vessel used to distribute wine to congregants during *communion*. Chalices are usually made from pottery, or from fine metals, including silver and gold.

Chalice Veil

A square piece of fabric used to cover the *chalice* during *communion*.

Chancel

The area within a worship space that contains the *table (altar)* and the *pulpit*. This area is usually elevated a step or more to provide visibility for those in the seats or pews. The word comes from a Latin term that referred to a railing or screen that separated the *nave* from the front portion of the worship space.

Chant

From the Latin word for "to sing." The recitation of a *liturgical* or biblical text according to a melodic formula in free rhythm. The simplest chant has the leader intone the text on a single note. Monastic chant eventually developed simple melodies and countermelodies sung by monastic communities at prayer.

Chasuble

A garment resembling a poncho that is worn on top of the *alb* and *stole* by the person presiding over *communion*. Its color usually reflects the season of the *church year*. From the Latin word for "little house," it was originally used as an extra layer of protection from the weather in cold climates.

Choir

An ensemble of singers who perform anthems and lead congregations in worship. The first purpose of the choir is to assist the congregation in their participation in worship. The secondary purpose is to rehearse and sing songs for the *assembly* that the people cannot sing for themselves.

Chorale

A stately, traditional musical setting of a hymn text. Associated most with the Lutheran tradition and homophonic hymn settings (arrangements), such as those of J. S. Bach.

Chrism

From the Greek title for Christ, the "Anointed One." The oil used in baptismal anointing. See *baptismal oil.*

Chrismation

In *baptism*, the act of anointing the newly baptized with oil. It represents a sealing of the person with the power of the Holy Spirit. It was part of the church's earliest three-part baptismal practice of baptizing with water, anointing with oil (also known as *confirmation*), and receiving *communion*.

Christ the King Sunday

A liturgical celebration held on the last Sunday of the *church year*. The following Sunday is the first Sunday of *Advent*. Thematically, the day emphasizes the kingly rule of

Christ in heaven and his dominion over the reign of God on earth. It is also known in some traditions as the Reign of Christ.

Christmas

The day commemorating the birth of Jesus. Western (Julian) calendars place it on December 25. In the Orthodox Church, the day falls on or near the same date (though it is calculated as January 7 on the Gregorian calendar). Christmas is also known as the Feast of the Nativity, or the Feast of the Incarnation. Christmas day begins a twelve-day season of Christmas and is followed by *Epiphany season.*

Christmas Cycle

This term refers to the first three seasons of the church calendar, *Advent, Christmas,* and *Epiphany.*

Christmas Season

The twelve-day period in which the Incarnation of Christ is celebrated, beginning December 25 and lasting until January 5th. The following day is the feast of *Epiphany.*

Church Year

Also known as the liturgical year. The term refers to a calendrical organization of the days, weeks, seasons, festivals, and commemorations of the church at worship. The year is divided into two parts. The first commemorates Jesus' coming, his life, death, resurrection, *ascension,* and second coming. The second follows the Day of *Pentecost* and commemorates the life of the church on earth. This portion of the church year is also known as *ordinary time.* Scripture readings are assigned for all days and festivals of the year according to a *lectionary.* See "On the Use of a Lectionary (FAQs)" in the Essays and Resources section of this book (p. 300).

Ciborium

A cup that holds bread for communion, from the Latin word for "food."

Cincture (or rope)

A cord with a knot at each end that is worn as a belt on the *alb.* From the Latin word for "to gird."

Collect

A prescribed form of prayer that collects themes of worship. For a detailed explanation and examples, see "The Collect" in the Essays and Resources section of this book (pp. 276–279).

Colors, Liturgical

The colors appointed as visual symbols for use on *paraments* and *vestments* in worship. Each season and special day in the *church year* has an appointed color. See the liturgical calendar on the back cover of this book.

Advent	blue or purple
Christmas	white
Epiphany of Our Lord	white
Baptism of Our Lord	white
Sundays after Epiphany	green
Transfiguration Day	white
Ash Wednesday	black or purple
Lent	purple
Holy Week	scarlet or purple
Maundy Thursday	scarlet or white
Good Friday	none, scarlet, or black
Vigil of Easter	white
Easter Day	white or gold
Sundays of Easter	white
Day of Pentecost	red
The Holy Trinity	white
Sundays after Pentecost	green
Christ the King	white

Communion, Holy

Celebration of the *Eucharist* or the *Lord's Supper*. Communion is one of the seven *sacraments* in the Roman Catholic Church and one of two sacraments (or *ordinances*) in the Protestant church.

Bread and wine are consecrated through prayer and served to the assembly in remembrance of Jesus eating his last meal with his disciples.

Compline

A form of evening prayer. See the Daily Office portion of the Essays and Resources section in this book (pp. 290–291).

Confession

The act of admitting sin, indicating remorse, and expressing a desire for forgiveness of sins. Confession can be done privately, alone, or with a clergy person. It is also done in corporate worship. Confession is always followed *liturgically* by a pronouncement of *absolution* or *pardon*.

Confirmation

Usually following a period of teaching (or *catechesis*), confirmation is a ceremony in which a person *baptized* as an infant affirms their baptismal vows. The term originates from the three-part rite of Christian initiation in the early church. Confirmation, in that setting, involved a local bishop anointing the newly baptized with oil as a sign of protection by the Holy Spirit.

Consecration

The term associated with blessing the bread and wine (or grape juice) during *communion*.

Corporal

Cloth that is placed under a *communion chalice*, like a placemat. From the Latin word meaning "body."

Corporate Confession and Forgiveness

A rite celebrated during corporate worship, whereby the people speak together a congregational statement confessing sins, followed by a pastor or leader's pronouncement of God's forgiveness. See *absolution* and *pardon*.

Creche

From the French word for "crib," a creche is nativity scene typically populated by statues of Jesus in a manger, his parents, three wise men (or magi), shepherds, angels, and animals.

Credence Table

From the Latin word for "sideboard," the credence table is situated to the side of the *chancel*, near the *communion table* and is used for holding *communion* vessels and offering plates.

Credo

The phrase is Latin for *creed*. This term usually refers to the Latin text of the Nicene Creed, one of the five elements of the *ordinary* of the *Mass*. (See pp. 330–331.)

Creed

A statement of one's beliefs, usually spoken together by an assembly at worship. The three creeds most associated with the Christian church are the Apostles, Nicene, and

Athanasian Creeds. See "Ecumenical Texts of the Church" in the Essays and Resources section of this book (pp. 320–333).

Cross, Pectoral

A cross that hangs across the chest, held by a chain. It is worn during worship and often associated with the office of bishop.

Cross, Processional

A large cross or *crucifix* attached to a processional staff. It is usually placed near the communion table after a *liturgical* procession. In processions (at the beginning of worship) and recessions (at its conclusion), the cross traditionally leads the way.

Cross, Sign of the

The sign of the cross is a *liturgical* gesture made by tracing the shape of the cross from one's forehead to the chest and from one shoulder to another with the hand. It is associated with the Trinitarian formula, "In the name of the Father, and of the Son, and of the Holy Spirit."

Crucifer

An *acolyte* who carries the *processional cross*.

Crucifix

A cross with the figure of Jesus crucified upon it. It is typically found in Roman Catholic use because of that church's strong theology emphasizing the sacrifice of Jesus upon the cross. Protestant churches typically have empty crosses, emphasizing that Christ has been raised from death.

D

Dismissal

The final act of worship whereby a pastor or leader dismisses the congregation. It is also known as the *sending*, where God's people are sent out into mission in their work and life.

Doxology

From the Greek word meaning "to honor," it is a form of praise directed toward the Trinity. It usually begins with the word "glory," and praises the "Father, Son, and Holy Spirit."

E

Easter Day

Easter is the greatest celebration of the *church year*, celebrating the resurrection of Christ. It follows the season of *Lent*, which culminates with *Holy Week* and the commemoration of Jesus' final days and death.

Easter Season

Easter season begins the evening before *Easter Day* with the *Easter Vigil*. It lasts for fifty days and ends on the day of *Pentecost*. Also known as the Great Fifty Days, the season historically emphasized teaching about the faith (*catechesis*) to new converts *baptized* at the Easter Vigil.

Easter Vigil

Known historically as "the mother of all vigils," the Easter Vigil is generally celebrated at nightfall on Holy Saturday. Usually long, with numerous readings from Scripture that recount the history of God's saving acts, as it moves through the night the vigil eventually commemorates the baptism of God's people. In Roman Catholic, Orthodox, and Episcopal churches, the vigil is the traditional time for baptisms. The extensive *liturgy* of the Easter Vigil includes 1) a service of light, 2) a service of the Word, 3) the *commemoration of baptism* and *baptism* of new converts, and 4) holy *communion*.

Epiclesis

From the Greek word meaning "to call down," the epiclesis is a prayer that invokes the Holy Spirit. Such a prayer occurs in *Eucharistic Prayers*, in baptism rites, and other places. While associated with formal liturgies, it is also found in Charismatic and Pentecostal churches, where prayer for the presence of the Holy Spirit is a common liturgical practice.

Epiphany of Our Lord, The

From the Greek word meaning "manifestation" or "appearance," the day of Epiphany is January 6 (in the Western church). The day is devoted to celebrating the manifestation of Jesus as the Christ. The story of the magi (or wise men) from Matt 2:1–12 is the appointed text for the day. Epiphany occurs on the thirteenth day after Christmas, and thus ends the twelve-day Christmas season.

Epiphany Season

This season with its associated texts continues celebration of the manifestation of Jesus as the Christ. It begins on the 6th of January, *the Epiphany of Our Lord*, and lasts until the Transfiguration of Our Lord, the Sunday before *Ash Wednesday*. Because the date of Eater varies, as does the date for Ash Wednesday, the Epiphany season varies in its number of Sundays. (Note: In Roman Catholic tradition, the Feast of the Transfiguration does not occur in Epiphany, but on August 6.)

Eucharist

The term refers to and is synonymous with *holy communion* and the *Lord's Supper*. The word derives from the Greek word for "thanksgiving." The *Eucharistic Prayer* incorporates a prayer of thanksgiving.

Eucharistic Prayer

This is the prayer said during the *communion liturgy*, as part of the *consecration* of the bread and wine (or grape juice). It incorporates a prayer of thanksgiving for God's saving acts, which is known as the *Great Thanksgiving*. See *anaphora*.

Eucharistic Vestments

Garments worn by ministers, priests, and assistants during *communion*. For *presiding ministers*, a *chasuble* is sometimes worn over an *alb* and *stole*. In the Reformed tradition, a *preaching gown* is sometimes worn by the *presider*. See *vestments*.

Eulogy

Often spoken by members of the deceased person's friends or family, this is a funeral oration in memory or praise of the deceased. The funeral *homily*, or sermon, is different in that it is typically spoken by the presiding minister and based on Scripture or God's promises in the Bible.

Evening Prayer

A worship service performed in the evening or at sunset, it is sometimes called *Vespers*. See "The Daily Office (Praying the Hours)" in the Essays and Resources section of this book (pp. 290–291).

F

Fasting

To refrain, for spiritual and devotional reasons, from eating. Some Christians fast for a meal or a day, especially during the season of *Lent*. It can also refer to refraining from eating certain foods for a period. Traditional Roman Catholic practice calls for fasting from eating meat on Fridays, making seafood the preferred meal.

Flagon

From the Latin word for "bottle" or "flask," this is a large pitcher that holds the sacramental wine (or grape juice).

Flood Prayer

A prayer of thanksgiving for water, originating with Martin Luther, used in some *baptismal* rites. See the Prayer section in this book (pp. 222–223).

Font

See *baptismal font or pool,* and *baptistery.*

Fraction

See *breaking of the bread.*

Funeral Pall

White fabric that covers the coffin during a funeral. It is reminiscent of the white robe of baptism. See *alb,* and *baptismal garment.*

G

Gathering

The term refers both to the *assembly* of the faithful for worship, and to the portion of worship that draws people together liturgically. It is the first part of the four-part movement of worship: gathering, word, *sacraments,* and *sending.*

Gloria in Excelsis

Latin for "Glory to God in the Highest," this is the first line of one of the songs of the *ordinary* of the *Mass.* It derives from the angels' song in Luke 2:14. It is also known as the greater doxology. (See p. 329.)

Gloria Patri

Latin for "Glory to the Father," this is the first line from the Trinitarian *doxology,* known as the lesser *doxology.* See "Ecumenical Texts of the Church" in the Essays and Resources section of this book (p. 323).

Godparents

Persons who vow to share responsibility for the spiritual development of a child in baptism. Also known as baptismal sponsors.

Good Friday

The sixth day of *Holy Week.* The second day of the *Triduum,* it commemorates the day of Christ's crucifixion.

Gospel Procession

A procession of the Bible, its bearer, and its reader, from the *lectern* to the center of the *assembly*. It occurs in formal liturgies at the reading of the Gospel lesson.

Great Fifty Days

See *Easter Season*.

Great "O" Antiphons

The Advent *antiphons* that begin with "O." They are traditionally sung during the seven days preceding Christmas Eve. Each antiphon recounts one of the attributes of Christ. The *stanzas* of the *Advent* hymn "O Come, O Come, Emmanuel" derive from these.

> December 17: "O Wisdom"
>
> December 18: "O Adonai"
>
> December 19: "O Root of Jesse"
>
> December 20: "O Key of David"
>
> December 21: "O Dayspring"
>
> December 22: "O King of the Nations"
>
> December 23: "O Emmanuel"

Great Thanksgiving

This term refers to the portion of the *communion liturgy* that includes the *Preface* Dialog, the *Proper* Preface, the *Sanctus*, and the *Eucharistic Prayer*. See *Eucharist*.

H

High Liturgy

The term refers to churches and traditions that incorporate highly traditional and ritualized forms into their regular services of public worship. For example, the Roman Catholic Church and its *Mass* would be considered a form of high liturgy. Anglicans, Episcopalians, Lutherans, and others also frequently use high forms of *liturgy*, especially on festival days. Low liturgy, correspondingly, refers to worship traditions that keep to simple *liturgies* with limited ritual.

Holy, Holy, Holy

See *Sanctus*.

Holy Saturday

The seventh day of *Holy Week*. It is the final day of the *Triduum*. The *Easter Vigil* generally begins on the evening of Holy Saturday.

Holy Week

The week before *Easter*. It begins with *Palm Sunday* (also known as *Passion Sunday*) and concludes on Easter Eve (*Holy Saturday*).

Homily

Another term for sermon, it sometimes is used to indicate a brief form; for example, a wedding homily.

Host

A term for the bread used in *communion*.

Hymn

A sacred poetic song set to music in a measured rhythm.

Hymn or Song of the Day

This refers to a hymn or song selected to correspond to the Scripture reading(s) and sermon within a service of worship. Typically, it precedes or follows the sermon. Also known as the sermon hymn.

Hymnal

A collection of hymns bound together in an organized book. Some hymnals (such as this one) contain other worship materials including *liturgies*, prayers, *lectionaries*, and indexes.

I

Immersion, Baptism by

A baptismal practice whereby the entire body of the convert is immersed in water. Common in free church practice (such as Baptist and Pentecostal), it is historically and theologically appropriate in all Christian traditions.

Imposition of Ashes

Ashes drawn in the shape of a cross on the forehead as part of the Ash Wednesday ritual. The action is usually accompanied by the words, "Remember that you are dust and to dust you shall return." See *ashes*.

Incense

Fragrant resins that are burned for ceremonial or liturgical purposes. As indicated in Ps 141:2, the smoke that rises represents prayers ascending to God. See *thurible*.

Institution Narrative

The words of Christ at the Last Supper. Various versions are found in the New Testament: Matt 16:26–29; Mark 14:22–25; Luke 22:15–20; and 1 Cor 11:23–24. These words form a central part of the Eucharistic Prayer in the communion liturgy. Also known as the Words of Institution.

Intercessions

A type of prayer in which petitions are made on behalf of persons, nations, the church, and the world.

Interment

The act of laying to rest or entombing the remains of the deceased, whether the remains are in the form of a body or have been cremated.

Intinction

The practice of distributing wine during communion by dipping the *host* (bread) into the *chalice*.

Introit

From the Latin word for "entrance," this term refers to a psalm or *liturgical* text sung as part of the entrance rite in worship.

K

Kiss of Peace

As early as the second century, a ritualized kiss found a place in Christian Eucharistic *liturgies*. Today, the kiss is often replaced by a spoken greeting (such as, "The peace of Christ be with you") accompanied by a handshake or hug.

Kyrie or Kyrie Eleison

From the Greek for "Lord," or "Lord have mercy," this Latin term refers to a prayer that is part of the *ordinary* of the *Mass*. Its full text in English is "Lord have mercy, Christ have mercy, Lord have mercy." Traditionally, it is sung three times. The text is also used as a refrain for hymns used during the gathering time in worship. (See p. 328.)

L

Lamb of God

See *Agnus Dei.*

Lectern

From the Latin word "reader," this refers to a stand or podium from which scriptural lessons are read during worship. It can also be used for preaching. See *ambo* and *pulpit.*

Lectionary

From the Latin word for "reading." See "On the Use of a Lectionary (FAQs)" in the Essays and Resources portion of this book (pp. 300–303).

Lector

A person appointed to read biblical lessons during worship.

Lent

From the Anglo-Saxon word for "spring," this is a forty-day (excluding Sundays) season that begins with *Ash Wednesday* and concludes at *Easter*. Lenten themes are repentance and *catechesis*, or preparation for *baptism*.

Litany

A form of prayer that contains repeated responses. See the Prayer section in the Essays and Resources portion of this book (pp. 279–283).

Liturgy

The term refers to any established form of worship. While some churches (such as Roman Catholic, Anglican, Episcopalian, Lutheran, and Eastern Orthodox) have formal, traditional liturgies, all churches have preferred forms of worship that are rightly called liturgies. From the Greek, the term originally referred to public good works performed by the citizenry. Today, it implies the corporate work of all people praising God in worship.

Liturgy of the Word

The portion of worship that attends to the reading and proclamation of the Word of God. It includes those elements (such as a *Prayer for Illumination* or Gospel *acclamation*) that precede readings and preaching, as well as those (such as a *hymn or song of the day*, a *creed*, or prayers) that follow the sermon.

Lord's Day

The first day of the week (Sunday) when most Christian churches elect to hold services of worship. The reference is to Christ being raised from death on Sunday, making that the Lord's Day and a fitting day for worship. In contrast, some churches (such as the Seventh Day Adventist Church) join the Jewish custom of offering principle worship services on the Sabbath, that is, on Saturday.

Lord's Supper

The term is used by Paul in 1 Cor 11:20 as a term for *holy communion*.

Lord's Table or Table

See *altar*.

M

Magnificat

Latin title for the *canticle,* "My soul proclaims the greatness of the Lord," from Luke 1:46–55. (See pp. 326–327.)

Mass

The traditional name of the Roman Catholic service of Holy Communion. Historically, the Mass has had a set text (see *ordinary*) as well as elements that are particular to the day of celebration. See *propers*.

Matins

A form of morning prayer. It is sometimes called Lauds. See "The Daily Office (Praying the Hours)" in the Essays and Resources section in this book (pp. 290–291).

Maundy Thursday

The term refers to Thursday of Holy Week. The word Maundy derives from Latin for mandate. It refers to the "new commandment" of Jesus, given on the night of his betrayal, for the disciples to love one another (John 13:34).

Memorial Service

The term applied to a service of worship that commemorates a person who has died. It differs from a funeral service principally in that the remains of the deceased are not present. Accordingly, memorial services are not necessarily held immediately near to the time of death.

Missal

Principally used in the Roman Catholic tradition, this refers to a book containing *liturgies* for the *Mass*. The missal especially includes the *proper* prayers and texts for given Sundays and celebrations.

N

Narthex

An ante-chamber, porch, or foyer that leads worshipers into the *nave* (or *sanctuary*) of a church building. It is traditionally located on the west side of the building.

Nave

From Latin for "ship," the nave is the central part of a church building and the principle place of public worship. The nave is so called because in Gothic architecture, as one looks at the ceiling, its lofty arches resemble looking into the framework of a wooden ship. See *sanctuary*.

Neophytes

The term refers to those newly converted and initiated (*baptized*) into the Christian faith.

Nicene Creed

See "Ecumenical Texts of the Church" in the Essays and Resources section of this book (pp. 330–331).

Nunc Dimittis

Latin for what is known as Simeon's Song, the *canticle*, "Lord, now let your servant go in peace," from Luke 2:29-32.

O

Occasional Services

Services of worship relating to occasional commemorations or celebrations such as baptisms, funerals, weddings, and Thanksgiving services.

Offering

The term refers both to tithes and contributions made by a worshiping assembly and to bread and wine (or grape juice) brought forth from the community for use in *holy communion*. Such gifts are regularly solicited from and/or brought forth to the chancel during the offering portion of worship.

Offertory

A musical response that accompanies *offering* gifts being brought forward.

Orans

A posture for prayer where arms are presented outward and slightly to the side, with palms upward. It is often used when a leader presents a prayer on behalf of the people. It can also be used as a posture for giving a *benediction*. In many churches, the posture is also used by the people when they pray or sing in public worship.

Ordinance

Another term for *sacrament*. It is used primarily in communities where there is little emphasis on the presence of Christ in *communion* and *baptism*. The term emphasizes that Jesus ordered his disciples to "do this in remembrance of me," and to "go and baptize."

Ordinary, Ordinaries

Services of worship consist of elements enacted regularly, week by week (that is, ordinarily), and elements enacted specially for each particular week or occasion (see *Propers*). For example, the Lord's Prayer might be said by a community each time it gathers. The texts for a given day, however, are selected according to the theme or season of worship. Those things done ordinarily are known as the ordinaries. In Roman Catholic usage, the ordinaries of the *Mass* include five texts (usually set to music) that include the *Kyrie*, the *Gloria*, the *Credo*, the *Sanctus* and *Benedictus*, and the *Agnus Dei*. These ordinaries have been set to music by church musicians and classical composers through the ages. Bach's Mass in B Minor is an example of the latter.

Ordinary Time

There are two periods on the liturgical calendar known as Ordinary Time. The first occurs during the weeks following the feast of *Epiphany*. This is a period variable in length, given the shifting date of *Easter* and *Lent* each year. The second occurs during the months following the feast of *Pentecost*. This, too, varies according to the placement of Easter. The first is also known as the season of *Epiphany*; the second is also known as the season following *Pentecost*.

Ordination

A service wherein persons are set apart as official clergy within a denomination or tradition. Ordained clergy are also known as pastors, and officially designated as The Rev. (Name). The term also refers to the consecratory act of ordaining clergy.

P

Pall

See *Funeral Pall*

Paraments

Cloth coverings for communion *tables*, *pulpits*, and *lecterns*. They are usually colored to match the liturgical season and decorated with Christian symbols. See *colors, liturgy*.

Pardon

A statement that reassures people of forgiveness. Usually spoken by a worship leader following corporate *confession* of sins.

Paschal Candle

A large candle associated with the *Easter Vigil*. It usually is decorated with the sign of the cross (sometimes with the figure of the crucified Christ upon it) and five nails (or pieces of incense) signifying the wounds of Christ. The candle represents Christ who is the light of the world. Paschal comes from the Hebrew word "pesach", meaning Passover. In some traditions, a new Paschal candle is blessed each year and is lit only during the Easter season and on special occasions, such as baptisms and funerals.

Passion Sunday or Palm Sunday

The Sunday before *Easter*. Lectionaries usually assign the full Passion narratives from one of the Gospels to this day. It is sometimes also called Palm Sunday because it is associated with Jesus' triumphal entry into Jerusalem on the days before his Passion (betrayal, suffering, crucifixion, and death).

Paten

A plate or bowl containing bread used in *holy communion*.

Pentecost

The day recorded in Acts 2 where the Holy Spirit comes upon Jesus' disciples. It is known as the birthday of the Church of Christ. It fell on the Jewish day of Pentecost (from Greek for "fiftieth day"). In the Christian calendar, Pentecost falls seven weeks after *Easter*, or on the fiftieth day after Easter. Thus, the season of Easter is also known as the Great Fifty Days.

Prayer for Illumination

A prayer offered by a leader prior to reading Scripture in public worship. The prayer typically calls upon the Holy Spirit to make the hearing of God's word plain as it is read and proclaimed.

Preaching Gown

A gown worn by preachers and worship leaders, especially in churches that follow the Reformed (Calvin and Zwingli) traditions. Resembling robes worn by scholars and judges, it is also known as a Geneva gown.

Preface

The *Eucharistic Prayer* begins with a preface, a proclamation of thanksgiving and praise that is appropriate to the day or season. See *propers*.

Presiding Minister

The minister, pastor, or priest who presides over a service of worship. In services of *holy communion*, the presider is usually an *ordained* minister.

Prime

See the Daily Office portion of the Essays and Resources section in this book (pp. 290–291).

Procession

An ordered progress of *liturgical* leaders and people into the place of worship. It is usually performed on festive occasions (such as *Easter* or *Pentecost*) and employs choirs and *acolytes* carrying a *crucifix* (see *crucifer*), *banners*, and a processional Bible. Services of worship that begin with processions usually conclude with recessions, where the order of people and elements is identical, entering and exiting. The *processional cross* is usually the first element in a procession and the *presiding minister* is usually the last person in a procession. In cases where a bishop is present, the bishop is properly the last person in a procession.

Propers

Elements of a worship service that are specially selected or appointed for the particular day of celebration. See *ordinary, ordinaries*.

Pulpit

A podium generally used for preaching. See *ambo* and *lectern*.

Pyx

A container used for transporting *communion* elements from worship to those who are homebound.

R

Rubric

From the Latin word for "red," rubrics are *liturgical* instructions printed in service books and *missals*. The rubrics are traditionally printed in red. The "negrics," (words printed in black) are the text of the worship service, words intended to be spoken by a leader or the gathered people.

S

Sacrament

From the Latin term for "mystery," a sacrament is a ritual that celebrates the mysteries of God's grace-filled interaction with believers. The Roman Catholic Church settled on seven rites that it considers sacramental: *baptism, holy communion*, penance, marriage, *confirmation*, last rites, and *ordination*. Since the Reformation, the Protestant Church has typically designated only two such rites as sacraments: *baptism* and *communion*. Following Luther, Protestants consider sacraments to be rituals that have been instituted (or ordered; see *ordinance*) by Jesus in Scripture and that make use of earthly elements (water, bread, and wine).

Sanctuary

A term referring either (especially in medieval usage) to the innermost part of the *chancel* where the *altar* (*table*) is located. Today it more generally refers to the entire space appointed for gatherings of corporate worship.

Sanctus

From the Latin for "holy," this term refers to a song that is part of the *ordinary* of the *Mass*. Its text derives from Isa 6:3, "Holy, holy, holy." The song is part of the Eucharistic Prayer in Roman Catholic and other churches with high *communion liturgies*. (See p. 331.)

Sending

The final portion of a service of corporate worship wherein the gathered people are ritually sent from the assembly into the world. It is also known as the *dismissal*, although this term suggests an adjournment of worship, while sending retains the sense that worship continues as people are sent into service in the world.

Stanza

As a convention in hymnody (the use and study of hymns), the word stanza is used to refer to the verses of the hymn text. The term "verse" is used in reference to portions of scriptural passages, to units in poems, and in song sections. Typically, the only persons aware of the distinction between stanza and verse, or that care to promote it, are hymn writers and hymnologists.

Stations of the Cross

This refers to fourteen scenes or depictions of the journey that Jesus made from Pilate's house to Calvary. Medieval pilgrims and crusaders brought images of the stations home to Europe after walking the "way of the cross" while visiting Jerusalem. The practice continues today, especially in Roman Catholic and Episcopal churches, where pictorial displays of the fourteen stations are displayed. The faithful pause for meditation at each of the stations as a *Lenten* or Paschal devotion. See *Paschal candle.*

Stole

One of the vestments that designates its wearer as an *ordained* member of the ministry. It is a long, narrow band of cloth that is worn over an *alb*, placed behind the neck and falling forward over the shoulders. Its ends drape down the front of the minister's robe. The stole is usually made of colored cloth matching the color of the church season, and is sometimes decorated with Christian symbols. In some traditions, deacons and non-*ordained* ministers wear a stole that is placed over the right shoulder and falls diagonally (in the front and back) to the left waist; it is secured with a *cincture.*

T

Table, Communion

The furnishing upon which is placed bread and wine (or grape juice) for *holy communion.* (See *altar.*)

Thurible

A metal vessel or censer, suspended by chains, in which incense is burned during religious ceremonies, most often found in Eastern Orthodox and Roman Catholic worship. The altar server who carries the thurible is the thurifer.

Triduum

The scholarly term for the three-day period, beginning with the celebration of *holy communion* on *Maundy Thursday* of *Holy Week* and concluding at the *Easter Vigil* on *Holy Saturday.*

V

Venite

From Latin for "O come," *venite* refers to a historic chant that derives from Ps 95:1–7 and Ps 96:9, 13.

Vespers

A form of *evening prayer*. See "The Daily Office (Praying the Hours)" in the Essays and Resources section in this book (pp. 290–291).

Vestments

The term refers to the special robes and garments worn by people leading worship. Their purpose is not to set the leaders apart from others, hierarchically. They are used as a sign of hospitality, indicating to worship participants the roles played by various persons in leadership roles. They include garments such as *albs, stoles, chasubles,* choir robes, and ushers' gloves.

Vestry

This refers to the room, usually located near the *chancel,* where clergy and other worship leaders store their *vestments* and dress for worship. It is also often the site of prayer among worship leaders before they commence their roles.

Acknowledgments and Permissions

Part II

Orders for Daily Prayer
   Joseph A. Novak and Clayton J. Schmit

Fuller Morning Prayer
   Clayton J. Schmit

Part III

"Lessons from St. Paul on Corporate Worship"
   Todd E. Johnson

"Biblical Foundations for Worship"
   Joseph A. Novak

"The Ecumenical Shape of Corporate Worship"
   Joseph A. Novak

"The Four-Fold Pattern of Worship"
   Clayton J. Schmit

"Principles for Worship Planning"
   Edwin M. Willmington and Clayton J. Schmit

"Shaping the Liturgy for the 21st Century: Utilizing the Ritual Process Model"
   C. E. Weber

"Scripture Reading in Worship"
   Clayton J. Schmit

"Principles for Leading in Public Prayer"
   Clayton J. Schmit

"Forms and Practices of Public Prayer"
   Jeffrey Frymire and Clayton J. Schmit

"The Daily Office (or Praying the Hours)"
   Clayton J. Schmit

"Using Choirs and Musical Ensembles in Worship"
Edwin M. Willmington, Jennifer Hill, and Clayton J. Schmit

"Hymn and Song Selection in Worship: Singing the Faithful to Life"
Amy C. Schifrin

"On the Use of a Lectionary (FAQs)"
Joseph A. Novak

"The Academic Calendar and Lectionary"
Clayton J. Schmit and Joseph A. Novak

"Ecumenical Texts of the Church"
Joseph A. Novak
Special permission to use these ecumenical texts has been
granted by the English Language Liturgical Consultation